THE APOSTOLIC PREACHING OF THE CROSS

The
Apostolic Preaching
of the Cross

by

T H E R E V. LEON MORRIS, B.Sc., M.Th., Ph.D.

Vice-Principal, Ridley College, Melbourne

LONDON

THE TYNDALE PRESS

39, Bedford Square, W.C.1

First Edition   – – – September, 1955

Second Edition   – – – October, 1960

PRINTED IN GREAT BRITAIN AT THE PITMAN PRESS, BATH

CONTENTS

ABBREVIATIONS

Customary abbreviations are used for the names of the books of the Bible, and also for the names of the tractates of the Mishnah (as given, for example, in Danby's translation) and the Talmud. Where 'b' is prefixed to the name of a Talmudic tractate it signifies that it is the Babylonian Talmud that is in question. Some books which are referred to often are abbreviated in accordance with the following list:

BDB. Brown, Driver and Briggs: *A Hebrew and English Lexicon of the Old Testament*

ET. The Expository Times

Enc. Bib. Encyclopaedia Biblica

HDAC. J. Hastings (ed.): *A Dictionary of the Apostolic Church*

HDB. J. Hastings (ed.): *A Dictionary of the Bible*

HDCG. J. Hastings (ed.): *A Dictionary of Christ and the Gospels*

H & R. Hatch and Redpath: *Concordance to the Septuagint*

I.C.C. The International Critical Commentary

LXX. The Septuagint

JTS. The Journal of Theological Studies

MM. Moulton and Milligan: *The Vocabulary of the Greek Testament*

MNTC. Moffatt New Testament Commentary

Prin. Theol. Rev. The Princeton Theological Review

SB. Strack-Billerbeck: *Kommentar zum Neuen Testament aus Talmud und Midrasch*

TWBB. A. Richardson (ed.): *A Theological Word Book of the Bible*

TWNT. G. Kittel: *Theologisches Wörterbuch zum Neuen Testament*

WH. Westcott and Hort: *The New Testament in the Original Greek*

INTRODUCTION

W HEN the present writer first began to read seriously on the atonement he discovered that some of the great theological words such as 'redemption', 'propitiation', and 'justification' are often used in a way which seems to indicate that they mean different things to different people. If we may take redemption, the subject of our opening chapter, as an example, some writers, as we there point out, practically equate it with deliverance; others see in it a reference to a substitutionary transaction; while others use it as a comprehensive term for the whole Christian salvation. For some it has a backward reference, pointing to the satisfaction for sin made on the cross, while for others it is essentially forward-looking and gives expression to the liberation from sin's bondage which enables the believer to live the Christ-like life. There is similar uncertainty and ambiguity attaching to the use of some other terms.

Now it ought to be possible to discover what the characteristic Christian expressions mean. One line of inquiry starts from the fact that the New Testament writers were steeped in the language and ideas of the Old Testament. An examination of the relevant Old Testament passages will reveal to us one of the influences which moulded the thinking of our writers, and which must, therefore, help us as we seek to understand their language.

Again, since the New Testament was written in the ordinary speech of ordinary men (and not the classical language of the scholar or literary man), the flood of light which has been thrown on this type of speech by modern discoveries of papyri, ostraka and inscriptions must illuminate many New Testament expressions. This, then, is a further field for investigation.

A third source is ancient Jewish literature. While the Christians vigorously repudiated many Rabbinic conclusions they yet discussed many of the same problems, and made use of the same terminology. Therefore it will usually repay us to examine the way the Rabbis used any term we are investigating.

This book, then, is not a full scale study of the atonement, but a necessary preliminary. It is an attempt to understand certain key words, words which are crucial to the New Testament picture of the atonement, by seeing them against the background of the Greek Old Testament, the papyri and the Rabbinic writings. Armed with our discoveries, we then proceed to examine them in their New Testament setting, always bearing in mind the possibility that the early Christians may modify or enrich any terms they may borrow.

L.M.

ACKNOWLEDGMENTS

In this volume I have incorporated the substance, and sometimes the actual wording of a number of articles written previously for various journals. These are as follows: 'The Use of ἱλάσκεσθαι etc. in Biblical Greek' (*The Expository Times*, Vol. LXII, No. 8); 'The Wrath of God' (*The Expository Times*, Vol. LXIII, No. 5); 'The Biblical Use of the term "Blood"' (*The Journal of Theological Studies*, New Series Vol. III, Pt. 2;) 'Justification by Faith: The Old Testament and Rabbinic Anticipation' (*The Evangelical Quarterly*, Vol. XXIV, No. 1); 'The Idea of Redemption in the Old Testament' (*The Reformed Theological Review*, Vol. XI, No. 3); 'The Biblical Idea of Atonement' (*The Australian Biblical Review*, Vol. II, Nos. 3–4).

To the editors of these journals I would express my indebtedness for their ready permission to republish.

Many friends have assisted me at various points, and it is difficult to acknowledge all my indebtedness. But especially would I mention the Rev. Dr. Newton Flew, who discussed many of these chapters with me, the late Rev. H. W. Oldham, who advised me constantly during the earlier part of my labours, and also my colleague, Mr. F. I. Andersen, who has very kindly compiled the Index. Finally, I would like to place on record my gratitude to the publishers for all the help they have given during the various stages of production.

L.M.

CHAPTER I

REDEMPTION

I. ETYMOLOGICAL CONSIDERATIONS

THE idea of redemption is usually conveyed in the New Testament by using λύτρον (ransom) and its associated word group, sometimes also by words connected with purchase like ἀγοράζω or περιποιέω. We examine these word groups in order.

λύτρον and its derivatives go back ultimately to the verb λύω which means basically 'to loose, loosen', and was used of such processes as unbinding clothes, armour, etc. By a natural extension of use the verb was applied to living beings, as in the unyoking of horses, and then with regard to men, when it signified the loosing of the bonds of the prisoner so that he became free. Quite often it was used in contexts where a ransom was supplied as the condition of release, and in this way came to signify 'to release on receipt of a ransom'. Liddell and Scott cite passages showing this use from Homer onwards.

It is from this use of the verb that the noun λύτρον is derived. The suffix -τρον denotes basically the means whereby an action is performed, being in common use for names of implements (e.g. ἄροτρον, 'a plough'). Debrunner[1] thinks of a second stage when the suffix denoted locality (θέατρον, 'a theatre'), and of a third stage later still when payment was the meaning (θρέπτρα, 'payment for rearing'). It is under this last head that λύτρον, a comparatively late word, is to be classed, and it denotes accordingly 'payment for loosing', i.e. ransom price.

From this noun a new word group developed. λύω conveyed no necessary significance of ransoming, being merely a general term for loosing, but when the verb λυτρόω was developed from

---

[1] Griechische Wortbildungslehre, Heidelberg, 1917, pp. 176f., and cf. J. H. Moulton and W. F. Howard, A Grammar of the Greek New Testament, Edinburgh, 1929, II, pp. 368f.

λύτρον it was in order that there might be a word which conveyed in its essence, and not fortuitously as an inference from the context, the idea of release by payment of ransom. The active signified 'to hold to ransom, to release on receipt of ransom', while the middle gave the idea 'to redeem by payment of ransom'. From this, again, other words evolved like λύτρωσις, and compounds like ἀπολυτρόω, which in turn gave rise to derivatives. All these words go back ultimately to λύτρον, and in all there is to be discerned the fundamental idea of a process involving release by payment of a ransom price, which process seems implied in the use of the word group throughout the whole range of profane Greek. It is only in biblical Greek that there is any question of another significance to be attached to the words, and the importance of the unwavering usage of profane authors must not be overlooked. The non-biblical use leaves us in no doubt as to what the words signified in themselves, in their essential meaning.

II. THE λύτρον WORD GROUP IN THE SEPTUAGINT

The use of λύτρον itself in the LXX is perfectly straightforward as in each case it signifies simply a ransom price, a typical example of its use being in the account of the institution of the tax of a half shekel when the census was taken: 'When thou takest the sum of the children of Israel, according to those that are numbered of them, then shall they give every man a ransom for his soul unto the Lord, when thou numberest them; that there be no plague among them, when thou numberest them' (Ex. xxx. 12). Congruous with this usage is that of other words from this group which, though not occurring in the New Testament, are worth noting since they help to give the significance of the word group. Thus the adjective λυτρωτός occurs twice (Lv. xxv. 31, 32) to indicate that certain houses were at all times open to redemption, and the verb ἀπολυτρόω is found twice also (Ex. xxi. 8; Zp. iii. 1), the thought of ransom being implicit in both places. Similarly the compound ἐκλύτρωσις is found in Nu. iii. 49 where the money paid for the ransoming is explicitly mentioned.

The position seems to be much the same in the single occurrence of ἀπολύτρωσις (Dn. iv. 30), where king Nebuchadnezzar says 'And at the completion of seven years the time of my redemption came'. This might be interpreted as an example of simple deliverance[1] if it did not plainly refer back to verse 24 where Daniel exhorts the king : 'pray to him concerning thy sins, and redeem all thy iniquities with almsgiving'. When this redemption is spoken of as actually accomplished, though we may well feel that the emphasis is on the result rather than the process, yet we cannot ignore the express mention of a ransom price.

In all the words thus far noted there is a clear and consistent usage; whenever any of them occurs there is a process of ransoming in view, with a definite price paid for release. When we come to consider the verb λυτρόω, however, the position is more complicated. We meet the characteristic use of the word for release by ransom on many occasions; but, in addition, a new usage makes its appearance where there seems neither ransom nor, indeed, any place for ransom, as when we read: 'For thus saith the Lord . . . ye shall be redeemed without money', 'for the Lord hath comforted his people, he hath redeemed Jerusalem' (Is. lii. 3, 9). So also the noun λύτρωσις, which occurs eight times, has no necessary implication of a ransom on three occasions, and the same is probably true of the two occurrences of λυτρωτής. It is this usage which leads Westcott to affirm that in the LXX 'the idea of a ransom received by the power from which the captive is delivered is practically lost in λυτροῦσθαι, etc.'[2] But the question is not an easy one, and the usage of the verb will bear more detailed examination.

λυτρόω occurs ninety-nine times in the canonical Old Testament. Where there is a Hebrew base it is the translation of g'l forty-five times, of pdh forty-two times, while no other root is represented more than four or five times. Thus there are two important Hebrew roots to be considered, and these will be found to underlie almost all the occurrences of the other words from this root, except that λύτρον

---

[1] As is done for example by Büchsel, TWNT., IV, p. 354.

[2] *Hebrews*, p. 298. Abbott on Eph. i. 7 (I.C.C.) gives a similar verdict on the LXX usage.

introduces another Hebrew root, being the translation of *kopher* on six occasions. From all this it appears that if we are to understand the LXX meaning of redemption we must examine the significance of these three Hebrew roots.

a. g'l
The primary sense of this root is given thus by S. R. Driver: '*g'l* is properly *to resume a claim or right* which has lapsed, *to reclaim, re-vindicate*.'[1] But this does not seem to bring out the essential significance of the word as well as does the short definition in the Oxford Lexicon, 'redeem, act as a kinsman'; for as Procksch says '*g'l* is a concept in family-law'.[2] The word has about it a family air, and this is never quite lost in the various shades of meaning which it ultimately embraces.

We see the basic meaning of the root in passages where the participle is used simply to denote a kinsman, as when we read that Zimri 'smote all the house of Baasha: he left him not a single man child, neither of his kinsfolks (*go'alayw*), nor of his friends' (1 Ki. xvi. 11, and cf. Ru. ii. 20, iii. 9, 12; Nu. v. 8, etc.). It is this meaning in Jb. iii. 5 where the patriarch utters his desire that 'darkness and the shadow of death' should *g'l*, i.e. 'claim as a kinsman', the day of his birth.

A kinsman is responsible for playing his part in maintaining the family honour and in preserving the family's possessions, and from this various obligations arise. Supremely is this so when one of the family has been done to death by an outsider. Then it devolves on the kinsman to avenge the family honour, and so we find the kinsman *par excellence*, the 'avenger of blood', making his appearance. See Nu. xxxv. 19, 21, 24, 25, 27; Dt. xix. 6, 12; Jos. xx. 3, 5, 9; 2 Sa. xiv. 11. In all these places a strong family sense is manifested and it cannot be doubted that this gives us the basic significance of the word.[3]

---

[1] On Dt. vii. 8 (I.C.C.).

[2] TWNT., IV, p. 331.

[3] C. Ryder Smith says that, of the various translations of the verb, ' "to do the part of a kinsman" is nearest to the Hebrew', and he adds, 'One could wish that there were some such English word as " to kinsman " ' (*The Bible Doctrine of Salvation*, London, 1941, p. 34).

In pursuance of his family obligation the kinsman might be called upon to perform other duties, such as marrying the widow of a deceased relative (Ru. iii. 13), or buying one of the family out of the slavery into which he has fallen (Lv. xxv. 48f.), or reclaiming the field of such a one (Lv. xxv. 26, 33; Ru. iv. 4, 6). From the usage for redeeming slaves and fields further applications of the term could find entrance, and thus, when the original owner wanted back again something he had sanctified to the Lord, he was said to redeem it (Lv. xxvii. 13, 15, 19, 20, 27, 28, 31, 33; see also Lv. xxvii. 28, 33 for things which could not in this way be redeemed).

Thus in the Old Testament use of the word we find two distinct ideas. The primary thought is the general one of family obligation, and arising out of this is the narrower concept of the payment of price, of redemption. The transition is an easy one, and the Hebrew term continued to be used for either idea; but the LXX translators made a distinction, for they use only the λύτρον word group as a rendering for g'l when a ransom is involved. There is no place where a member of the λύτρον group translates g'l with a human subject without a ransom being mentioned or implied. g'l may justly be held to involve a family obligation, but it is not this so much as the paying of a redemption price as a consequence of this relationship which the LXX translators seek to express by λυτρόω.

There are some very important passages wherein Yahweh is the subject of the verb g'l. In these we are to think of God as the great Kinsman of His people, to whom they could look for succour in times of distress, and in particular, upon occasions when their liberty was lost or in jeopardy. Pre-eminently is this the case with the rescue of the people from their bondage in Egypt. 'I am Jehovah, and I will bring you out from under the burdens of the Egyptians, and I will rid you out of their bondage, and I will redeem you with a stretched out arm, and with great judgments: and I will take you to me for a people, and I will be to you a God' (Ex. vi. 6; see also Ex. xv. 13; Pss. lxxiv. 2, lxxvii. 16 (15), lxxviii. 35, cvi. 10). This deliverance furnished the pattern for describing the later deliverance from Babylon as a redemption, which we find in Ps. cvii. 2; Is. xliii. 1, xliv. 22, 23, xlviii. 20, lii. 3, 9, lxiii. 9; Je. xxxi. 11; Ho. xiii. 14; Mi. iv. 10. It is in exactly similar vein that we have Yahweh spoken of as Redeemer (*go'el*) thirteen times over in Is. xl–lxvi, and the people referred to as 'the redeemed' in a number of passages (Ps. cvii. 2; Is. xxxv. 9, etc.). Yahweh's redemptive activity is not confined to great national deliverances, for we find Jacob invoking 'the God which hath fed me all my life long unto this day, the angel which hath redeemed me from all evil' (Gn. xlviii. 15, 16), and the psalmist thinks of a God who 'redeemeth thy life from destruction' (Ps. ciii. 4; cf. also Pss. lxix. 18, lxxii. 14, cxix. 154).

It is sometimes argued from this usage that the verb has lost its original significance and means simply 'to deliver'; but this does not seem quite to square up with the facts. Thus, if it is simply a term indicating deliverance, we should expect it to be used now and then of human deliverance without ransom, but such is not the case. Wherever the verb is used with a human subject the deliverance is always by payment of ransom. In other words the word itself does not come to mean 'deliver' rather than 'redeem with a price', but it gets this meaning from the fact that Yahweh is its subject.

Examination of the passages in which Yahweh is the subject reveals the interesting fact that in many places the redemption He effects is not regarded as something He performs with effortless ease, although in other passages, sometimes not far from the redemption ones, the idea is put forward that all the might of the nations is but a puny thing, a thing of nought, in His sight. But though they accept this thought, when the Bible writers think of Yahweh as Redeemer they prefer to think of Him as putting forth a strong effort. Thus we read 'I will redeem you with a stretched out arm' (Ex. vi. 6); 'Thou art the God that doest wonders: Thou hast made known thy strength among the peoples. Thou hast with thine arm redeemed thy people' (Ps. lxxvii. 14, 15); 'Enter not into the fields of the fatherless: for their redeemer is strong' (Pr. xxiii. 10, 11); 'Their redeemer is strong; the Lord of hosts is his name: he shall throughly plead their cause' (Je. l. 34). This stress on Yahweh's effort seems to be the reason for applying the redemption terminology to His dealings, for it is regarded as the 'price' which gives point to the metaphor. Yahweh's action is at cost to Himself. While He could, so to speak, cope with the situation with a small expenditure of effort, yet because He loves His people He 'hath made bare his holy arm in the eyes of all the nations' (Is. lii. 10).[1]

b. pdh

The ground meaning of this root is undoubtedly that of 'ransom by the payment of a price', indicating something in the nature of a commercial transaction without any obligation arising from kinship or the like which we have seen to be implied in g'l. A typical use of the verb is found in the passage describing the procedure to be adopted with regard to the firstborn, 'Thou shalt set apart unto the Lord all that openeth the womb, and every firstling which thou hast that cometh of a beast; the males shall be the Lord's. And every firstling of an ass thou shalt redeem with a lamb; and if thou wilt not redeem it, then thou shalt break its neck: and all the firstborn of man among thy sons shalt thou redeem' (Ex. xiii. 12f.; cf. Nu. xviii. 15–17). The firstborn belong to the Lord; they should be sacrificed to Him upon the altar. But in certain cases it is permitted, or required, to offer a substitute in lieu of the forfeited life, and this idea of a substitute is basic to pdh. All the other uses may be seen to arise out of this one.

Arising out of Yahweh's claim to the firstborn is the taking of the Levites in the stead of the firstborn (Nu. iii. 40ff.). As there were more firstborn Israelites than Levites, the excess, numbering 273, were redeemed by a payment of five shekels apiece (Nu. iii. 46). There can be no doubt as to the substitutionary nature of the transaction, 'And thou shalt take the Levites for me (I am the Lord) instead of (tahath; LXX ἀντί) all the firstborn among the children of Israel' (Nu. iii. 41).

It is quite in harmony with this usage that we find the word applied to the redemption of a slave-concubine, Ex. xxi. 8; Lv. xix. 20. The Exodus passage says that, when a man is displeased with such a concubine, 'then shall he let her be redeemed', and the contention that this means he shall simply release her seems to

---

[1] Cf. Westcott on Hebrews, p. 298: 'It cannot be said that God paid to the Egyptian oppressor any price for the redemption of His people. On the other hand the idea of the exertion of a mighty force, the idea that the "redemption" costs much, is everywhere present. The force may be represented by divine might, or love, or self-sacrifice which become finally indentical'. So also F. J. Taylor: 'the idea of payment is not wholly forgotten' (TWBB, p. 186).

be negatived by the alternative way in which she may become free mentioned in verse 11 where it is expressly said that it is 'for nothing, without money'.

In many of these cases it is open to the individual concerned to redeem or not as he sees fit. There is no element of obligation, as there would be in *g'l* (which implies that there is a family duty to be performed). In line with this, anyone at all can perform the redemption indicated by *pdh* in almost every case, so that this verb may imply an element of grace.[1]

There are some passages where Yahweh is the subject of the verb, the deliverance from Egypt being thus described as in 2 Sa. vii. 23, '. . . thy people, which thou redeemedst to thee out of Egypt, from the nations and their gods'. (See also Dt. vii. 8, ix. 26, xiii. 5, xv. 15, xxiv. 18; 1 Ch. xvii. 21; Ps. lxxviii. 42, etc.). Redemption from the exile is not often referred to by this verb, but it does occur (see Is. xxxv. 10, li. 11). There are a number of passages where Yahweh's redemption is spoken of without any particular occasion being specified, as in Ho. vii. 13, 'Though I would redeem them, yet they have spoken lies against me' (see also Dt. xxi. 8; Ne. i. 10; Is. i. 27; Je. xxxi. 11). Similar are passages referring to redemption from 'the power of the grave' (Ho. xiii. 14), 'all his iniquities' (Ps. cxxx. 8), 'all his troubles' (Ps. xxv. 22). There are also places where the verb is used of redemption of the individual, as 2 Sa. iv. 9; Jb. v. 20, xxxiii. 28; Pss. xxxi. 5, lxix. 18, cxix. 134, etc.

A superficial reading of these passages might lead to the conclusion that redemption here means nothing more than deliverance but, as we saw in the case of *g'l*, there is usually the underlying thought that Yahweh is bestirring Himself on His people's behalf; it is no ordinary activity that is thought of. Thus the psalmist complains, 'They remembered not his hand, nor the day when he redeemed them from the adversary. How he set his signs in Egypt, and his wonders in the field of Zoan' (Ps. lxxviii. 42, 43); Nehemiah prays, 'Now these are thy servants and thy people, whom thou hast redeemed by thy great power, and by thy strong hand' (Ne. i. 10); and David can say, 'What one

---

[1] Cf. TWNT, IV, p. 333. Yet this element of grace ought not to be set in too sharp an antithesis to the obligation implied in *g'l*. From Ru. iii. 13, iv. 4–6, it is clear that the *go'el* might refuse to carry out the act of redemption.

nation in the earth is like thy people, even like Israel, whom God went to redeem unto himself for a people, and to make him a name, and to do great things for you, and terrible things for thy land. . . .?' (2 Sa. vii. 23). Even more impressive than specific quotation is the general implication of many passages that Yahweh was putting forth His mighty power on behalf of those He loved when He redeemed them. In the face of this evidence it seems impossible to deduce that the word has become a mere synonym for 'deliver', though it may well be held that the thought of deliverance is prominent. We must feel that there was a real reason for the choice of this word to describe the divine activity, and this might be given in the words of the Oxford Lexicon, that when Yahweh is the subject there is the 'underlying thought of payment'.[1]

c. Kopher

The noun *kopher* means a ransom price, and upon every occasion on which it is used it can be shown that there is the thought of a payment to be made. In its biblical usage it refers to the sum paid to redeem a forfeited life. The only places where this meaning is not compelled by the context are 1 Sa. xii. 3 and Am. v. 12, both of which refer to bribes; and even here Herrmann would keep open the possibility that not bribes in general are meant, but the wrongful reception of ransom from those whose lives were forfeit.[2]

---

[1] The meaning of the word may be illustrated by its treatment by the LXX translators. They render it by λυτρόω forty-three times, and a further four times by its cognates (λύτρον twice, λύτρωσις and ἀπολυτρόω once each), by ἀλλάσσω three times, by ῥύομαι four times, by ἀφορίζω once, while in Nu. xviii. 16 it is not translated, and in 1 Sa. xiv. 45 προσηύξατο looks like a paraphrase. The overwhelming preponderance for λυτρόω, etc., indicates clearly that they recognized the meaning 'redeem' as the essential meaning of the root.

There are a few other words from the same root, but they simply confirm the picture gained from *pdh*. Thus the noun *pedhuth*, defined by BDB as 'ransom', occurs four times, of which Ex. viii. 23 seems a textual error (the verse reads 'and I will set *pedhuth* between my people and thy people'), and the other three (Pss. cxi. 9, cxxx. 7; Is. l. 2) are all used of Yahweh's redemption of His people. *Pidhyon* (Ex. xxi. 30; Ps. xlix. 9) and *pidhyom* (Nu. iii. 49 and perhaps 51) both refer clearly to the payment of a ransom price for deliverance.

[2] His words are, 'When in 1 Sa. xii. 3 the aged Samuel can testify that he has taken no *kopher* (LXX: ἐξίλασμα), it is not at all certain from the context whether there is meant here also "atonement money for a condemned life", but at the least it says nothing to the contrary. The same is true of Am. v. 12'.

2

The first occurrence of the noun shows us a typical usage, for we read in Ex. xxi. 28ff. of the man whose ox has gored another man, and whose life is forfeit in accordance with the ruling 'the ox shall be stoned, and his owner also shall be put to death', but who is permitted to redeem his life by paying a *kopher*, a sum of money 'laid on him'. We see the essential meaning also in the account of the institution of the half shekel tax at the census. 'When thou takest the sum of the children of Israel, according to those that are numbered of them, then shall they give every man a *kopher* for his soul unto the Lord' (Ex. xxx. 12). Here the thought is that there would be plague among the people unless the command of Yahweh was complied with—the *kopher* was accepted as substitute for the life that would otherwise perish in the plague. Similar examples are Jb. xxxiii. 24, where the imagery points us to a *kopher* which delivers from 'going down to the pit' ('the price paid in lieu of forfeiting life'[1]); Jb. xxxvi. 18, with the difference that the sufferings of the patriarch are here thought of as the payment which delivers ('the severity of your sufferings, which form the ransom or price, which God will accept in lieu of your life'[2]); Pr. xiii. 8, where a man's riches are thought of as the ransom of his life; Pr. xxi. 18, where 'the wicked is a ransom for the righteous'[3]; and Is. xliii. 3, noteworthy as the one occasion when the word is used of Yahweh's deliverance of His people, and where the ransom price is explicitly mentioned, 'I have given Egypt as thy ransom, Ethiopia and Seba for thee'. The thought of substitution is plain, as Herrmann notes: 'In Is. xliii. 3, 4 the thought of substitution is clearly bound up with *kopher*; Egypt and the neighbouring kingdoms serve as substitutionary ransom price (*substitutives Lösegeld*) for Israel; that life for life is thereby meant is expressly said in verse 4'.[4]

[1] Driver and Gray (I.C.C.), p. 291.

[2] *Op. cit.*, p. 313; similarly Gibson quotes Delitzsch as referring to 'the ransom which is required of him as the price of restoration'. Comm. *in loc.*

[3] Toy (I.C.C.) says: 'The form of the couplet suggests the sense that the righteous would, in the ordinary course of justice, be punished, but that God takes the wicked as his substitute' (p. 406). He rejects that as 'too crude a conception', but he insists that the passage speaks of a 'substitution' thus bringing out the force of the *kopher*.

[4] TWNT, III, p. 303.

For the sake of completeness we must notice that there are some circumstances wherein no *kopher* can avail. Thus '. . . ye shall take no *kopher* for the life of a manslayer, which is guilty of death: but he shall surely be put to death' (Nu. xxxv. 31); and again, when a man who has fled to a city of refuge after an accidental killing wants to return to his possession, 'ye shall take no *kopher* for him' (Nu. xxxv. 32). The impossibility of a man finding a ransom which would deliver from death is the thought behind the *kopher* in Ps. xlix. 8, while in a different sphere, an outraged husband will not accept a *kopher* from the adulterer (Pr. vi. 35).

From these examples we see that this word necessarily involves thought of a ransom price, a substitute, this being demanded by every occurrence of the term. The force of this should not be overlooked in estimating the significance of λύτρον in the LXX, for, as Procksch remarks: 'As translation of *kopher*, then, λύτρον (α) always means a substitute-gift (*Ersatzgabe*), whose worth avails as covering for a debt, so that the debt is not simply struck out'.[1]

The investigation of the ideas conveyed by the three main word groups which the λύτρον words translate in the LXX shows us that redemption consistently signifies deliverance by payment of a price. There may be other ideas, like that of family obligation in *g'l*, or the element of grace in *pdh*, but as a stubborn substratum in every case is the basic price-paying conception.

We saw that the idea of the price paid tends to fade when Yahweh is the subject of the verb, but that, nevertheless, it does not disappear, for there is reference to price in the insistence that Yahweh's redemption is at the cost of the exertion of His mighty power. Moreover it should not be overlooked that, now and then, the thought of the ransom comes to the surface. Thus in Is. xliii. 1ff. we read, 'Fear not, for I have redeemed thee; . . . For I am the Lord thy God, the Holy One of Israel, thy saviour; I have given Egypt as thy ransom, Ethiopia and Seba for thee', and in verse 4 comes 'I will give men for thee'. So in Ps. lxxiii (lxxiv). 2, 'Remember thy synagogue which thou acquiredst (or perhaps, purchasedst, ἐκτήσω) in the beginning; thou redeemedst the

[1] TWNT, IV, p. 330.

rod of thine inheritance', and Is. lii. 3, 'For thus saith the Lord, you were sold for nothing, and you will not be redeemed with money'. In these last two passages it would seem that it is just as impossible to have redemption without a price as a sale. Both terms may be used metaphorically, but that should not blind us to their essential significance, which is what gives them their force in these metaphorical passages.

The general picture then is quite clear. The LXX usage is such as to leave us in no doubt but that λύτρον and its cognates are properly applied to redemption by payment of price, and though the idea of price might fade when God is the subject, it never disappears. Particularly clear is the connection of λύτρον itself with price, for there is no occurrence of the word in the LXX without a price being expressed or clearly implied. We can confidently say that, in as far as the New Testament writers were imbued with the LXX outlook, they must have had in their minds some idea of deliverance by payment of price when they used the words of this word group.

III. REDEMPTION IN JUDAISM

All three Hebrew roots that we have seen employed in the Old Testament to express the idea of redemption are employed in much the same way in the Rabbinic literature. Thus $g'l$ is in use for redemption of property (Arak. ix. 1, 2, 3, 4, etc.) and for things dedicated to the Lord (Arak. vii. 3, 4, 5, etc.). If anything, the use of the term with regard to the deliverances effected by the Lord increases, and we find mention not only of past deliverances such as that from Egypt (e.g. Pes. x. 6), but also there is frequent mention of a future deliverance when Israel's troubles will be over. We might cite the seventh of the Eighteen Benedictions as a typical example of this. 'Look but upon our affliction and fight our fight and redeem us speedily for the sake of Thy name: for Thou art a strong redeemer. Blessed art Thou, O Lord, the Redeemer of Israel'. Here we can discern the same idea of cost in the exercise of mighty power that we have already noted in the Old Testament; but it must be admitted that the use of the term tended to become conventionalized, so that it is not always possible to insist upon this. A feature of the usage which cannot fail to have influenced Christian terminology is its association with the Messiah, who is often seen as the great Redeemer of the glorious future.[1]

Pdh is in regular use for redemption of various kinds. Thus it refers to redemption of produce (Men. x. 4), spoil (Sanh. x. 6), second tithe (B.M. iv. 8), dedicated goods generally (Arak. vi. 2), goods belonging to the Temple (Meil. vi. 2), animal offerings (Hul. x. 2). It was also the regular word for ransoming persons, especially prisoners of war, a duty which the Jews rated highly (see Kid. iii. 8; Git. iv. 9; A. Zar. iii. 9; Ket. i. 2, etc.).

Kopher features largely in certain parts of the Talmud as the technical term for the ransom price which a man must pay to redeem his life when it becomes forfeit after his ox has gored a man (Ex. xxi. 30), and in other similar cases. The idea of providing a *kopher* for the release of another may lie behind the recurring expression 'May I be an atonement for you', wherein one expresses his readiness to suffer on behalf of another. That the idea of payment for release had penetrated deeply into the Jewish consciousness is shown in the interpretation of Dt. xxv. 11, which, as Danby points out, was 'the basis of the imposition of damages for "indignity". The penalty "thou shalt cut off her hand" is interpreted to mean, "she shall pay a money-fine".'[2]

It is true that in some Jewish writings the idea of redemption by payment seems to have receded somewhat. Thus Sirach uses the verb five times, and in none of them can we say that a payment is necessary, although possibly there is still the idea of God redeeming by the expenditure of effort regarded as a cost (see Sir. li. 2, 3). But that the words of this group still retained their essential significance is seen, for example, by the frequency with which such a writer as Josephus uses λύτρον for the ransom paid for the redemption of prisoners of war.[3] There is an interesting use of the ransom idea in En. xcviii. 10, 'wherefore do not hope to live, ye sinners, but ye shall depart and die; for you know no ransom', a passage reminiscent of Ps. xlix. 7–9.

---

[1] Cf. G. F. Moore, *Judaism*, Harvard, 1927–30, II, p. 298, and *Jewish Encyclopedia*, Art. Go'el.

[2] *The Mishnah*, Oxford, 1933, p. 342, n. 8.

[3] See for example the passages listed in TWNT, IV, p. 341.

Summing up then, we may say that Judaism, subsequent to the Old Testament, continued to use the three redemption word groups we found in the Old Testament in much the same manner as the canonical books, while the writers in Greek recall the usage of the LXX, although there is a tendency sometimes to use the words with more emphasis on deliverance than on payment of price. Development there was, and extension of usage in both Greek and Hebrew terms, but the basic thought in most writings continues to be that of deliverance by payment of price.

IV. THE λύτρον WORD GROUP IN NON-BIBLICAL GREEK

Both in classical authors and in common speech the words of this group were closely associated with the redemption of prisoners of war, the release of slaves and similar processes. So common was this that Deissmann can say 'when anybody heard the Greek word λύτρον, "ransom", in the first century, it was natural for him to think of the purchase-money for manumitting slaves'.[1] Deissmann refers to the practice of fictitious purchase of the slave by a god, whereby the slave himself provided the price of his release out of his own meagre earnings, first paying it into the temple treasury, and then being bought by the god. Technically he was still slave to the god, and sometimes a few pious obligations were laid upon him to remind him of the fact, but as far as men were concerned he was free. Deissmann gives the usual formula in such manumissions:

'Date. "N.N. sold to the Pythian Apollo a male slave named X.Y. at a price of —— minae, for freedom (or on condition that he shall be free, etc.)." Then follow any special arrangements and the names of the witnesses'.[2]

The actual term λύτρον does not usually occur in these inscriptions but it was in regular use to describe the price paid.

Another form of manumission was by simple purchase, and Grenfell and Hunt describe the procedure as follows: 'The terms of freedom having been agreed upon by master and slave, a notification of the details of the transaction was sent to the

---

[1] *Light from the Ancient East*, London, 1927, p. 327.

[2] *Op. cit.*, p. 322.

agoranomus by the banker through whom the purchase money was paid, accompanied perhaps by his receipt for the payment. The slave was then presumably declared by the agoranomus to be free'.[1] A typical document of this type, dated A.D. 86, is translated by them thus:

'Chaeremon to the agoranomus, greeting. Grant freedom to Euphrosyne, a slave, aged about 35 years, born in her owner's house of the slave Demetrous. She is being set at liberty under Zeus, Earth, Sun, by ransom (ἐπὶ λύτροι[ς]) by her mistress Aloine, daughter of Komon, son of Dionysius, of Oxyrhyncus, under the wardship of Komon, the son of Aloine's deceased brother Dioscorus. The price paid is 10 drachmae of coined silver and 10 talents, 3,000 drachmae of copper. Farewell'.[2] Here we have explicit mention of the ransom, and the same is true of similar manumissions in documents 49, 722, in the same series.

It is quite obvious that manumission in its various forms was widely known throughout the world of the first century, and that λύτρον was in common use to describe the price paid for freeing a slave, and that this would be the most familiar usage of the term to Gentiles to whom much of the New Testament was originally written. Büchsel's criticism of Deissmann for thinking that Paul's use of redemption is to be found in the realms of manumissions,[3] must not be taken too seriously, for while it is true that if we are to understand the apostle's use we must examine his Epistles, it still remains that we cannot pass over contemporary usage. Nobody, writing to a group of Gentile Christians, could afford to overlook associations that would inevitably be evoked by the terminology used.[4]

Other usages of the term occur. Naturally enough it is used for the redemption of things as well as people, but this hardly calls for comment. An interesting use is that for an expiatory offering in the cultus of more than one deity, the idea being that sin had involved the worshipper in destruction, and he must redeem himself. Examples of this use are cited by Liddell and Scott,

[1] *The Oxyrhyncus Papyri*, London, 1898, I, p. 106.

[2] *Op. cit.*, p. 106.

[3] TWNT, IV, p. 358, n. 23.

[4] See also below, p. 49.

Ramsay, Steinleitner, etc. Rarely the word comes to mean 'recompense', but this is a metaphorical use easy to be understood in the light of the foregoing. Metaphorical uses occur also in Philo as when he speaks of the wise man as the 'ransom for the fool' (De Sac. xxxvii) or ' the aspirations of the reason to wisdom and knowledge' as 'ransom and first-born' for the man's life (Ibid. Loeb translation). But he brings out the force of ransom in the first passage by adding that the fool's existence 'could not endure for an hour, did not the wise provide for his preservation by compassion and forethought', and in the second the force of λύτρα is just as little destroyed by the metaphorical use as is that of πρωτοτόκος. In other words, while Philo is an incurable allegorizer he knows what λύτρον really signifies.

The derivative verb λυτρόω in the active usually conveys the meaning of 'to release on receipt of ransom' or it may mean 'to hold to ransom', while in the middle the sense is rather 'to secure release by payment of ransom, to redeem'. Moulton and Milligan note that this 'verb and its kindred are well established in the vernacular', and they quote a catena of passages ranging from P. Eleph. xix. 8 (Ptol.) and P. Par. xxii. 18 (c. B.C. 165) to a late fourth century A.D. Christian prayer. The meaning at bottom is the giving of a price in exchange for something, mostly that which was one's own and has somehow found its way into some-one else's possession. The derived noun λύτρωσις is rare in non-biblical Greek, and the lexicons cite but three occurrences, wherein the word seems to fit in with the general sense of the word group.

The compound ἀπολύτρωσις is likewise a rare word, and it is not cited, for example, in Moulton and Milligan. But for our purpose it is an important word since it is the characteristic New Testament word for redemption, and accordingly it will be well to examine the passages in which it does occur.

Plutarch uses the word in Pompey 24; 'Pipes and songs and drunkennesses all along the shore, and seizings of the persons of officers, and ransomings of captured cities were a reproach to the Roman governorship'. Here the word plainly means the accepting of money for the release of captured cities. There are two examples in the Epistle of Aristeas (12, 33), and in both cases it is the release of prisoners of war that is indicated, the ransom price being given in section 22 as twenty drachmas per man. We see the same sort of process in view when Philo tells us of a Laconian boy carried into captivity who 'judged that death was a happier lot than his present valueless life, and despairing of ransom, gladly put an end to himself' (Quod Omn. Prob. lib., 114, Loeb translation). It is not otherwise with the passage in Josephus where we read that 'the cost of ransoming them was more than four hundred talents' (Ant. xii. 27), the force of the word being made plain by the express mention of the ransom price. In Diod. Frag. lib. 37. v. 3 there is a reference to a manumission being arranged in an agreement between a slave and his masters, but before he could be liberated Scaevola intervened, and 'anticipating the ransoming . . . crucified him'.[2] The word is found in another record of manumission, namely in an inscription from Cos[1] dealing with the liberation of a slave, and here it is sometimes said that the word means only 'deliverance' because the same transaction is described also as ἀπελευθέρωσις. But this seems to be reading too much into it. Looked at from one point of view the manumission might well be called a liberation, but it is a liberation of a particular kind, namely by paying a ransom, and thus it may be defined with greater precision as an ἀπολύτρωσις. In view of the fact that the release takes place only after payment of a price there is no reason for thinking that the word has any other than its usual meaning here.

The only other passage I have been able to find in which the word occurs is Dn. iv. 30 which we dealt with earlier,[3] when we saw that a ransom price is mentioned in the context. Thus we see that in every one of the occurrences of this word outside the New Testament there is a ransom expressed or implied, and the word invariably denotes a process whereby a release takes place after a ransom price has been paid. There are no grounds for thinking that the word can be reduced to 'deliverance' in any of its occurrences outside the New Testament.

The corresponding verb ἀπολυτρόω is rarely met with. In form it would be well adapted to expressing the deliverance aspect of

---

[1] W. R. Paton and E. L. Hicks, *The Inscriptions of Cos*, Oxford, 1891, no. 29, p. 52.

[2] See also below, pp. 39f.   [3] See above, p. 11.

redemption, but in actual practice the word seems to differ little from λυτρόω, if anything the idea of ransoming being retained more definitely. Thus Warfield cites eight occurrences in non-biblical passages,[1] and shows that in the context in every case a ransom price is mentioned. The usage is similar in the LXX (Ex. xxi. 8; Zp. iii. 1), and in the letter of Aristeas (20). Thus in every passage in which the verb occurs it plainly bears the meaning 'to ransom'.

We see then, that in the Old Testament, in Rabbinic writers, and in profane authors, the basic idea of redemption is the paying of a ransom price to secure a liberation. Circumstances may vary for the word applies to the freeing of a prisoner of war, or of a man under sentence of death because his ox has gored a man, or of articles in pawn, or of a slave seeking manumission; but always there is the idea of payment of a ransom to secure the desired effect.

When God is the subject of the verb we noticed a difference, for it is inconceivable that He should pay a ransom to men, and in these passages there tends to be a greater stress on the idea of deliverance than on the means by which it is brought about. Yet even here we saw that the Old Testament writers were not unmindful of the meaning of the words they were applying to God's dealings with His people, for they think of Him as delivering at some cost. Clearly the metaphor was one with point.

V. THE λύτρον WORD GROUP IN THE NEW TESTAMENT

a. λύτρον

λύτρον is found twice only in the New Testament, namely Mt. xx. 28; Mk. x. 45, the latter passage reading 'For verily the Son of man came not to be ministered unto, but to minister, and to give his life a ransom for many (λύτρον ἀντὶ πολλῶν)'. The Matthean passage is essentially the same, there being but one unimportant verbal alteration.

---

[1] Plato, *Laws*, 919A; Demosthenes, 159, 15; Polybius 2.6.6, 22.21.8; Lucian (passage not documented); Plutarch, Pompey 24; Pantaenus, Strat. V. 40; Julian, Imp. Grat. vi, Teubner, I, 253.

The genuineness of the saying has been denied by some, in the face of the fact of its occurrence in Mark, generally admitted to be the oldest of the Gospels, and of the absence of textual doubts. Hastings Rashdall vigorously assails the passage,[1] and offers four main objections to its authenticity: (1) The critical words about ransom are absent from Lk. xxii. 26, 27. (2) The passage has every appearance of being an ecclesiastical or doctrinal gloss. (3) It is irrelevant to its context (this he regards as the strongest objection). (4) It is out of harmony with Christ's teaching as a whole. As other objectors do not seem to have anything of importance to add to this, we will take Rashdall's as the case against the passage.

The first point loses its force when we notice that Luke is not reporting the same incident as Mark. The Lukan narrative has to do with a dispute in the upper room as to which of the disciples was to be accounted the greatest; the Markan refers to the request of the sons of Zebedee for the chief places for themselves. Unless we can be sure that Luke is basing his narrative on that of Mark's different incident, or on another report of that incident, his employment or omission of the ransom terminology is completely irrelevant to the genuineness of the Markan passage. It must first be proved that Lk. xxii. 26, 27 and Mk. x. 45 go back ultimately to the same saying of Jesus, and this has not been done. That there are resemblances between the two is accounted for sufficiently by the likeness between the two occasions.[2]

The second objection is highly subjective, for what appears to be definitely a gloss to one mind, may well have the stamp of authenticity to another. Branscomb gives some evidence for the idea of a gloss with his contention that the ransom idea is 'almost completely absent from the Gospels elsewhere', and 'so frequent in Paul's writings as to account adequately for its expression here.'[3] But that the idea is not common in the Gospels need mean only that it is not the central point in Jesus' teaching about His death;

---

[1] *The Idea of Atonement in Christian Theology*, London, 1925, pp. 29–37, 49–56.

[2] Branscomb remarks: 'this was one of Jesus' most constant themes judging from the number of times and slightly varying forms in which the teaching occurs in the Gospels' (MNTC, *Mark*, p. 190).

[3] *Op. cit.*, p. 190f.

it certainly does not carry the implication that this saying cannot be authentic. The suggestion that the ransom idea is common in the Pauline writings can be received only with qualification. St. Paul never uses the word λύτρον in the extant Epistles, and, while he does make use of the redemption category, it is not as common as some would think, not nearly as common, for example, as that of justification. Another small point is that the language used is not what we should have expected in a doctrinal insertion, for the New Testament writers commonly use expressions like 'the blood' or 'the death' of Christ, rather than referring to the offering of life.

But Rashdall regards the next point as the strongest objection and we give it in his own words: 'Our Lord has been speaking of His death as a kind of service—a service which His disciples were to imitate. There is a sudden transition to a different order of ideas—which is then immediately dropped and in no way followed up or explained'.[1] But in the first place this is to demand in the words of Jesus a sense of rigid logic which is foreign to the atmosphere of the Gospels, and can be insisted upon only rarely if at all; and, in the second, the statement in the form given by Rashdall cannot stand, for our Lord has not been speaking of His death as a kind of service. He has been speaking of the necessity for humble service on the part of the disciples; 'whosoever would be first among you, shall be servant of all'. This He drives home by an appeal to His own purpose in coming to earth, namely that He might minister to others and ransom them at the cost of His life. If Jesus thinks of His death as service it does not seem illogical that He should explain, if only briefly, in what the service consisted, i.e. in being a ransom for many. The words about ransom may not be required by the immediately preceding words, but they follow on quite naturally.

The objection that the ransom saying is out of harmony with the teaching of Jesus as a whole does not seem tenable these days, if only because there is considerable agreement that Jesus saw in the prophecy of the suffering servant a picture of His vocation. If He thought of His mission as in any way comparable to that described in Is. liii then, clearly, it is congruous to refer to it as a

[1] Op cit., p. 51. He goes on to note that Loisy says: 'The idea of a life given in ransom belongs to another course than that of service'.

process of ransom. There are other relevant considerations, such as the repeated predictions of His death by Jesus, and the whole attitude that finally led to Calvary, so that this objection cannot be said to have any great weight.

Thus none of the objections urged against the saying can be said to be decisive. While it may be true, as W. Manson says, that 'It is not in our power to prove the authenticity of *any* word which tradition has ascribed to Jesus',[1] yet at the very least we can say, in the words of the same scholar, 'it will not do to pronounce it impossible or unlikely that Jesus, who saw his work and teaching to be fraught with critical significance for his nation, should think of his sacrifice in terms of an '*asham* for many, as completing and consummating the work—the conversion and redemption of the many—which he had sought by his life to effect.'[2] Most of us will feel that the authenticity of the ransom saying is as well established as the facts of the case make possible.

We now turn to the meaning of the terms used. We have seen that λύτρον in the LXX consistently denotes the payment of a ransom price substitutionary in character,[3] and the same we saw to be true of almost all the usages met with outside the Bible. While it is not impossible for the word to be used in a metaphorical sense, yet it should be recognized that this is rather unusual, and we are justified in demanding the strongest of evidence to remove a substitutionary meaning from a passage containing it.[4] In this case, so far from the context removing the substitutionary meaning, it actually reinforces it.

[1] *Jesus the Messiah*, London, 1943, p. 132.

[2] *Op. cit.*, p. 133. Manson's examination of the evidence (p. 131ff.) affords strong reason for accepting the genuineness of the ransom saying.

[3] Cf. MM.: 'It may be noted that in the LXX the word is always used to denote an equivalent'.

[4] Thus Steinleitner says that the sense of λύτρον in this passage is that of 'Loskaufgeld' (*Die Beicht in Zusammenhange*, Leipzig, 1913, p. 37). Similarly L. Pullan, 'The word "ransom" emphasizes not only the idea of freedom gained for the believer and the great value of the price paid, but also the truth that His life is a substitute offered for our life in profound sympathy. Nothing short of this will satisfy the natural sense of the words employed' (*The Atonement*, London, 1907, p. 101).

Scholars who have gone into the Semitic background of the ransom saying bring further evidence for the substitutionary conception, whether we regard the Semitic equivalent for λύτρον in this passage as *pidhyon* with Dalman,[1] or as *kopher* with Procksch.[2] For Dalman understands ransom as 'substitute for the forfeited life', and Procksch speaks of a substitution-idea (*Stellvertretungsgedanke*) 'which is always given with *kopher*,[3] and again he says that by the equation *kopher*=λύτρον there is always meant 'a substitutionary-offering for a human life.'[4]

The preposition ἀντί characteristically has the meaning 'in the place of', 'instead of', whether in the classics or in the κοινή[5]. This remains true for biblical Greek, and Dana and Mantey draw attention to LXX passages such as 'and offered him up for a burnt offering in the stead of (ἀντί) his son' (Gn. xxii. 13), 'Let thy servant, I pray thee, abide instead of (ἀντί) the lad a bondman to my lord' (Gn. xliv. 33), and 'I have taken the Levites from among the children of Israel instead of (ἀντί) all the firstborn' (Nu. iii. 12). This usage they point out is continued in the New Testament; and they cite the statement that Archelaus reigned instead of (ἀντί) Herod (Mt. ii. 22), and the following phrases: 'and he for (ἀντί) a fish give him a serpent (Lk. xi. 11), 'for her hair is given her for (ἀντί) a covering (1 Cor. xi. 15), 'Jesus . . . who for (ἀντί) the joy that was set before him endured the cross' (Heb. xii. 2).[6] There are other passages which Dana and Mantey do not mention where the translation 'instead of' is more difficult, as in the 'evil for evil' passages (Rom. xii. 17; 1 Pet. iii. 9; 1 Thes. v. 15); though Büchsel would render the word even here by '*anstatt*',[7] or where ἀνθ᾽ ὧν or ἀντὶ τούτου are found. But

---

[1] *Jesus-Jeshua*, London, 1929, p. 118.

[2] TWNT, IV, p. 331, So, too, Orr in HDCG, II, 468, and he adds, 'most admit the connection'.

[3] *Op. cit.*, p. 330,

[4] *Op. cit.*, p. 330,

[5] See Liddell and Scott for the classical use, and MM for the κοινή. Cf. MM.: 'By far the commonest meaning of ἀντί is the simple "instead of".'

[6] *A Manual Grammar of the Greek New Testament*, 3rd Ed., reprinted, Edinburgh, 1944.

[7] TWNT, I, p. 373.

when full allowance has been made for passages of this sort it still remains that the most common meaning of the preposition, both inside the New Testament and out, is 'instead of' or 'in exchange for'.

The force of this is denied by some scholars. Thus C. Ryder Smith points out that ἀντί does not always denote substitution,[1] which may be granted, although it should be qualified by saying that such cases are comparatively rare, and must be regarded as the exceptions and not the rule. Rather strangely H. Wheeler Robinson says that 'the preposition *anti* means simply 'for',[2] but he may mean only that this is the meaning of the word in the ransom saying. Otherwise he has the lexicographers against him, and the usage in the overwhelming majority of the places where the word is found. He draws attention to Mt. xvii. 27 in support of his contention, but this is clearly an exceptional case. No one could deny that a weakening of the substitutionary force of the word occasionally occurs. But it cannot be too strongly insisted that, in order to determine the meaning of a word, we must take it in its habitual usage and not fasten our attention exclusively on unusual cases (here on one case only). If the term is to be emptied of substitutionary force in the ransom saying this will be done, not by showing that in unusual circumstances ἀντί may occur without stress on substitution, but only by bringing forward reasons for thinking that this passage uses the term in an unusual way. But in point of fact its use is perfectly normal, and there seems no reason for disputing the conclusion reached by Dana and Mantey when they say that, in the ransom saying, ἀντί must mean either 'instead of' or 'in exchange for', and 'each implies substitution'. They add *'The obscurity of this passage is not the result of linguistic ambiguity, but of theological controversy'.*[3]

But in any case even if, with Wheeler Robinson, we take the substitutionary meaning out of the preposition, we have not taken it out of the passage, for the situation envisaged is one in which the many are condemned, their lives are forfeit. If Jesus

[1] *The Bible Doctrine of Salvation*, London, 1941, p. 189.

[2] *Redemption and Revelation*, London, 1942, p. 229.

[3] *Ibid* (italics ours). Similarly F. J. Taylor says that the preposition 'suggests a substitutionary idea which is elsewhere expressed by reference to what Christ bore for men' (TWBB, p. 187).

gives His life 'a ransom for many' and thereby they are released from their condemnation, then a substitutionary transaction has taken place, understand the individual words as we will.[1]

The expression λύτρον ἀντί can be paralleled from Josephus who says, with reference to the visit of Crassus to the Temple, that a priest named Eleazar, seeing the Roman intent on plundering the sanctuary, gave him a bar of gold, λύτρον ἀντὶ πάντων (Ant. xiv. 107). There can be no doubt but that here a substitutionary meaning is to be attached to the expression—the bar of gold was to be a substitute for the treasures of the Temple. It is true that we are dealing in this situation with inanimate objects, but otherwise the saying is closely parallel to that in the Gospels, and it gives a presumption in favour of the substitutionary meaning.

Thus we have seen that there is no substantial reason for doubting the authenticity of the passage, and that the words, taken at their face value, contain a substitutionary meaning, indicating the offering of life for life quite in the style of Lv. xvii. 11.[2] Swete sees the key to the saying in Lv. xxiv. 18, 'The Lord contemplates a λύτρον which is ψυχὴ ἀντὶ ψυχῆς (Lv. xxiv. 18), His own ψυχή (xiv. 34) given as a ransom for the ψυχαί of men.'[3]

The force of the passage is sometimes evaded even by those who feel the force of the language. Thus Büchsel correctly gives the sense of the ransom saying: 'The ransom saying in any case includes a substitutionary concept. For one might interpret ἀντί as 'in place of' or 'for the benefit of': when Jesus gives Himself in

[1] This is brought out by Büchsel's comment: 'In Mk. x. 45: δοῦναι τὴν ψυχὴν αὐτοῦ λύτρον ἀντὶ πολλῶν the setting of ἀντὶ πολλῶν is dependent on λύτρον not on δοῦναι. Therefore ἀντί has the meaning a not b in the sense of Mt. xvii. 27 (He has already given the meaning a as 'instead of' and b as 'for the benefit of'). The life of Jesus thus given is the sufficient price for the ransoming of the many. But if one were to connect ἀντὶ πολλῶν with δοῦναι and understand it in sense b the saying retains the actuality of a substitutionary conception. For that which the many are condemned to forfeit is not a cherished possession, but their life, their self; and what Jesus gives is His life, His self. For their advantage He does nothing other than stand in their place' (TWNT, I, p. 373).

[2] Lods' comment on Lv. xvii. 11 reminds us of the ransom saying. 'It would seem from this passage that the life ("the soul") of the sinner is threatened by the holiness of God; he must give, as an equivalent, blood, that is a soul, a life. There is a ransom, a redemption, a death by proxy' (The Prophets and the Rise of Judaism, London, 1937, p. 294).

[3] Comm. in loc.

death there happens to Him what should happen to the many, He stands in their place. The saying clearly looks back to Mk. viii. 37, Mt. xvi. 26'.[1] Yet later he denies any objective equivalence between the death of Jesus and that which the many owe, and proceeds: 'The equivalence for God is to be sought in this, that Jesus' giving of life is the proof of His complete obedience, and as such, as power in mankind, overcomes sin.'[2] It is not called in question that Jesus' death is the proof of His full obedience to the Father, nor that this is important for the understanding of the atonement; but the point is that the passage does not say this. It cannot be derived thence by exegesis. The point of the saying is not that Jesus was obedient, and that this obedience is what benefits sinners, but that the life of Jesus was given up to ransom them.

Others again strongly dispute this interpretation on the grounds of context, which speaks of service, and they go on to suggest that any action here ascribed to Jesus must be such as can be emulated by His followers. Thus Gould likens the death of Jesus to that of the martyrs,[3] and Rashdall denies that there is anything to suggest that the benefit procured by the death of Christ 'was anything *sui generis*—different in kind from the benefit which the sufferings of other righteous men might obtain for them, or that the way in which it was to operate was by constituting an expiatory or substitutionary sacrifice'.[4] But such interpretation seems to lean too heavily on the context. For, after all, the context of a saying, while undoubtedly important, can indicate only in a

[1] TWNT, IV, p. 344, There are other strong statements about substitution in the same article, e.g. pp. 345, 346.

[2] *Op. cit.*, p. 348.

[3] Comm. *in loc.* (I.C.C.). His words are 'All that is required by the statement ... is that his life becomes the price by which men are freed from their bondage. The soldiers in the American civil war gave their lives as a λύτρον for the slaves, and every martyr's death is a λύτρον. There may be more than this involved in the death of the Redeemer, but more than this is not involved in his words here.'

[4] *Op. cit.*, pp. 35f. Similarly W. Russell Maltby: 'He lived and died serving; and the supreme service which He did for mankind was to die for them. In that context then, it was fitting to speak of His dying as the supreme example for us all to follow. But in all this there is no expiatory reference' (*Christ and His Cross*, London, 1936, p. 136). It may be freely admitted that Christ's death is 'the supreme service' but that does not mean that there is no thought of substitutionary ransom.

general way the drift of the saying; it cannot finally determine its meaning in detail. Moreover in this case there seems to be a tendency to undue limitation. If the death of Jesus is *sui generis* that does not mean that there are no aspects in which it can be imitated. There seems no particular reason why our Lord should not have directed the attention of the disciples to the aspects of self-abnegation and of service to others which are seen in His death, and then have gone on to indicate also that the supreme service lay elsewhere.

But the language used rules out such interpretations as those of Gould and Rashdall, as Montefiore recognizes; for though he rejects the ransom saying he gives its meaning thus: 'It is true that to give your life for others is the highest possible service (McNeile), but the word '*lutron*' seems to imply something more. Cf. 4 Macc. vi. 29, xviii. 22, i. 11, 2 Macc. vii. 37. God somehow makes the death of Jesus help in the salvation of others. It is in this more special sense that Jesus gives his own life for the sake of many lives.'[1] While we are not satisfied that this fully explains the passage, it yet carries a recognition that the interpretations we have been discussing will not fit the words used. As with λύτρον so with ἀντί;[2] both imply substitution, and we must interpret the passage in a highly unnatural manner if we are to overlook this. Again, the aorist tenses 'indicate that the allusion is not to a lifelong sacrifice but to one definitive act of self-surrender',[3] and this may be of importance. Finally, it is not seriously disputed that the critical words evoke memories of Is. liii and of the servant who suffered for many, and in this Old Testament passage the thought of substitutionary suffering is plain.[4]

---

[1] *The Synoptic Gospels*, London, 1927, I, 253.

[2] Cf. A. M. Hunter: 'It would be rash to find here a doctrine of the Atonement; yet the preposition used (ἀντί, "instead of") clearly implies substitution. . . . At the very least then, we must say (it seems to me) that the death of Jesus takes the place of " the many" ' (*The Work and Words of Jesus*, London, 1950).

[3] W. Manson, *op, cit.,* p. 131.

[4] 'The Idea of substitution which is prominent in Is. liii. 6, appears in the ransom saying' (A. M. Hunter, *op. cit.,* p. 100). Similarly W. Manson: 'The Son of Man here means Jesus on earth . . . and the claim is that he fulfils his vocation by accepting the sacrificial function of the Servant of the Lord who gives his life "in compensation for the sins of the people, interposing for them as their substitute" ' (*op. cit.* p. 131). The quotation is from BDB, p. 80.

To bring this discussion to a close: the natural meaning of the ransom saying is that Jesus' death was in the stead of the many, He was to give His life instead of their lives, and we see no reason for abandoning this interpretation. It may or may not be easy to integrate this into some theory of the way the atonement works, but either way we are not justified in evading the plain sense of the Greek.

b. λυτρόω

The first λυτρόω passage in the New Testament is the conversation on the way to Emmaus, where the two disciples say, with reference to Jesus, 'we hoped that it was he which should redeem Israel' (Lk. xxiv. 21). They clearly are using 'redeem' in the typically Jewish manner of the long awaited intervention by Almighty God, when His power would free His people from all their enemies and bring in a period of blessing and prosperity. The passage is not of first importance for our purposes; for clearly a redemption rendered impossible by the cross can tell us little about the redemption effected by the cross.

In Tit. ii. 14, however, we have a specifically Christian reference to redemption, for Christ, we read, 'gave himself for us, that he might redeem us from all iniquity'. The fairly obvious reference to the ransom saying of Mk. x. 45 points in the direction of substitution, and this is supported by the general usage of λυτρόω and by the specific mention of the ransom price ('gave himself').

Even clearer is the remaining passage, 1 Pet. i. 18, 19, for here the price of our redemption, which is given as 'the precious blood, as of a lamb without blemish and without spot, even the blood of Christ', is contrasted with such prices as 'gold or silver', so that there is no possibility of missing the reference to a normal process of redemption.[1]

It seems clear that only special pleading can rid these two passages of the thought of a ransoming. In each case we find the price mentioned and an evil condition from which the ransoming

---

[1] It should also be noted here that the manner of introducing the ransom price, 'the precious blood of Christ as of a lamb without blemish and without spot', brings us into the sphere of sacrificial thought. Whether the writer thought of sacrifice in general as in the nature of a ransom, he certainly conceived that the death of Christ was both a ransom price and a sacrificial offering.

has freed us. There is a substitutionary thought, for it is Christ, not the sinners, who has paid the price, so that He is acting in their stead in His redeeming death.

c. λύτρωσις

λύτρωσις like λυτρόω occurs three times in the New Testament, namely at Lk. i. 68, ii. 38 and Heb. ix. 12. The two former occurrences are used in the Jewish sense, just as we have seen is the case in Lk. xxiv. 21. Neither of these passages is of great importance for our present purpose.

When we turn to Heb. ix. 12 we find ourselves in a different sphere of thought altogether. Christ is pictured as a High Priest who, not 'through the blood of goats and calves, but through his own blood, entered in once for all into the holy place, having obtained eternal redemption', which brings us into the realm of sacrifice. But the sacrificial conception is blended with that of redemption, and 'his own blood' must be regarded as indicating the price of redemption, as well as pointing to the sacrificial process (cf. 1 Pet. i. 18, 19 for this blending of the sacrificial with the redemptive concept).

It may be well to notice here that, although the writer to the Hebrews does not speak often of redemption, yet the thought of cost to Christ in the securing of our salvation is one which is frequently met with in the Epistle. Perhaps this is nowhere more forcefully put than in Heb. v. 7, 8; 'in the days of his flesh, having offered up prayers and supplications with strong crying and tears unto him that was able to save him from death . . . learned obedience by the things which he suffered', a passage which, referring primarily to the agony in Gethsemane,[1] brings out strongly the cost element in the process of salvation. Our redemption was not purchased cheaply. This thought is to be discerned in the statement that 'it became him . . . in bringing many sons unto glory, to make the author of their salvation perfect through sufferings' (Heb. ii. 10). Again, there is the thought that Christ suffered through temptation (Heb. ii. 18 and see iv. 15), and it is said that He 'suffered without the gate' (Heb. xiii. 12). In similar vein are passages stressing the humiliation of the incarnation; He was made lower than the angels for the tasting of death

---

[1] See, for example, Westcott *in loc.*

(Heb. ii.9), He endured the cross despising its shame, and again, He endured the gainsaying of sinners (Heb. xii. 2, 3). Thus from many directions we see a stress laid on the cost of our salvation, and this should be borne in mind in estimating the thought of the writer with regard to redemption. Even when he is not using that exact term, he has the idea of cost that it denotes.

d. ἀπολύτρωσις

ἀπολύτρωσις is a very rare word, there being as far as we have been able to ascertain, only eight examples of its use outside the New Testament. Its structure could well give the thought of a 'ransoming away' with a corresponding emphasis on the result, the effective deliverance, rather than the mode whereby this is brought about, as Chrysostom notes.[1] But this cannot be pressed; for on the one hand we have the well-known fondness for compounded forms which characterizes the κοινή writers, and on the other λύτρωσις may be used for the most effective deliverance. See, for example, Heb. ix. 12, where the deliverance is as final as is possible, being 'eternal redemption'. Moreover the actual usage of ἀπολύτρωσις shows 'ransoming' rather than 'deliverance' to be the essential meaning of the word. In an earlier section we examined all the non-biblical passages in which the word occurs, and on each occasion we found that it signifies a process of obtaining release by payment of ransom, a process also indicated in every occurrence of the corresponding verb ἀπολυτρόω. This creates a presumption that in the New Testament it will continue to signify such a process.

The paucity of the occurrences of ἀπολύτρωσις in literature generally is somewhat in contrast with the New Testament where it appears as the typical term for redemption. It occurs ten times as against nine times for all the other words from the same root put together. This is in contrast too, with the usage of the LXX where ἀπολύτρωσις occurs but once, and that in a passage where there is no corresponding Hebrew word in the Massoretic text.

---

[1] Cf. his often quoted remark on Rom. iii. 24, καὶ οὐχ ἁπλῶς εἶπε λυτρώσεως, ἀλλ' ἀπολυτρώσεως, ὡς μηκέτι ἡμᾶς ἐπανελθεῖν πάλιν ἐπὶ τὴν αὐτὴν δουλείαν: 'And he said not simply "ransoming", but "ransoming away", so that we no more come again into the same slavery.' Chrysostom is not concerned here so much with the process as the result, and thus he stresses the preposition.

At the same time λυτρόομαι which is the characteristic representative of this family in the LXX with its ninety-nine occurrences, is found but three times in the New Testament, and one of these is not in the specifically Christian sense. This difference in terminology is not always noticed, and it is difficult to account for. We have noted in the section on the LXX that the usage there is a little away from the general run of Greek literature in that we have a number of passages (with God as the subject) where λυτρόομαι, etc., are used without a ransom being expressly implied. Accordingly it is just possible that the New Testament writers felt that the LXX usage was not quite what they wanted when they wished to express the redemption idea. Whether that is the explanation or not, it is beyond dispute that the terminology *is* different, and, therefore, to assume that the New Testament follows the LXX, as some writers do, is not justified. The New Testament must be allowed to speak for itself.

When we turn to the ten occurrences of the term ἀπολύτρωσις in the New Testament we find that the price is expressed three times and implied twice, on three occasions a future redemption with a certain eschatological significance is referred to, on one occasion the reference is perfectly general and there is one passage referring to a non-Christian redemption. Some writers (e.g. Büchsel, Abbott) make their point of departure one or other of the exceptional cases, but since we have seen a perfectly uniform usage outside the New Testament it would seem preferable to deal first of all with passages which conform to this general scheme.

The three clearest passages are Rom. iii. 24, Eph. i. 7 and Heb. ix. 15. There has been discussion about each of these, of course, and it would be an overstatement to say that there is a generally accepted conclusion in any one of them. Nevertheless it is a fact that there is a redemption price mentioned in each case, and accordingly, unless the strongest of reasons can be put forward, we must conclude that here again we have the typical usage of the word group coming forward.

In Eph. i. 7 we read of Christ 'in whom we have the redemption through his blood, the remission of sins, according to the riches of his grace . . .' One would have thought that 'redemption through his blood' is a plain enough indication of the payment of a ransom price, but we find, for example, Abbott disputing this.

He says, rightly, that the verb ἀπολυτρόω 'signifies properly, not "to redeem" (λυτροῦσθαι), but to release on receiving a ransom' (though he should have noted that ἀπολυτροῦσθαι, as well as λυτροῦσθαι, means 'to redeem'). But when he goes on to consider the derived noun ἀπολύτρωσις, he cites a number of instances apparently to show that it is used to take up the sense of the active[1] and not of the middle, and says: 'As far as usage goes, then, it would seem that if we are to attach to ἀπολύτρωσις the idea of ransom, the word will mean "holding to ransom" or "release on receipt of ransom", not "payment of ransom".' But this is in error. To begin with the derived noun can just as well take up the sense of the middle as the active,[2] and there is no particular reason for thinking that the active will be favoured. Then Abbott has not subjected his examples to a sufficiently close scrutiny, for the passage he cites from Philo is clearly a case of the middle sense. When Philo says ἀπογνοὺς ἀπολύτρωσιν ἄσμενος ἑαυτὸν διεχρήσατο the meaning plainly is 'despairing of ransoming he cheerfully slew himself'. It cannot mean 'despairing of holding to ransom' because it is himself that is to be ransomed, not someone in his power. A similar criticism may be made of Abbott's failure to notice that Dn. iv. 30, ὁ χρόνος μου τῆς ἀπολυτρώσεως ἦλθε also bears witness to the release by payment of ransom[3] rather than by receiving ransom. Nebuchadnezzar was not holding anyone to ransom, but was referring to his own release from trouble when he used the words, and thus the sense is definitely that of the middle. Abbott also cites Diod. Frag. lib. 37. v. 3 where, after a

---

[1] The passages he notes are Plutarch, Pomp. 24, 2; Josephus, Ant. xii, 2, 3; Philo, Quod Omn. Prob. lib. 17; Diod. Frag. lib. 37, 5, 3; Dn. iv. 30.

[2] Thus Zahn says: 'It is not to be overlooked that according to circumstances the regular meaning of the act. λυτροῦν, ἀπολυτροῦν (dimittere) or that of the mid. λυτροῦσθαι, ἀπολυτροῦσθαι (redimere) lies at the basis, also the derived substantive denotes either the action of him who discharges, releases the imprisoned man from the hold, or the action of him who through the payment of a ransom price or even without this accomplishes the freeing of another who is in custody whether person or thing' (Der Brief des Paulus an die Römer, p. 179f.). Although he speaks of freeing without payment of a ransom it is noteworthy that he cites no examples of this, and it may be doubted whether there are such. Procksch also points out the dual meaning of ἀπολύτρωσις and gives it as his verdict that, in the Bible, it is used following the sense of the middle (TWNT, IV, p. 336).

[3] The ransom, namely almsgiving, is referred to in verse 24. See also above, p. 11.

certain slave had agreed with his owners for his manumission, Scaevola intervened, φθάσας τὴν ἀπολύτρωσιν . . . ἀνεσταύρωσεν. The meaning of ἀπολύτρωσιν here is doubtful, it makes quite good sense to understand 'anticipating release on receipt of ransom' i.e. interpreting ἀπολύτρωσιν from the point of view of the owners; but it can also be understood quite well in this context from the point of view of the slave, 'anticipating release by paying ransom'. The most that can be said is that this passage is congruous with the former meaning; it certainly does not establish it. The difficulty in determining which meaning is the correct one is illustrated by the fact that Abbott seems to take Jos. *Ant.* xii. 27[1] in the sense of the active, and Warfield[2] in the sense of the middle. Occurrences not treated in Abbott include the two references in Ep. Arist., both of which are probably in the middle sense, and the inscription from Cos dealing with a slave's manumission where, again, the middle gives good sense.

It does not seem possible, then, to maintain Abbott's position. The undisputed instances of ἀπολύτρωσις in the sense of 'holding to ransom, release on receipt of ransom' are reduced to the passage he cites from Plutarch, while all the other examples can bear the sense of 'release by payment of ransom', and some positively demand it. This being so, there remains no obstacle to interpreting Eph. i. 7 in the natural way and to understanding the passage as referring to Christ's redemption of believers through the price of His blood. Perhaps we may find a clue to the right interpretation in the passage from Romeo and Juliet which Abbott adduces, 'Before the time that Romeo come to redeem me'. Here unquestionably the word means 'deliver' and there is no thought of payment of price, but equally unquestionably it is not the normal English usage. The passage can be understood, but it is not a reliable guide to the understanding of the English verb. So is it with the idea of redemption in Greek. The basic meaning of the root is concerned with release by payment of a price, and while a metaphorical usage may appear it cannot be regarded as the standard. The price-paying conception is still in the background and it is this that gives force to the metaphor.

[1] Which, however, he cites as *Ant.* xii. 2, 3.

[2] *Princ. Theol. Rev.*, Apr. 1917, p. 213, n. 40.

The occurrence of ἄφεσιν in apposition with ἀπολύτρωσιν does not really alter this seriously, for it only indicates that there were many ways of looking at the work of Christ and that no one way was by itself satisfactory. We have already had occasion to notice that in some passages there is a conjunction of references to redemption and sacrifice (e.g. Heb. ix. 12, 1 Pet. i. 18, 19) and here we have a similar conjunction of redemption and forgiveness.[1]

Another attempt to evade the force of the passage is by referring τὴν ἀπολύτρωσιν here to the final eschatological deliverance. Concerning this it may be said that even if that is the interpretation of the passage it does not empty ἀπολύτρωσιν of its force. Rather it would emphasize that the eschatological aspect of redemption is dependent on the price paid on Calvary. The time of the redemption does not seem to have any real effect on the presence or otherwise of the implication of a ransom price. But is there any real reason for understanding this passage in an eschatological sense? It would seem not. The writer uses the present tense (ἔχομεν) and appears to be thinking of a redemption already brought about so that it is the present possession of the believer. There is no more reason for thinking that redemption here signifies something in the far future than there is for understanding remission of sins (to which it is joined) in the same way. It is, of course, true that redemption has a final aspect, and that we cannot regard our redemption as fully consummated here and now. Its final perfection must await the advent of the Lord. But it is just as true that the New Testament does not regard redemption as something that is only in the future (cf. 'ye were redeemed', 1 Pet. i. 18), and it is redemption as the present possession of the believer which occupies the attention of the writer here.

Rom. iii. 24 comes in a context which presents difficult problems, but as far as ἀπολύτρωσις is concerned the meaning seems to be clear. Paul is here making use of the redemption metaphor again, and once more we have the price mentioned in the context,

---

[1] Cf. the comment of C. H. Dodd on Rom. iii. 21-26; 'We find that he is combining three metaphors: the first taken from the law court—the metaphor of justification; the second taken from the institution of slavery—that of emancipation; the third taken from the sacrificial ritual of ancient religion—that of expiation by blood. Under all three metaphors he describes an act of God for men' (MNTC).

though in this case it is not formally joined to ἀπολύτρωσις. 'Being justified freely by his grace,' says the apostle, 'through the redemption that is in Christ Jesus: whom God set forth to be a propitiation, through faith, by his blood . . .' It is true that 'his blood' is more directly connected here with propitiation than with redemption, but there can be no doubt that there is also an indirect glance at the price paid, so that Moffatt is justified when he translates ἀπολυτρώσεως by 'ransom'. Sanday and Headlam come to a similar conclusion when on the idea of ἀπολυτρώσεως they say, '. . . we can hardly resist the conclusion that the idea of the λύτρον retains its full force, that it is identical with the τιμή, and that both are ways of describing the Death of Christ. The emphasis is on the *cost* of man's redemption.'[1]

The third passage where the thought of price is clear is Heb. ix. 15 where we read of a death taking place 'for the redemption of the transgressions that were under the first covenant'. The expression 'redemption of the transgressions' is unusual, but it does not modify the central thought, namely that the redemption spoken of is the result of the death which has taken place; indeed, the death took place for the very purpose of effecting this redemption. Thus the idea that Christ has paid the price of our freedom in His death is present in this passage also.[2]

[1] Comm. *in loc.* G. O. Griffith says: 'The idea of deliverance contained in the Pauline term is not merely the idea of liberation or release, but of deliverance effected on the initiative, and by the action, of Another' (*St. Paul's Gospel to the Romans*, Oxford, 1949, p. 80). This is a helpful comment, but in my judgment it needs to be supplemented by the thought that the deliverance is by that Other's taking the initiative in paying the price.

[2] The expression 'redemption of the transgressions' calls for some comment, and strange conclusions have sometimes been drawn from it as, for example, by Hofmann: 'It is the transgressions themselves which are regarded as having fallen under the wrath of God, and so liable to punishment, and as delivered from this fall and liability by the work of the Redeemer' (quoted by Delitzsch *in loc.*). But in Greek the genitive can express various relationships. Thus it has often been noted that τὴν μετοικεσίαν Βαβυλῶνος in Mt. i. 12 merely signifies 'a Babylon-removal', whether of, to or from Babylon the form does not and cannot say. But the context and our general knowledge of the position clears up any indefiniteness and the expression is seen to mean 'to Babylon'. So is it here. What is spoken of is a 'transgressions-redemption', and our knowledge of the general Christian context enables us to say that this means a redemption *from* transgressions. It is the transgressors, not the transgressions which are redeemed. Delitzsch has a helpful note *in loc.*

Of the other passages where the word occurs Eph. i. 14 must be taken in conjunction with Eph. i. 7. It is hardly conceivable that our author should use the one word in two completely different ways in the same context. (Actually, since the style is somewhat involved, the two occurrences of ἀπολύτρωσις are in successive sentences.) That is to say, since ἀπολύτρωσις bears its usual meaning in Eph. i. 7 it would be captious to urge that it has a different meaning in verse 14 unless some cogent reason can be found. But such does not appear.

The case is not otherwise with Col. i. 14 for this verse, as far as the reference to redemption is concerned, merely repeats Eph. i. 7, with the omission of the words referring to the price paid. If there is some compelling reason, we can of course say that the omission is significant and that ἀπολύτρωσις bears a different meaning here, but such a reason is not apparent. Indeed, the context favours a strict application of the ransom idea, for the metaphor of deliverance from captivity at the hand of a powerful enemy is being followed out. In verse 13 this takes place by the intervention of a stronger power defeating and overcoming the foe, but in verse 14 the metaphor changes from 'the victor who rescues the captive by force of arms (verse 13 ἐρύσατο) to the philanthropist who releases him by the payment of a ransom'.[1] There can be no reasonable doubt in view of the usage of Eph. i. 7 and the context in these other two passages that in these two cases also we are to think of a ransom being paid.

There are three passages wherein the thought is eschatological, namely Lk. xxi. 28, 'But when these things begin to come to pass, look up, and lift up your heads; because your redemption draweth nigh'; Rom. viii. 23, '. . . but ourselves also, which have the firstfruits of the Spirit, even we ourselves groan within ourselves, waiting for our adoption, to wit, the redemption of our body'; Eph. iv. 30, 'And grieve not the holy Spirit of God, in whom ye were sealed unto the day of redemption'. There can be no doubt that in each of these cases the redemption spoken of is something more than what believers have already experienced. Just as the Jews of that day (and of all succeeding ages right down to our own) looked forward to a 'redemption', so did the Christians. One day

---

[1] Lightfoot, *in loc.*

their Messiah would return to the earth and thus there would be a great 'redemption' which would be of the greatest concern to them all. The resemblances to the Jewish conception are striking. The wording, the assurance of deliverance, the association of the deliverance with the Messiah, the earnest looking forward to it, in all these points we have resemblance to the Jewish idea.

But before we conclude that this is just another example of the Jewish usage and equate ἀπολύτρωσις in these passages with deliverance, there are certain factors which must be considered. The first of these reminds us of the difference in terminology. The Jewish conception is expressed usually by λυτρόομαι, which, in two of its three New Testament occurrences, indicates clearly a ransoming with the price explicitly mentioned. The noun λύτρωσις would accord better with the Jewish idea, but the word used of this eschatological redemption is not λύτρωσις but ἀπολύτρωσις. This difference in terminology may or may not amount to much, but it is there, and as far as it goes it signifies a different idea.

But the great obstacle to believing that these passages refer simply to a final deliverance along purely Jewish lines lies in the fact that between the Old and the New Testaments stands the cross. The older writers spoke of a coming redemption, but without any precise idea of how God's Messiah would bring it about. The New Testament writers had in view a redemption purchased at the price of the precious blood. The words we have quoted must be interpreted in the light of the whole Christian experience of God's mighty intervention for man's salvation and not in isolation from it. As we read, for example, the glowing words of St. Paul it is impossible not to be struck by the fact that for him everything is to be estimated in the light of the cross which for him has made all things new. It is difficult to think of a reason why redemption in two passages should form an exception to this. On the contrary, it must surely be presumed that Paul could think of the Christian redemption only in the light of the cross, all the more so when there are undoubted examples in his writings of this sort of thinking.

It is, moreover, a definite strand in Christian teaching that salvation, although it is a present reality and not something which may, if all goes well, eventually be given to the believer, is nevertheless not capable of being realized in all its fulness here and now. Now we enjoy 'the earnest' of the Spirit, but only in the hereafter will the complete experience be possible. 'Beloved, now are we children of God, and it is not yet made manifest what we shall be' (1 Jn. iii. 2) is typical New Testament teaching, and it has its application to the concept of redemption. To speak of a future redemption is not to imply that there awaits us a redemption which has no relationship to that accomplished at Calvary, being simply a deliverance from some outward enemy in the typical Jewish style. On the contrary, the future redemption is the consummation, the outworking of the redemption which, viewed from another angle, was accomplished once for all by the death of the Redeemer. While there is no reason to doubt that the three passages we have quoted point to some further tremendous action of divine power, yet it still remains that it is only by taking them out of their context in Christian life and thought that they can be separated from the atonement wrought by Christ. The New Testament consistently bases our redemption on the payment of the price in the death on Calvary.[1]

There remain for consideration only 1 Cor. i. 30 and Heb. xi. 35. The former passage tells us that 'of him are ye in Christ Jesus, who was made unto us wisdom from God, and righteousness and sanctification, and redemption: that, according as it is written, He that glorieth, let him glory in the Lord'. There is nothing here which absolutely determines the sense of ἀπολύτρωσις, and we must take the meaning from general considerations, and from its meaning in other passages. If we are convinced from such other passages that ἀπολύτρωσις means nothing more than deliverance, then we shall naturally take the same meaning here,[2] but if we, from the other occurrences, feel that the word has a fuller meaning we shall find nothing to forbid us applying that fuller meaning in this context. Indeed, in the concluding words, with their

---

[1] Orr well remarks; 'Alike in his (i.e. St. Paul's) thought and that of St. Peter (cf. 1 Pet. i. 18f.), the idea of a λύτρον is involved in the conception of ἀπολύτρωσις. Redemption has the two aspects, which can never be separated—redemption by "ransom", i.e. from sin's guilt and condemnation; and redemption by power, from sin's bondage and other evil effects. The apostolic gospel comprehended both' (HDCG, II, p. 469).

[2] As Johannes Weiss does in his commentary, 'It is approximately=σωτηρία.'

implication of man's total inability to do anything meritorious in the sight of God, we shall find positive encouragement for thinking of a full meaning in redemption.[1]

The final passage deals with times of persecution, and speaks of various tortures which were inflicted upon the sufferers. The fate of individuals, however, varied, and the writer speaks of women receiving their dead by resurrection. But there were others who 'were tortured, not accepting the redemption', and this has been interpreted as simply meaning 'deliverance'. In the context this interpretation is not impossible, but it is certainly not demanded. There is no thought that the sufferers received an unconditional offer of freedom. On the contrary, their refusal of the redemption 'that they might obtain a better resurrection' certainly implies that there were conditions laid down, and such conditions as made it difficult or impossible to preserve their standing in the sight of God. In a word the context leads us to think that deliverance was offered to them only on condition of apostasy.

The kind of situation that is meant is found in the stories in 2 Macc. of the death of Eleazar (vi. 18f.) and of the seven brothers (vii. 1f.) The case of the youngest of these is especially to the point, and may even have been in the mind of the writer to the Hebrews. After six of the brothers had died refusing to accept deliverance at the price of apostasy, the tyrant exhorted the lad's mother to urge him to save his life. She, instead, urged him to remain constant, and finished her exhortation with the words: 'Fear not this butcher, but, proving thyself worthy of thy brethren, accept thy death, that in the mercy of God I may receive thee again with thy brethren' (2 Macc. vii. 29).[2] If it was this kind of choice the writer had in mind when he spoke of refusing the redemption in order to obtain a better resurrection, then his choice of the word ἀπολύτρωσις is peculiarly apt, for such a deliverance could be

---

[1] A. Schlatter speaks of ἀπολύτρωσις here as 'the ransom (*Loskauf*)', and follows out the metaphor by saying 'through which the condemnation to death is taken from the congregation' (*Paulus der Bote Jesu*, Stuttgart, 1934, p. 97).

[2] Cf. the last words of the second brother: 'Thou cursed miscreant! Thou dost despatch us from this life, but the King of the world shall raise us up, who have died for his laws, and revive us to life everlasting'. (verse 9).

bought only at a considerable price. It appears then, that there is nothing in this passage to disturb the conclusions we have hitherto reached.

From our examination of the occurrences of ἀπολύτρωσις it would seem then, that everything depends on the way we approach the question. If we forget the intrinsic meaning of the word, and begin with one of the more metaphorical examples we may be able to build up quite a case for believing that in the New Testament the word has been emasculated.[1] But if, rather, we seek first to find out what the word means in itself, and then approach the New Testament to see whether it uses the term in the usual fashion or whether it whittles down its significance, it appears that the first Christians were no less colourful in their language than other men, and that in every case ἀπολύτρωσις may be allowed to have its natural meaning. This latter seems the better way of proceeding.

It is sometimes urged in support of the idea that redemption is a rather colourless conception for the early Christians that it has become a technical term for them, and that thereby it has taken to itself a meaning which it holds nowhere else. Thus Büchsel says: 'The word ἀπολύτρωσις has become in early Christianity an expression with a religious content and has thus acquired a special meaning which is not found outside the same', and he goes on to speak of ἀπολύτρωσις as a 'terminus technicus'.[2] But it is difficult to see how this position can be made good. After all a technical term, to be understood, must be accepted by those to whom it is addressed as a technical term. It must be in use in the entire circle, or if used by one man only it must be explained by him, or, at the very least, used by him so frequently in the technical sense that there can be no doubt as to his meaning. He just cannot take a word with a known significance, give it a new meaning all his own, and use it occasionally in the new sense without explanation.

---

[1] Cf. Büchsel's comment that the etymological meaning of ἀπολύτρωσις is 'in Biblical usage "wiped out" ' (TWNT, IV, p. 358). So too, C. Anderson Scott says, 'for the most part the meaning is weakened to simple deliverance' (*Christianity According to St. Paul*, Cambridge, 1927, p. 28).

[2] TWNT, IV, p. 358.

But if Büchsel is right, it is precisely this of which we must accuse Paul! What sort of technical term is it about which it can be said (in Büchsel's own words) 'ἀπολύτρωσις does not belong to the leading ideas of the first Christian preaching and teaching. It is completely absent from Mk.-Mt., John, the Catholic epistles and the Apocalypse. Its occurrence in Lk. is rare. In Paul it cannot compare in importance with δικαιοσύνη or καταλλαγή'? To take up such a position seems to be to avoid the issues raised by the redemption idea. There can be no doubt as to the significance of this word group, and there can be no doubt that the normal significance will fit in well with the New Testament passages.

e. ἀντιλύτρον

This word occurs but once in the New Testament and its only known occurrences outside the Scripture are later. In meaning it does not seem to differ greatly from the simple λύτρον, but the preposition emphasizes the thought of substitution; it is a 'substitute-ransom' that is signified. Such a term well suits the context, for we read of Christ 'who gave himself on behalf of all' (1 Tim. ii. 6). The thought clearly resembles that of Mk. x. 45[1], i.e. that Jesus has died in the stead of those who deserved death.[2] If the thought of substitution is there, we find it here to an even greater degree in view of the addition of the preposition which emphasizes substitution.

The position then appears to be that the words associated with λύτρον consistently express the ransom idea. They remind us of a conception that has disappeared, at least in large measure, from the modern scene, but which appealed to the early Christians as of value in illustrating one aspect of a vast and complex subject. Viewed from this aspect the atonement looked to them like a process of ransoming. Christians were men who had been under

---

[1] Cf. Büchsel, TWNT, IV, p. 351.

[2] Cf. Orr in HDCG, II, p. 469: ' "Ransom" has here its true and proper sense of "a price paid in exchange", and the ideas of "ransom" and expiatory sacrifice flow together in the unity of the thought of redemption through Christ's reconciling death'.

sentence of death (Rom. vi. 23), they had been enslaved to sin (Jn. viii. 34; Rom. vi. 17, vii. 14); but now they were ransomed from the death sentence (free 'from the law of death', Rom. viii. 2, and cf. I Cor. xv. 54f.; I Jn. iii. 14; 2 Tim. i. 10, etc.).[1] Processes which were familiar to them from their ordinary daily life gave a vivid picture of what had been happening in the spiritual realm when the Saviour gave His life for them.

Deissmann brings out the force of the redemption terminology for an ordinary man of the first century thus:

'A Christian slave of Corinth going up the path to the Acrocorinthus about Eastertide, when St. Paul's letter arrived, would see towards the north west the snowy peak of Parnassus rising clearer and clearer before him, and everyone knew that within the circuit of that commanding summit lay the shrines at which Apollo or Serapis or Asclepius the Healer *bought slaves with a price, for freedom.* Then in the evening assembly was read the letter lately received from Ephesus, and straightway the new Healer was present in spirit with His worshippers, giving them freedom from another slavery, *redeeming with a price* the bondmen of sin and the law—and that price no pious fiction, first received by Him out of the hard earned denarii of the slave, but paid by Himself with the redemption money of His daily new self-sacrifice, rousing up *for freedom* those who languished in slavery'.[2]

There is no need to water down the language of the biblical writers, to reduce their colourful metaphors to a uniform drabness. They did not intend ransom to be taken as a full and sufficient statement of what the atonement was and did, but as far as it goes it gives a picture of one aspect of that great work. It is a metaphor which involves the payment of a price which is plainly stated in several places and understood in others to be the death of Christ. From the very nature of the imagery being used this involves a substitutionary idea; instead of our death there is His, instead of our slavery there is His blood, and all our verbal juggling cannot remove this from the New Testament.

[1] In the Scripture men are spoken of as slaves with regard to sin (Rom. vi. 17), to men (I Cor. vii. 23), corruption (Rom. viii. 20), the rudiments or elemental spirits of the world (Gal. iv. 3), while the Gentiles are said in addition to be slaves to their gods (Gal. iv. 8).

[2] *Light from the Ancient East*, London, 1927, p. 329.

VI. THE USE OF ἀγοράζω

The word originally meant 'to frequent the forum' from which eventually the meaning 'to acquire, to buy in the forum' evolved, and this remains the standard meaning of the verb (though the connection with place, the forum, disappears). It is a usual word for 'to buy', and in this sense it is used in the New Testament twenty-four times with reference to such matters as a field (Mt. xiii. 44) or food (Lk. ix. 13). But on six occasions Christians are said to be 'bought' and our concern is with these passages.

The Septuagint does not appear to help us greatly, as all the references there seem to be to simple commercial purchase of such items as food (Gn. xli. 57, xlii. 5, 7, etc.), a threshing floor (1 Ch. xxi. 24), etc. It translates the Hebrew roots *shbr* and *qnh* mainly, with one or two sporadic appearances of other roots which shed no light on our inquiry.

In Hellenistic Greek the usage for purchasing in general is quite common and a particular application which calls for comment is that in which the word refers to the buying of slaves (see for example P. Oxy. 1149), a close parallel to the New Testament passages we are considering. The word does not occur as far as I know in connection with manumissions, but τιμῆς (price) which is used with this verb in 1 Cor. vi. 20, vii. 23, is so frequently used in this connection that Deissmann can call it 'quite a stereotyped expression'.[1]

If the conception that Christians have been bought fits in with the customs of the Greek-speaking world, it is no less at home in a Jewish setting as the following parable from the Midrash Sifre on Numbers shows. 'It can be likened unto a king whose friend's son was taken prisoner. The king redeemed him, but expressly upon the understanding that he should become his slave, so that at any time, if he should disobey the king, the latter could say: "Thou art my slave!" As soon as they came into a country, the king said to him: "Put my sandals on for me! Take my clothes to the bathhouse!" That son (of the king's friend) began to protest. And the king took out the bill of sale and said to him: "Thou art my slave!"'[2] The Midrash goes on to point out that in similar

---

[1] *Op. cit.*, p. 324, n. 2.
[2] *Midrash Sifre* on Numbers 115 (trans. P. Levertoff, p. 110).

fashion Jehovah did not redeem the Israelites 'with the view that they should be (His) sons, but (His) slaves'.

When Paul then says, 'ye are not your own; for ye were bought with a price' (1 Cor. vi. 19, 20), or again, 'he that was called, being free, is Christ's slave. Ye were bought with a price; become not slaves of men' (1 Cor. vii. 22, 23), he is not drawing our attention to quite the same aspect of the Christian life as when he uses the redemption words we have considered hitherto. With them the emphasis is on the final freedom of the redeemed; here it is rather on the truth that the redeemed are paradoxically slaves, the slaves of God, for they were bought with a price. This thought is a necessary supplement to the former one, for the Christian idea of redemption is not that believers are brought into a liberty of selfish ease. Rather, since they have been bought by God at terrible cost, they have become God's slaves, to do His will.

This conception is used to bring out the heinousness of sin in 2 Pet. ii. 1 where the writer denounces false prophets 'who shall privily bring in destructive heresies, denying even the Master that bought them'. Having been bought by the Master, they were His and their lives should have been lived to His glory, and it is only against this background that their sin can be seen in all its vileness. There is also probably a contrast between their faithlessness and the love of Christ who paid such a price in love for them.

The divine ownership as a result of purchase comes out also in Rev. v. 9, 10, 'thou wast slain, and didst purchase unto God with thy blood men of every tribe, and tongue, and people, and nation, and madest them to be unto our God a kingdom and priests', while the one hundred and forty four thousand are redeemed 'from the earth' and 'from among men', and are spoken of as 'the firstfruits unto God and unto the Lamb' (Rev. xiv. 3, 4). In each case it is clear that those so purchased are in a special relationship to God, and it is this which determines their conduct.[1] In passing we might note that this thought is to be found in many passages

---

[1] The Hebrew *be*, denoting price, is probably behind the ascription in Rev. i. 5, 'to him that loves us and loosed us from our sins ἐν τῷ αἵματι αὐτοῦ', in which case the sense of the passage is as Denney says, 'Christ's blood was the cost of our liberation, the ransom price which He paid' (*The Death of Christ*,
[continued on p. 52]

which do not make explicit use of the redemption or purchase terminology, as for example when Christians are said to be 'slaves' of God or of Christ.

This way of regarding the atonement stresses the new life in Christ. It is because we are Christ's slaves that we are introduced into this way of living, and we are His slaves because we were bought by Him. There is no stress on substitution in this conception except to the extent that a price paid is an equivalent for the thing purchased. The main emphasis is on the fact that the redeemed are God's.

VII. THE USE OF ἐξαγοράζω

The preposition modifies the force of the uncompounded verb and we find ἐξαγοράζω used broadly in two senses, the one 'to redeem' (occurring for example in Diod. xxxvi. 1 with reference to the redemption of a handmaid)[1] and the other 'to buy up', but this need not detain us as it is the former usage that we have in the two New Testament passages in which this verb is used of the atonement.

The first of these is Gal. iii. 13: 'Christ redeemed us from the curse of the law, having become a curse for us'. Two questions in particular are raised here, namely, how the curse is considered to rest upon men, and how it is thought of as resting on Christ.

The first question is comparatively easy of solution for κατάρας in verse 13 plainly refers back to Paul's earlier use of the same word in verse 10. There he says that those who are 'of works of law', i.e. those who base their hopes for eternity on living in conformity with law, are under a curse, and he proceeds to quote the LXX version of Dt. xxvii. 26 with slight modifications which make his point a little clearer, but do not affect the sense of the LXX. The point of that passage is, as Paul says, 'Cursed is every one

---

[1] Cf. Burton, who gives the meaning of the verb as 'to redeem, to deliver at cost of some sort to the deliverer' (I.C.C. on Gal. iii. 13).

London, 1951, p. 134). Charles supports this, and he quotes WH's explanation of the variant reading λούσαντι for λύσαντι as 'due to failure to understand the Hebraic use of ἐν to denote a price . . . and a certain misapplication of vii. 14' (Comm. *in loc.*).

which continueth not in all things that are written in the book of the law to do them'. He is affirming that no man can be pleasing in the sight of God by his own efforts. Rather, the best that he can do will result only in disaster because the Scripture pronounces a curse on all who fail to keep the law in its entirety. Since no man does that, then all are under the curse.

How, then, does Paul conceive of Christ's removing the curse from men? Christ, he says, became a curse for us, and this is linked with a curse pronounced by the law on 'everyone that hangeth upon a tree'. A curse rests on everyone who does not fulfil the law; Christ died in such a way as to bear or be a curse; we who should have been accursed now go free.

The expression 'having become a curse for us' seems to rest on a Hebraic mode of thought like the similar expression in 2 Cor. v. 21 where Christ is said to have been 'made sin for us'. Lightfoot draws attention to Protev. Jac. 3 where Anna is said to have become a curse, κατάρα ἐγενήθην ἐγὼ ἐνώπιον τῶν υἱῶν ᾽Ισραήλ, which he thinks may be partly explained by the paucity of adjectives in Hebrew, 'but still more by the religious conception which it involves. The victim is regarded as bearing the sins of those for whom atonement is made. The curse is transferred from them to it. It becomes in a certain sense the impersonation of the sin and of the curse'.[1] He adduces also the scapegoat, the use of ἁμαρτία (Lv. iv. 25) and ἁμάρτημα (Lv. iv. 29) to indicate the sin-offering as well as the sin, and the similar usage with the Heb. ḥṭ'th, as well as identical modes of thought among other nations. Identification seems to run through and through Hebrew religion and thought. Thus the prophetic action and the event which it foreshadows (as for example in Je. xix or Ezk. iv) are in some

---

[1] Comm. *in loc.* Cf. his paraphrase: 'Christ ransomed us from this curse pronounced by the law, Himself taking our place and becoming a curse for our sakes.' V. F. Storr's comment is of importance, because although he does not accept such an idea himself he yet recognizes that Paul's language teaches it: 'Like a black thundercloud the Law hung over men's heads, and they looked up to it in fear that at any minute the lightning of the divine judgment might flame out from its heart. What could be done? God took the initiative. Christ came and on the Cross bore for us the doom which sin involved . . . Christ bore the penalty which in strict justice we ought to have borne . . . Death was the curse of Law, and that curse Christ took upon Himself' (*The Problem of the Cross*, London, 1924, p. 55).

way one, the name and the person are not separate, and so on. The identification of Christ and the curse then becomes a picturesque way of saying that He took our curse upon Himself, and we bear it no more.[1]

Much is sometimes made of Paul's omission of the words ὑπὸ θεοῦ in his citation of Dt. xxi. 23, and Sydney Cave can say: 'Whatever be the meaning of the words "He became a curse for us," it is clear from their context that the curse is not the curse of God but of the law'.[2] But it is extremely doubtful whether such a sharp antithesis can be justified in the case of such a writer as Paul. A study of the way he cites the Old Testament indicates plainly that he regarded its statements as of divine origin; and while a modern writer might distinguish between a curse of God and a curse of the law, accepting the latter while rejecting the former, it is hard to imagine Paul taking such a course. Lightfoot says: 'He (i.e. Christ) had undergone that punishment, which under the law betokened the curse of God. So far He had become κατάρα. But He was in no literal sense κατάρατος ὑπὸ θεοῦ and St. Paul instinctively omits those words which do not strictly apply, and

---

[1] Similar interpretations are endorsed by many scholars of various periods, as Delitzsch: 'He so takes our curse upon Him, that He in person represents the executed curse' (Comm. on Hebrews, II, 426). D. W. Simon describes the action of Christ in this verse as 'assuming the position or relationship of one who is under the curse' (The Redemption of Man, London, 1906, p. 267); while even H. Bushnell says: 'Probably the expression "being made a curse for us", does imply that He somehow comes under the retributive consequences of our sin' (The Vicarious Sacrifice, London, 1866, p. 121). J. Scott Lidgett comments: 'His being made a curse is His entering into the whole of those evil consequences which are the mark of the displeasure of the law' (The Spiritual Principle of the Atonement, London, 1898, p. 47). Similarly W. Manson can speak of Jesus 'taking the curse of their sin upon his Spirit' (Jesus the Messiah, London, 1943, p. 165), and H. G. G. Herklots says: 'A curse indeed lay upon the one whom they hanged upon a tree; but it was the curse of man's sin borne freely by one in whom dwelt all the fulness of the Godhead bodily' (A Fresh Approach to the New Testament, London, 1950, p. 23).

[2] The Doctrine of the Work of Christ, London, 1937, p. 45, and cf. Burton: 'The curse of the law was, therefore, an actual curse in the sense that it expressed the verdict of legalism, but not in the sense that he on whom it fell was accursed of God' (Comm. in loc.); and again, commenting on Gal. iii. 10, 'The curse of which the verse speaks is not the curse of God, but as Paul expressly calls it in verse 13, the curse of the law'.

which, if added, would have required some qualification'.[1] But this seems as far as we can go. Although Paul has some strong things to say about the law, they really boil down to this: the law can never bring salvation. If there is a curse of the law, then that ultimately, in Pauline thought, comes from God, and represents the divine judgment on sin.[2] It could not possibly to his way of thinking come from man, and to represent the law as a hypostatized entity is to misrepresent Paul. When, therefore, Paul speaks of Christ having borne the curse of the law, he speaks of our removal from the legal plight into which we were fallen through our failure to keep the law of God. As Büchsel says: 'The essential meaning of this freeing from the curse of the Law is that He gives not only an actual, but a legally based freedom'.[3] The law of God has no more claim on us.

This involves a definitely substitutionary idea. If I should have been under a curse, but instead Christ was made a curse, so that now I am free, redeemed from the curse, then His action is of a substitutionary kind as H. Wheeler Robinson recognizes when he finds in this passage 'one of the clearest indications that St. Paul conceived the death of Christ as both substitutionary and penal'.[4]

[1] Comm. *in loc.* H. L. Goudge does not shrink from speaking of 'the curse of God', saying, 'Thus, that Jesus had died upon the cross had meant to St. Paul that He had died under the curse of God' (*Glorying in the Cross*, London, 1940, p. 97).

[2] Cf. Duncan: 'And if Paul does not say in so many words that the curse was imposed by God, he nevertheless believed, as his subsequent argument shows, that the Law which brought the curse in its train was introduced in order to further the divine purpose of redemption; and in so far as God was behind the giving of the Law, so far also was He a party to the curse' (MNTC, *Galatians*, p. 101).

[3] TWNT, I, p. 126.

[4] *Redemption and Revelation*, London, 1942, p. 231. He also says 'Christ *actually* bears a part of the universal curse (in its consequences) and thus enables God graciously to remove it altogether' (*Ibid*). H. A. A. Kennedy with reference to this verse speaks of 'that redemption in which Christ became accursed . . . for our sakes' and goes on to refer to Christ as 'the Redeemer and Substitute of His people' (*The Expositor*, Eighth Series, x, p. 405). Similarly F. V. Filson puts Gal. iii. 13 at the head of a list of passages which show that 'From one aspect this death is thought of as a substitutionary suffering by Christ of the penalty due to men for their sins' (*St. Paul's Conception of Recompense*, Leipzig, 1931, p. 15).

There may be more to it than substitution, but we cannot dismiss the substitutionary aspect without doing violence to the words.[1]

The second verse, Gal. iv. 4, adds little to what the first one says. Here there is the thought that God sent forth His Son, 'born under the law, that he might redeem them which were under the law', which indicates that the redemption spoken of was the whole purpose of the sending forth of the Son, and that the manner of the redemption included the Son coming Himself 'under the law'.

It is worthy of note, especially in view of the fact that the uncompounded verb ἀγοράζω seems to include the thought of the state into which the Christian is bought as an integral part of the conception of being bought by Christ, that on both occasions when ἐξαγοράζω is used there is added an expression indicative of the resultant state of the believer. In Gal. iii. 14 we learn that the redemption was 'that upon the Gentiles might come the blessing of Abraham in Christ Jesus; that we might receive the promise of the Spirit through faith', while Gal. iv. 5 tells us that we were redeemed 'that we might receive the adoption of sons (υἱοθεσίαν).' It is wrong to separate the legal status, gained by the complete discharge of the claims the law had upon us, from the resultant life. The only redemption Paul knew was one in which the redeemed had received the gift of the Holy Spirit, and in which they lived as those who had been adopted into the family of God.

VIII. THE USE OF περιποιοῦμαι

There is one New Testament passage where this verb is used with reference to the atonement, namely Paul's speech to the elders at Miletus during the course of which he said to them: 'Take heed unto yourselves, and to all the flock, in the which the Holy Ghost hath made you bishops, to feed the church of God, which he purchased with his own blood' (Acts xx. 28). The verb gives a thought allied to those of the passages we have considered in the earlier sections, but with an emphasis of its own.

περιποιέω really means 'to make to remain over', hence 'to keep safe, to preserve'. In the middle it signifies 'to keep or save for oneself', and thus 'to acquire, gain possession of'. In the LXX it has the meaning 'to save, preserve alive, let live' more often than any

---

[1] See additional note on this passage on p. 59.

other (cf. Lk. xvii. 33), but there are a number of passages where 'to acquire' is clearly required (e.g., Gn. xxxi. 18, xxxvi. 6; Je. xlviii. 36, etc.). Lake and Cadbury translate the verb in Paul's speech by 'rescued',[1] taking the former meaning, but this seems to be a misunderstanding of the passage. The thought that man needs only 'saving alive' is not a New Testament idea. On the contrary, Scripture consistently thinks of him as completely lost until he is brought out of his sinful condition by the action of Christ. Some such sense as 'purchased' or 'acquired' is demanded by the context, and as the latter is a well attested meaning there seems no reason why it should not be accepted here. The sense then is that the Church was acquired by God διὰ τοῦ αἵματος τοῦ ἰδίου. Whether we adopt the suggestion of Lake and Cadbury and translate 'by the blood of his Own', or retain the RV 'with his own blood', the reference is clearly to the action of Christ in dying for man's redemption.

This verb seems to have about it a flavour of personal possession. Thus in 1 Tim. iii. 13 the deacons acquire the 'good standing' for themselves as their very own possession, and the noun περιποίησις seems to give the same idea in 1 Pet. ii. 9, where it corresponds to the Hebrew segullah, 'possession, property', in the Old Testament passage alluded to, namely Ex. xix. 5. If it is legitimate to assume that this idea is present in Acts xx. 28 we get the thought of the Church as being acquired by God to be a possession peculiarly His own, His treasured possession.[2]

Whether we can say that this is to be deduced from the passage or not, it is yet clear that it bears witness to the thought of the Church being acquired at the price of the blood of Christ. Once again we have the thought of the price paid; the shedding of blood takes place instead of the loss of the sinners.

IX. CONCLUSION

From the foregoing examination then we see that where the redemption category is employed there are three aspects of the process of atonement especially in view.

---

[1] In the translation given in The Beginnings of Christianity, Vol. IV.

[2] Cf. the conjunction of the terms ἀπολύτρωσις and περιποίησις in Eph. i. 14.

a. The state of sin out of which man is to be redeemed

This is likened to a slavery, a captivity which man cannot himself break, so that redemption represents the intervention of an outside Person who pays the price which man cannot pay. The Bible sometimes speaks of this slavery in set terms (e.g. Jn. viii. 34, Rom. vii. 14), but more often assumes it. It is a basic tenet of biblical theology that man is completely unable to grapple with the position created by the fact of his sin, and the redemption passages must be interpreted in this context.

b. The price which is paid

This has been too much neglected by many exegetes who have tended to see in the redemption words no more than another way of saying 'deliverance'. But our study has shown that this is erroneous, for both inside and outside the New Testament writings the payment of price is a necessary component of the redemption idea. When the New Testament speaks of redemption then, unless our linguistics are at fault, it means that Christ has paid the price of our redemption. To the extent that the price paid must be adequate for the purchase in question this indicates an equivalence, a substitution.

Sometimes, where redemption is conjoined with some other expression like 'redeemed from the curse', the thought goes further; and in the case of this expression it does seem as though what the apostle is saying is that Christ bore what we should have borne, that He is our Substitute. We have noted that many scholars subscribe to this interpretation, and their agreement is made the more impressive in that many who feel that this is a mistaken way of viewing the atonement yet recognize that this is the thought of the apostle. He found it necessary to bring in many categories to interpret what was done on Calvary, and it would seem impossible to escape the conclusion that substitution was one of them. The place and nature of the substitution may require careful definition, but that substitution is part of St. Paul's thought seems beyond reasonable doubt. And in view of such passages as the ransom saying of Mk. x. 45 we must hold that this substitutionary idea is not peculiar to St. Paul.

c. The resultant state of the believer

Holders of substitutionary ideas have sometimes been criticized as being indifferent to moral values, but this criticism cannot be urged against the biblical writers. In the Scripture we see the price paid, the curse borne, in order that those who are redeemed should be brought into the liberty of the sons of God, a liberty which may paradoxically be called slavery to God. The whole point of this redemption is that sin no longer has dominion; the redeemed are those saved to do the will of their Master.

ADDITIONAL NOTE ON GALATIANS III. 13

It seems likely that the preposition ὑπέρ here conveys a substitutionary thought. That it is capable of such a meaning is made clear by Mayser's note: 'Tolerably widespread is the use of ὑπέρ = instead of, in the place of, in substitution for someone, exclusively of persons, yet generally in such a way that it is not a simple, external, mechanical substitution, but there predominates a ground meaning "in the name, in the interest, for the benefit of someone". Yet there also occur cases in which ὑπέρ stands completely in the sense of ἀντί' (*Grammatik der Griechischen Papyri aus der Ptolemaerzeit*, Berlin and Leipzig, 1934, II. 2, 460). He cites examples from the papyri to prove his point.

In the New Testament a substitutionary sense seems necessary in 1 Cor. xv. 29, 'they that are baptized ὑπέρ the dead', however we translate the word. So is it in 2 Cor. v. 20 (A.V. 'in Christ's stead') and Philemon 13 where Goodspeed translates ὑπέρ σοῦ 'in your place'. In view of the resemblance between 1 Tim. ii. 6 and Mk. x. 45 the ὑπέρ of the former must be very nearly identical in meaning with the ἀντί of the latter. Other passages where the natural interpretation gives ὑπέρ a substitutionary meaning are Jn. x. 11, xi. 50; Rom. xvi. 4.

If this can be regarded as established there is no reason why a substitutionary meaning may not be given to ὑπέρ in some at least of the passages where Christ is said to have died ὑπέρ ἡμῶν. In the passage we are discussing such an interpretation has strong claims.

CHAPTER II

COVENANT

I. INTRODUCTION

THE thought of covenant is one of the leading conceptions of the Old Testament, and thus it is not surprising that the early Christians sought to interpret the new faith, in part at least, along the lines of this conception, all the more so since some of the prophets had envisaged a day when there would be a new covenant to replace the old. Of the thirty-three occurrences of the word διαθήκη in the New Testament sixteen refer to the new covenant and a seventeenth speaks of 'two covenants' contrasting the old with the new (Gal. iv. 24). Of the sixteen, six refer to 'the blood of the covenant' (or similar phrase) (Mt. xxvi. 28; Mk. xiv. 24; Lk. xxii. 20; 1 Cor. xi. 25; Heb. ix. 20, x. 29), thus reminding us of the relevance of this subject to the discussion of the atonement, two refer to the new covenant as a 'better covenant' (Heb. vii. 22, viii. 6), four bring out the specific note of the fulfilment of prophecy in the new covenant (Rom. xi. 27; Heb. viii. 8, 10, x. 16), one is a baffling reference to 'the ark of his covenant' in heaven (Rev. xi. 19) while the remaining three are more general (2 Cor. iii. 6; Heb. ix. 15, xii. 24).

It is of interest to notice that the covenant at Sinai seems to be alluded to eight times (including the 'two covenants' reference mentioned above) (2 Cor. iii. 14; Gal. iv. 24; Heb. viii. 9 (twice), ix. 4 (twice), 15, 20), and is probably included also in the plural 'covenants' in two other places (Rom. ix. 4; Eph. ii. 12); while the covenant with Abraham is spoken of four times (Lk. i. 72; Acts iii. 25, vii. 8; Gal. iii. 17), and there are three allusions to 'covenants of men' (Gal. iii. 15; Heb. ix. 16, 17).

The writer to the Hebrews seems to have been specially interested in this aspect of things Christian, for he uses the term διαθήκη seventeen times as against sixteen for the whole of the rest of the New Testament (which sixteen include four references to the words of institution of the Lord's Supper), and he refers freely both to the Sinai covenant and to the new covenant although, interestingly enough, he does not mention the covenant with Abraham.

The verb διατίθεμαι is found half a dozen times in the New Testament, but as it occurs in connection with the noun διαθήκη in every case except Lk. xxii. 19 (where it means 'appoint' rather than 'make a covenant'), there seems to be no necessity for giving it separate consideration.[1]

At the outset we notice that a big difficulty is posed by the fact that in the Septuagint the word διαθήκη is used regularly to translate the Hebrew *berith*, which is generally understood to signify 'covenant', whereas in non-biblical Greek διαθήκη almost invariably denotes a last will and testament. It is not easy to see which meaning should be understood as the New Testament meaning and there have not been wanting advocates of varying points of view. Thus Deissmann can say: 'no one in the Mediterranean world in the first century A.D. would have thought of finding in the word διαθήκη the idea of "covenant". St. Paul would not, and in fact did not'.[2] That this to him is a point of consequence appears from the statement which follows a little later: 'This one point concerns more than the merely superficial question whether we are to write "New Testament" or "New Covenant" on the title-page of the sacred volume; it becomes ultimately the great question of all religious history: a religion of grace, or a religion of works?'[3] On the other hand Lightfoot says: '. . . in the LXX it (i.e. διαθήκη) is as universally used of a covenant. . . . Nor in the New Testament is it ever found in any other sense, with one exception. Even in this exceptional case, Heb. ix. 15-17, the sacred writer starts from the sense of a "covenant", and glides into that of a "testament" '.[4] Westcott goes

---

[1] It is, however, possible that the verb gives us a clue to the way in which the noun διαθήκη is to be understood in the Supper narrative. If this is so, the meaning of the verb here, 'appoint', would indicate a meaning like 'authoritative disposition' in the noun. For a discussion of this point see Candlish, ET, IV, p. 21.

[2] *Light from the Ancient East*, London, 1927, p. 337.

[3] *Op. cit.*, pp. 337f.

[4] *Galatians*, p. 141.

further, and argues that even this passage is to be understood of a covenant.[1] It thus appears that the most widely divergent views of the meaning of the word in the New Testament are held, and held strongly.

II. THE IDEA OF COVENANT IN THE OLD TESTAMENT

a. *The derivation of berith*

Our first task will be to examine the idea in the Hebrew term *berith*. The derivation of the term is still rather obscure despite the optimistic statement of Henry S. Gehman: 'The etymology of the word in Hebrew is apparently quite clear: Akkadian *baru*, "to bind", "to fetter", and *biritu* "fettering", "fetters", suggest that Hebrew *berith* contains the sense of binding or a bond'.[2] This is no doubt an attractive derivation, but it is not the only one in the field. Thus Kautsch says: 'After the thoroughgoing investigations of J. P. Valeton and R. Kraetzschmar, there can be no doubt that *berith* belongs primarily to the secular vocabulary, and means 'cutting in pieces', namely of one or more sacrificial victims . . . '[3] Again, the form of the noun *berith* is that of a feminine from the root *bry* which directs our attention to *barah*, a verb which actually occurs in the sense 'to eat', as does the noun *biryah* 'food', and also the form *beruth*. The derivation suggested by this root would make the sacred meal the important feature of covenant. There are other suggested derivations, but the whole subject is so obscure that not much can be made of it. Accordingly we must turn to the usage of the term for our information as to its significance.

b. *The meaning of karath berith*

The word occurs frequently in conjunction with the verb *karath* in the expression 'to cut a covenant'. This would fit in with the derivation suggested by Kautsch, but it raises the question why a verb from another root is used, so not much weight can be laid on this. The thought of cutting is associated by Trumbull with the rite of blood brotherhood among primitive men and he says,

---

[1] *Hebrews*, pp. 300f.

[2] *Theology Today*, Apr., 1950, p. 27.

[3] HDB, v, p. 630b.

'the primitive rite of blood-covenanting was by cutting into the flesh in order to the tasting of the blood'.[1] On this view to speak of 'cutting a covenant' was to use an archaic form of expression referring to a rite which had in earlier days been universally practised at the making of a covenant, but which no longer was in use. This is possible; but on the whole it seems better to associate the expression with the cutting of sacrificial victims in pieces as mentioned in Gn. xv. 9f.; Je. xxxiv. 18, and which seems to have been an integral part of the making of a covenant, even though it is not often mentioned in the Old Testament. As Quell puts it: 'To cut something with the result that a *berith* appears, is concisely expressed by the formula "cut a *berith*" '.[2]

That the cutting of an animal in pieces was necessary to the making of a covenant seems clear enough (from Je. xxxiv. 18 it would seem that also the passing of the partners between the pieces was required); but why this should be thought necessary is not so certain. There is never an explanation of the ceremony, and we are left to draw our conclusion from the fact that such an action did take place. Some writers talk of the action symbolizing the fact that the partners enter into the mystical life of the victim;[3] but this is very difficult to accept. One wonders what meaning this would have to men like Laban or Abimelech (or for that matter to most men of today), and why this should solemnly seal the covenant. It is not sufficient to say that they thereby enter a common life, for the point is that, even if they do, it does not appear why being together in the life of an animal should consummate such a far-reaching compact as the *berith* evidently was.

The cutting of the animals in pieces seems more intelligible as an invocation of the same fate upon the partners should they be guilty of breaking their compact. Davidson supports this point of view when he says that a necessary element in the making of the covenant was 'the imprecation or curse . . . invoked by each party on himself in case of failure, this curse being, at the same time, symbolically expressed by passing between the pieces of the

[1] *The Blood Covenant*, London, 1887, p. 264.

[2] TWNT, III, p. 108.

[3] Cf. W. Robertson Smith quoted on pp. 69f. below.

slaughtered animal'.[1] Kautsch views the matter in a similar light,[2] and both men proceed to note that the Hebrew form of oath 'God do so to me and more also' probably connects with such ceremonies.

If we may cite a non-biblical text this is explicit in the account of a Babylonian Covenant, which mentions the sacrificing of a goat, and proceeds: 'This head is not the head of the goat . . . it is the head of Mati'-ilu. . . . If Mati'-ilu (breaks) this oath, as the head of this goat is cut off . . . so shall the head of Mati'-ilu be cut off. . . . This loin is not the loin of the goat, it is the loin of Mati'-ilu, etc.'[3] We could hardly have a more explicit statement as to the purpose of the cutting up of the animal, and this must be regarded as of importance, coming as it does from a land which had contact with the Hebrews at many points over centuries. Other rites could be cited from various lands to emphasize the same point, as is done for example by Trumbull (*The Blood Covenant*, pp. 44f., 53f.) The natural interpretation of the rite as described in the Bible, coupled with explicit interpretations of similar rites in non-Hebrew spheres, seems to show beyond reasonable doubt what the significance of the division of the animals is.

c. Actual Covenants

When we turn from considerations of the implications of the phrase *karath berith* to examples of actual covenants concluded in Old Testament days we notice immediately that the term is applied to agreements between men, and to those between God and men. Since it would seem that the term was taken from the secular sphere to illustrate relations between God and man, and not vice versa, we turn our attention first of all to human covenants.

(i) *Covenants between Men*. Most covenants of this kind are between representative persons, such as heads of clans, or rulers, there being, in the opinion of Quell,[4] only one covenant between

[1] HDB, i, p. 510.

[2] HDB, v, p. 630.

[3] Cited from A. Jeremias, *The Old Testament in the Light of the Ancient East*, London, 1911, ii, p. 49.

[4] TWNT, ii, p. 112.

purely private people in the whole Old Testament, namely that between David and Jonathan. This was a compact arising out of the mutual love of the pair, and its terms are not given, though David could say: 'Therefore deal kindly with thy servant; for thou hast brought thy servant into a covenant of the Lord with thee' (1 Sa. xx. 8) so that evidently it gave each of them at least a general claim on the other. Of the manner of making this covenant we know little; the only information being that, when the covenant was made, Jonathan gave David presents of his apparel and weapons (1 Sa. xviii. 4), a procedure which seems to have been widely observed in similar rites in other lands. That a religious element was involved, however, is evident from David's statement, quoted above, that it was 'a covenant of the Lord'.

This religious element comes out more prominently in other covenants, as for example in that between Jacob and Laban (Gn. xxxi. 44f.). Here we notice an oath which Jacob is explicitly said to have sworn 'by the Fear of his father Isaac', and a sacrifice together with a meal shared by the covenant brothers, evidently the sacrificial meal accompanying the peace offering. In this case we have the terms of the agreement recorded, as also the fact that a heap of stones was set up as a witness to the covenant. The witness in the covenant between Abraham and Abimelech is a group of seven ewe lambs (Gn. xxi. 30, and cf. the reference to the tamarisk tree in verse 33) and in the narrative of the making of this covenant the oath figures largely, though there is no mention of sacrifice or sacrificial meal. The omission, however, need not surprise us for, in fact, there are few if any places where we have the full ritual of covenant-making described. It is of interest in this connection that there is no mention of the dividing of the animals in pieces between the time of Abraham and that of Jeremiah, though we must hold that it continued throughout all those centuries. The men of antiquity knew quite well how a covenant was 'cut', and they did not write down unnecessary details.

Putting together the hints that we obtain from the various occasions on which human covenants are referred to we find that the following were important points in the making of a covenant: (1) The drawing up of terms of agreement. (2) The oath to keep the agreement. (3) The ritual slaughter of animals, including both the animal or animals to be divided and those to be offered up in sacrifice and consumed in the meal of fellowship. In addition there may have been other practices considered essential, such as the provision of witnesses in a heap of stones, a group of lambs, or a tree, each of which we have seen serving such a purpose.

(ii) *Covenants between God and Men.* The use of the term 'covenant' to describe the relationship existing between God and men goes back to the story of the flood in which we read the word of the Lord to Noah: 'But I will establish my covenant with thee; and thou shalt come into the ark, thou, and thy sons, and thy wife, and thy sons' wives with thee' (Gn. vi. 18). Here we notice that not only is the initiative with God, the whole 'covenant' is His. Noah is not represented as doing anything in the matter, either in the way of seeking a covenant, or of performing covenant obligations. Nothing is said here, or in subsequent passages which refer to this covenant, of the method whereby the covenant was established. There is, therefore, little that we can say about the procedure of covenant-making adopted. But we may notice that the covenant was made with Noah as a representative man rather than as an individual (Gn. ix. 9–10), that the terms were stated in the form of a promise (Gn. ix. 11), and that there was a witness or sign that the covenant would be kept, namely the rainbow (Gn. ix. 12–16). An important point is that the covenant is one of grace, with the Lord freely bestowing His blessing on His servant, and not granting it as a return for services rendered.

The next covenant referred to is that with Abraham. In response to the patriarch's query as to how he should know that he would subsequently (in his seed) inherit the land of Canaan, Yahweh commanded him to take certain animals and divide them in two, after which, 'when the sun was going down, a deep sleep fell upon Abram; and, lo, an horror of great darkness fell upon him' (Gn. xv. 12). The divine promise was then renewed to him, and 'when the sun went down, and it was dark, behold a smoking furnace, and a flaming torch that passed between these pieces' (Gn. xv. 17). There are some interesting features of this process of covenant making, the outstanding one being that again we see Yahweh as taking on Himself all the obligations. He alone symbolically passes through the pieces, probably because Abram was not taking upon himself any obligation. We see him in the position of a recipient of a boon, of a promise, rather than of a partner contracting to perform certain duties. Again, as in the case of the covenant with Noah, we notice that the covenant is with a representative man (Abraham's 'seed' are expressly mentioned), and the terms of the covenant are given in the form of the promise. On this occasion, however, there is nothing we can regard as a witness unless the smoking furnace and the flaming torch can be said to fulfil this requirement, which seems unlikely as they rather symbolize the divine presence.

Later on we do find certain duties assigned to Abraham and linked to the covenant. 'This is my covenant, which ye shall keep, between me and you and thy seed after thee; every male among you shall be circumcised . . . and my covenant shall be in your flesh for an everlasting covenant. And the uncircumcised male who is not circumcised in the flesh of his foreskin, that soul shall be cut off from his people; he hath broken my covenant' (Gn. xvii. 10–14). However, this hardly interferes with the principles of grace and of the divine initiative, for on the one hand circumcision is rather a sign, a seal, a badge of the covenant than a contractual obligation, and on the other it is a duty imposed by Yahweh and not assented to in free negotiation by Abraham. The absolute sovereignty of the divine will is apparent throughout the whole of this covenant.

From many such references in the Bible to covenants with Yahweh we must notice a third. In Ex. xxiv we read of a covenant made, not with representative individuals, but with the whole people of Israel. Again the initiative is with Yahweh who called Moses and others to Him to the mount, Moses being assigned a position of privilege (see verse 2). Before they went, Moses told the people 'all the words of the Lord, and all the judgments'; to this they responded: 'All the words which the Lord hath spoken will we do'. On a specially made altar burnt and peace offerings were offered up, not by priests, but by 'young men of the children of Israel', the blood being collected and divided into two portions, one of which Moses proceeded to throw on the altar. Then he read from 'the book of the covenant', and again the people agreed to obey the Lord: 'All that the Lord hath spoken will we do, and be obedient'. After this undertaking Moses took the other half of the blood and threw it over the people, saying, 'Behold the blood of the covenant which the Lord hath made with you concerning all these words'. The ceremonies concluded with Moses and other representatives of the people going up into the mount where 'they beheld God, and did eat and drink', evidently an allusion to the sacrificial meal.

This ceremony was of the utmost importance for the later history of the people, for from this time the nation stood in a peculiar relationship to Yahweh, a relationship shared by no other.

Attention must be called to three features of this new arrangement, namely the participation of the people, the 'blood of the covenant', and the obligations resting upon the people. Concerning the first of these, there is importance in the fact that this covenant was not made through some representative as had been the case with the earlier covenants we have noticed, but with the principals themselves.[1] This point is emphasized in Dt. v. 2f. where we read: 'The Lord our God made a covenant with us in Horeb. The Lord made not this covenant with our fathers, but with us, even us, who are all of us here alive this day'. On this verse H. H. Rowley comments: 'It is there implied that the Covenant with the patriarchs was not valid for the generation of the Exodus, but that only the Covenant into which they themselves entered could have validity and meaning for them. And by the same token their Covenant could not have automatic validity for the generations that followed'.[2] While we make no attempt to minimize the extent to which the fathers can claim the promise for their children, yet in the last resort, there seems to be a principle of personal participation involved. No one can live on the spiritual capital of his ancestors. Cf. also R. B. Y. Scott: 'The religious group which only carries on the momentum in belief and practice of an age which has passed away, and has not made its own the covenant of the fathers, will find that the covenant is no longer valid, and the living God has passed on to seek a new people for Himself'.[3]

[1] The narrative seems to stress the activity of the people themselves; see e.g. Ex. xxiv. 3, 7.

[2] The Biblical Doctrine of Election, London, 1950, p. 48.

[3] The Relevance of the Prophets, p. 210 (cited in Rowley op. cit., p. 139).

The blood is seen by some as the typical means of entering into blood brotherhood, a point of view which is well expressed by Trumbull: 'And now observe the celebration of the symbolic rite of the blood-covenant between the Lord and the Lord's people, with the substitute blood accepted on both sides, and with the covenant record agreed upon'.[1] Or again: 'When Israel was to be inducted into the privileges of this covenant of blood-friendship at Mount Sinai, half of the blood came from the one party, and half of the blood came from the other party, to the sacred compact; both portions being supplied from a common and a mutually accepted symbolic substitute'.[2] According to this view the blood is essentially the same as that used in the making of blood brothers, only whereas, originally at any rate, in the establishment of this bond the brothers shared each other's blood, on Mt. Sinai a mutually acceptable substitute provided the blood for both parties (such a provision of a substitute being not unknown in other places). Such a view stresses the closeness of the kinship between the two parties to the agreement, but it falls down at critical points. Thus there is nothing in the narrative to indicate that the blood was thought of by either party as a substitute for his or the other's blood; the idea has to be imported into the story. Again it gives rise to the concept of an equality of the partners which does not appear to be justified. Buber's summary of the position is better when he says: 'YHVH unites himself with Israel into a political, theo-political unity, within which the two partners bear the relations towards each other of a primitive wandering community and its *melek*'.[3] Throughout the chapter there is no question but that Yahweh is directing all things; it is His will that the covenant should come about, and it is established on His terms. The idea that the people acted independently does not appear to be established.

Robertson Smith regards the use of the blood as essentially the same as the division of the animal into two parts. 'We see from Ex. xxiv. 8, "this is the blood of the covenant which Jehovah hath cut with you", that the dividing of the sacrifice and the application

---

[1] *Op. cit.*, p. 239.

[2] *Op. cit.*, p. 240.

[3] *Moses*, Oxford, 1946, p. 115.

of the blood to both parties go together. The sacrifice presumably was divided into two parts (as in Ex. *l. c.* the blood is divided into two parts), when both parties joined in eating it; and when it ceased to be eaten, the parties stood between the pieces, as a symbol that they were taken within the mystical life of the victim'.[1] But this does not seem to fit into the picture very accurately. There is no reason to think that the sprinkling of the blood which we see here was characteristic of Hebrew covenants; in point of fact it is mentioned nowhere else in such a connection. Again, there appears no obvious reason for equating a sprinkling of blood with a division of corpses; the two actions seem distinct. And as we have already seen, the thought of being taken 'within the mystical life of the victim' is not one which we can readily credit to the typical Hebrew of antiquity. Moreover, in regarding this incident as a typical example of the blood covenant, Robertson Smith seems to miss the fact that this is a unique rite. To quote Buber again: 'This rite . . . though reminiscent of the Semitic custom of Blood Covenant, is nevertheless unique in character'.[2]

Others regard the rite as, in a measure at least, piacular. Thus Davidson quotes Robertson Smith's 'both parties having communion in the same blood' and comments: 'This may be; but in the main the sacrifice, being an offering to J", was piacular, atoning for and consecrating the people on their entering upon their new relation to J".'[3] This would be supported by the general piacular character of the sacrifices.[4] It has Jewish support, for Dalman remarks: 'Onkelos and Targum Yer. I remark also that the second half of the blood was poured out towards the altar, "in order to propitiate the people". They think thus of a propitiation of the blood'.[5] There is inherent probability in the suggestion, too, for men in their sinful state would not be suitable candidates for membership in a covenant with God, and the removal of sin

---

[1] *The Religion of the Semites*, London, 1927, p. 481.

[2] *Op. cit.*, p. 115.

[3] HDB, I, p. 512. See also L. Pullan, *The Atonement*, London, 1907, p. 110.

[4] Cf. Pedersen: 'Everything in any way connected with sacrifice acquired an expiatory power' (*Israel* III, IV, London, 1947, p. 364).

[5] *Jesus-Jeshua*, London, 1929.

by an atoning offering seems a logical step. The difficulty in the way of a full acceptance of this point of view is the treatment of the blood, for the sprinkling of the people in particular is difficult to explain in an atoning sacrifice.

The clue to the meaning of the sprinkling seems to be given in the only two other incidents in the Old Testament wherein we find men sprinkled with blood, namely, the consecration of Aaron and his sons to the priesthood, and the ceremony for the purification of the man healed of leprosy. In the former case we have an explicit statement of the effect of the sprinkling: 'And Moses took of the anointing oil, and of the blood which was upon the altar, and sprinkled it upon Aaron, upon his garments, and upon his sons, and upon his sons' garments with him; and sanctified (*wayeqaddesh*) Aaron . . .' (Lv. viii. 30). Here the blood is a part of a consecratory rite and the effect is to 'sanctify' those sprinkled. In the case of the healed leper we read that the priest is to take hyssop, etc., and he 'shall dip them . . . in the blood of the bird that was killed over the running water: and he shall sprinkle upon him that is to be cleansed from the leprosy seven times, and shall pronounce him clean' (Lv. xiv. 6–7). From this we see that the sprinkling of the blood had a purifying effect, being immediately followed by the priest's pronouncing the man clean. It is true that the cleansing here is from uncleanness rather than from sin, but in view of the close connection between the two in the Old Testament the use of the blood for such a purpose must be held to be significant.

From these two incidents, then, we get the principle that the sprinkling of blood is likely to signify the entry into a new state marked by cleansing from previous defilement and consecration to a holy purpose. It seems that both these thoughts are present in Ex. xxiv and that we are to regard the blood as both piacular and consecratory, cleansing the people from their sin and sanctifying them for their part in the covenant. As Hort puts it: 'The primary purpose of the sprinkling was to consecrate the covenant between Jehovah and the people, the invisible bond between them being indicated by the community of origin of the blood on the altar, as representing Jehovah, and the blood on the persons of the people . . . the sprinkling of the people with this blood was regarded as a consecration and symbolic purification of themselves'.[1] Eichrodt notices these two passages concerning Aaron and the healed leper, but, strangely enough, dismisses them since there the blood sprinkling 'has another meaning, namely that of consecration and cleansing'.[2] It is curious that he does not notice that it is precisely these ideas of consecration and purification that make the passages relevant.

In passing we note that Ps. l. 5 witnesses to the close connection between sacrifice and covenant with its 'Gather my saints together unto me; those that have made a covenant with me by sacrifice (*zabhah*)', whether we are to understand this as referring to such an event as the establishing of the Sinai covenant,[3] or whether it signifies that every sacrifice could be regarded as confirming the covenant.[4] The 'blood of the covenant' is also referred to in Zc. ix. 11, but the passage gives no indication as to the manner in which the blood was regarded and the significance that was attached to it.[5]

The people's promise of obedience next claims our attention, for as we have seen, there is nothing like it in the earlier covenants. The covenants made with Noah and with Abraham were covenants of sheer grace, with the promise of divine blessing upon the patriarchs and their seed but with no corresponding obligations mentioned as resting upon them. At first sight it appears that in the Sinai covenant the principle of grace has been abandoned, and that it is now necessary for the people to earn the divine blessing. Merit, not grace, seems to be the criterion, all the more so since the passage speaks of the people's obedience to Yahweh, but says nothing of any promise on His part. This last point, however,

---

[1] *The First Epistle of St. Peter*, p. 23.

[2] *Theologie des Alten Testaments*, Leipzig, 1933-9, I, p. 73, n.8.

[3] Mishna San. x. 3 refers this verse to the wilderness generation on the authority of R. Eliezer.

[4] Cf. F. W. Dillistone: 'from now onwards (i.e. the making of the covenant in Ex. xxiv) in the life of Israel the covenant and the sacrifice are indissolubly bound together. Only through sacrifice could the covenant be renewed and deepened; every offering of sacrifice was, at least ideally, a witness to the original covenant' (*The Significance of the Cross*, London, 1946, p. 59).

[5] Among the Rabbis this verse was sometimes at least understood as referring to the Passover, and Dalman adopts this interpretation (*op. cit.* pp. 166f.). But Lv. R. vi. 5 (Soncino trans., p. 85) understands it of the blood of the Sinai covenant.

cannot be held to be significant, for in other places we have made explicit what is implicit in Ex. xxiv, namely, that Yahweh will be Israel's God, and that He will give them His blessing. See, for example, Ex. xix. 5–6; Lv. xxvi. 9–12.

The place of the duties which devolved upon the people in the covenant should not be overstressed, for it is clear that the whole process of covenant-making in Ex. xxiv is regarded as taking place under divine direction. It is not a compact freely negotiated by independent parties with the people determining just how far they intend to go. Their part is an unconditional surrender to whatever might be the will of God, their absolute Ruler.[1] As Vos puts it: 'Notwithstanding all the emphasis placed upon the two-sidedness of the Berith, Scripture always so represents it that the Berith in its origin and in the determination of its content is not two-sided but based on the sovereignty of God.'[2] There is nothing in Ex. xxiv to indicate that the reason for God's choice of the people was their agreement to carry out His commands. Rather the picture we get is of God in His free grace choosing Israel to be His people, and having chosen them, imposing upon them His commands. But the choice is first and fundamental and in it we detect the element of grace.[3]

The difference between the process in Ex. xxiv and the conclusion of a bargain is readily seen if we compare a passage like Gn. xxviii. 20f. where Jacob says: 'If God will be with me, and will keep me in this way that I go, and will give me bread to eat,

---

[1] Dt. xxxiii. 5 might be translated, 'He became king in Jeshurun, when the heads of the people were gathered', in which case the covenant is being regarded as the people's acceptance of the kingship of Yahweh. Cf. Driver: 'Jehovah assumed, as it were, the sovereignty over Israel, when the tribes with their leaders (verse 21) were gathered about Him, on the "day of the assembly" (ix. 10, x. 4, xviii. 16) at Sinai' (Deuteronomy, I.C.C., p. 394); see also the Rabbinic views in section III below.

[2] Princ. Theol. Rev., July, 1913, p. 516.

[3] Cf. Snaith's comment on the covenant conception as we see it in Amos: 'Amos holds that God chose Israel in a special and unique way. "You only have I known of all the families of the earth", iii. 2. With this choice there are certain specific ethical demands . . . the choice comes first and the demands second. The prophet speaks first of the Divine Election of Israel, and, secondly, says: "Therefore I will visit upon you all your iniquities" ' (The Distinctive Ideas of the Old Testament, London, 1944, p. 108).

and raiment to put on, so that I come again to my father's house in peace, then shall the Lord be my God . . . and of all that thou shalt give me I will surely give the tenth unto thee'. Here we do find a process involving bargaining as its essence, so that Jacob's attitude might be summed up as 'If Thou wilt do these things for me, then will I do those things for Thee'. But the thought of Ex. xxiv is different. In that passage Yahweh has already been gracious to the people in delivering them from the power of Egypt—'. . . ye have seen what I did unto the Egyptians, and how I bare you on eagles' wings, and brought you unto myself' (Ex. xix. 4)— and the action of the nation is that of those who say: 'Thou, Lord, hast been gracious unto us. We acknowledge Thy goodness, and we pledge ourselves to be Thine, and to do Thy will'.

A. M. Stibbs has an interesting passage in which he compares the making of this covenant to a wedding: 'In the wilderness at Sinai the Lord confronted Israel with His purpose for them and with His demand for their co-operating response. He said, "I . . . brought you unto myself. Now therefore, if ye will obey my voice indeed, and keep my covenant, then ye shall be a peculiar treasure unto me above all people; . . . and ye shall be unto me a kingdom of priests and an holy nation". And all the people answered together and said, "All that the Lord hath spoken we will do". This scene of covenant making was very similar to a wedding ceremony, and the more so when later the covenant between God and Israel was visibly sealed in sprinkled blood; just as in the wedding ceremony the ring given and received is "a token and pledge of the vow and covenant betwixt them made". Like the bride answering, the Israelites solemnly said, "We will" '.[1]

---

[1] *The Church Universal and Local*, London, 1948, pp. 18f. Cf. Elmslie: 'The Hebrew People's Pledge at Horeb declared *their* confession that this God had never ceased to be faithful to His covenant with their fathers, and to the forgetful children of those fathers had manifested His abiding mercy. The Pledge was *their* acknowledgement of God's continuing grace—to which *they* now responded, vowing themselves to be faithful, willing now to trust in His guidance and henceforth to walk in His ways' (*How Came Our Faith*, Cambridge, 1948, p. 210). So also H. H. Rowley: 'To effect that deliverance they (i.e. the Israelites) did not have to do anything, save trust their leader and follow him. After the deliverance was achieved they committed themselves to God in the obedience of the covenant' (*The Enduring Gospel*, Ed. R. G. Smith, London, 1950, p. 28).

The covenant does not represent the people's endeavour to earn God's favour by performing meritorious works, but the people's acceptance of God's proffered grace, with all that that implies.

The implications of this are not unimportant. Among them is the fact that they were the people of God, and they must henceforth live up to the obligations inherent in this proud title. They were not chosen merely in order that they might be the recipients of His blessings, but that they might do Him service, that they might be 'a kingdom of priests, and an holy nation' (Ex. xix. 6). Spiritual privilege and spiritual obligation are inextricably interwoven, so that those who refuse to obey the commandments of God place themselves outside the sphere of His blessing. There is nothing automatic about the covenant, nothing which binds Yahweh to bless the nation henceforth irrespective of what they might do. It has often been pointed out that, among the other nations nearby, the concept of a physical kinship of the god with his people meant that the god rose or fell with his people, so that, in the last resort, he was bound to save them if he was to save himself, and that the concept of covenant delivered Israel from this error. If He chose them, He could also reject them; and the making of the keeping of His commandments integral to the covenant meant that He was insisting upon a certain way of life if the people were to receive His blessing. The keeping of the commandments of the Lord is thus not thought of as a peripheral thing (cf. Je. xi. 1ff.), but as of the very warp and woof of the whole covenant conception. Failure to walk in God's ways means the complete overthrow of the covenant, so that it may fittingly be described in terms of works, though this must not be understood in such a way as to overlook the element of grace which we have seen is so marked a feature.

Thus we reach something of a paradoxical conclusion that the covenant is of the free grace of God, but that nevertheless, having chosen the people, God imposed upon them ethical demands, and these can be spoken of as the people's part in the covenant without thereby derogating from the freeness of God's grace. Thus over and over we have the choice of the people explicitly said to be due to the love of God and not anything in them, thus placing an emphasis on the unconditioned love of God, and without any apparent sense of contradiction we have passages in which it is said that the people have broken the covenant and thereby have drawn down upon them the wrath and the punishment of God. Both aspects are important in an evaluation of Old Testament teaching.

It is not too much to say that the covenant conception came to dominate Israel's thought with regard to her relationship to God. She was Yahweh's people; He was Israel's God. And through the centuries the people have clung almost fiercely to this central teaching. Not that in Old Testament times this gave grounds for appealing to Yahweh for assistance in time of need. Very occasionally we find indication that the covenant relationship was pleaded, but this is exceptional, probably because of the very obvious fact that Israel had not kept her part of the covenant obligation, and accordingly could not very well insist that the covenant gave her grounds for a claim. Rather the tendency is for her to plead the nature of God Himself, and thus we come upon pleas that He will help of His great mercy, for His Name's sake, etc.

But if Israel had no reason to feel that she had done her part in the covenant, she was sure, or at least her most spiritual minds were sure, that Yahweh had certainly kept His. 'If we are faithless, he abideth faithful; for he cannot deny himself' (2 Tim. ii. 13) is a New Testament saying; but it represents an Old Testament thought. Thus Snaith speaks of 'God's sure love for Israel', and goes on: 'Because of this sure, unswerving love, the covenant can never be finally and completely broken. It takes two to make a covenant, and it also takes two to break it. Israel may have rejected God, but God has not rejected Israel'.[1] He is a covenant-keeping God, and His unwavering love to faithless Israel is one of the great Old Testament conceptions.

This thought of a God who is faithful to the covenant even though the people are not, should not, however, be so interpreted as to give the impression that Yahweh is indifferent to Israel's moral state. It is characteristic of the Old Testament point of view that Yahweh never for one moment relaxes His high ethical demands. This for ever stamps the religion of Israel as something

[1] *Op. cit.*, p. 112.

quite different from other religions of antiquity. It is not that Israel alone has the thought of covenant, for there is evidence that in other religions this conception found its place. We get a hint of this in the mention of Baal-berith in Jdg. viii. 33, etc., and Quell cites a number of religions in antiquity where the covenant idea finds a place.[1] But what gave the religion of Israel its peculiar quality is that the ethical demands which Yahweh made upon His people were both stringent and rigidly insisted upon. There is no hint of toning them down when it became apparent that the people would not be able to measure up to them.

It is true that the Old Testament envisages a replacement of the covenant by a new covenant, a thought which received its classical expression in Je. xxxi. 31ff., and is also to be found in other parts of the Old Testament. Even though it is here said that the new covenant will be 'not according to the covenant that I made with their fathers in the day that I took them by the hand to bring them out of the land of Egypt; which my covenant they brake, although I was an husband unto them, saith the Lord', yet in its ethical demands the new covenant was to be no less stringent than the old, for 'I will put my law in their inward parts, and in their heart will I write it'. As the sequel was to show, the new covenant would have some radically new thoughts, but in its ethical content we see nothing in the way of a whittling down of the divine requirements. Throughout the Old Testament the covenant idea is one which demands from the people a strenuous morality.

It remains to notice that there are some Scriptures which look forward to an association of a Person with the covenant, which must be the new covenant. Thus we read of the Servant in Is. xlii. 6, 'I the Lord . . . will . . . give thee for a covenant of the people, for a light of the Gentiles', and the thought is repeated in xlix. 8. Cheyne says: ' "A covenant of the people" means "the medium or mediator of a covenant between Jehovah and Israel." As the Servant is called "a light" in person, so he can be called "a covenant" in Person'.[2] Other passages which might be held to associate a Person with the inauguration of the new covenant are Mal. iii. 1

[1] TWNT, II, p. 121.
[2] *Isaiah*, I, p. 266.

(the coming of the 'messenger of the covenant') and Zc. ix. 11 (LXX), where in place of 'As for thee also, because of the blood of thy covenant I have sent forth thy prisoners out of the pit, etc.', we have καὶ σὺ ἐν αἵματι διαθήκης σοῦ ἐξαπέστειλας δεσμίους σοῦ ἐκ λάκκου κτλ, 'and thou, in the blood of thy covenant, didst send forth thy prisoners out of the pit', etc. The thought thus vaguely intimated in the Old Testament was to have a very full place in the New Testament reinterpretation of the covenant idea.

III. THE IDEA OF COVENANT IN JUDAISM

The Rabbinic references to covenant are such as to shed light on the Old and New Testament conceptions at a number of points. We deal with the more important of these in order.

a. The Blood of the Covenant

We have already noticed that there are some grounds for thinking that this blood was regarded as at least in part piacular, and there is Rabbinic support for this. Thus Strack-Billerbeck quote Targ. Onk. saying: 'In order to emphasize the atoning power of the blood Targ. Onk. does not translate "Moses sprinkled the blood on the people", but "Moses took the blood and sprinkled it on the altar to make atonement for the people, and he said: See, this is blood of the covenant which Jahve has concluded with you on the basis of all these words". Targ. Jerus. I is almost word for word the same'.[1] This is, of course, later than the Christian era, but it is interesting as showing the accepted line of Jewish interpretation. However, in other places this thought does not seem to be prominent, and, for example, it is not mentioned in a long section in Lv. R. dealing with the blood at Sinai. An interesting interpretation given in this passage suggests that the significance of the blood is a symbolical calling down of punishment if the covenant were broken: 'R. Isaac said: When a king administers an oath to his legions, he does so with a sword, the implication being: Whoever transgresses these conditions, let the sword pass over his neck. Similarly (at Sinai), *Moses took half of the blood*'.[2]

[1] Vol. 1, p. 991.

[2] Lv. R. vi. 5 (Soncino trans.), p. 83.

The blood of the covenant was sometimes interpreted in a quite different fashion, namely of the blood of circumcision whereby men were admitted into the covenant. Thus the Talmud reports a discussion between the rival schools of Shammai and Hillel: 'Beth Shammai maintain one must cause a few drops of the covenant blood to flow from him (i.e. that is born circumcised) while Beth Hillel rule: It is unnecessary. R. Simeon b. Eleazar said: Beth Shammai and Beth Hillel did not differ concerning him who is born circumcised that you must cause a few drops of the covenant blood to flow from him, etc'.[1] Of this manner of interpretation Strack-Billerbeck say: 'One commonly understands by "blood of the covenant" *dm bryth*, the circumcision blood'.[2] Not far removed in thought from this is the habit of referring to the 'covenant of circumcision'[3] and perhaps also of designating the Israelites as 'sons of the covenant',[4] although this latter usage may well be explained otherwise.

b. *The New Covenant*

In the New Testament the new covenant prophesied by Jeremiah is enthusiastically applied to the new conditions brought about by the death of Christ, but there seems little interest in the conception in the Rabbinic writings. One passage in Cant. R. says that the Israelites learnt from God and did not forget, then they learnt through Moses and forgot, so they came to Moses and said ' "Our master, Moses, would that God might be revealed to us a second time! Would that He would kiss us WITH THE KISSES OF HIS LIPS! Would that He would fix the knowledge of the Torah in our hearts as it was!" He replied to them: "This cannot be now, but it will be in the days to come", as it says, *I will put my law in*

[1] Shab. 135, a (Soncino trans.).

[2] Vol. I, p. 991. They quote only one passage, but indicate that it is repeated in a number of parallel passages.

[3] Although it should be noted that this designation is often referred directly to the covenant with Abraham, without mention being made of the Sinai covenant and its blood (see SB ii, p. 671). The expression is found once in the New Testament, namely Acts vii. 8.

[4] Cf. Acts iii. 25 on which SB say: "Sons of the covenant" (=υἱοὶ τῆς διαθήκης) means, when used absolutely, "sons of the covenant of circumcision" and designates Israelites in opposition to non-Israelites' (II, p. 627).

their inward parts and in their heart will I write it'.[1] This passage evidently refers the new covenant to the messianic days in the indefinite future, which seems to be the usual way in which the Rabbis understood the fulfilment of this prophecy. There is an interesting passage in Cant. R. i. 14 which affirms the permanency of the covenant with Abraham, and is evidently a polemic against the Christian view. While this passage is late, it nevertheless indicates the typical Rabbinic interest in the first covenant, and unreadiness to pay much attention to the new covenant.

c. The Covenant with Abraham

The passage just referred to stresses the permanence of the agreement between God and Abraham, and contains God's assurance that He will see to it that this covenant is not superseded. This continuance of the Abrahamic covenant is seen also in most of the passages referring to the 'sons of the covenant' referred to above, as also to the 'covenant of circumcision'. The unique place given to Abraham comes out in many places, such as: 'Five possessions did the Holy One, blessed is he, take to Himself in his world; and these are they: the Law is one possession, and the heaven and earth are one possession, Abraham is one possession, Israel is one possession, and the Temple is one possession'.[2] There can be no doubt that, just as the Christians thought of Abraham as showing the right method of approach to God, and of the covenant with Abraham as being of continuing force, so also did the Rabbis, although they interpreted both these points differently.

d. The concept of Testament

In Old Testament times there does not seem to have been in existence among the Hebrews the practice of disposing of one's goods by means of a last will and testament, the matter being controlled by the laws of inheritance. But in later times the practice of testamentary disposition came into vogue, and the Greek word διαθήκη was transliterated into Hebrew to give the word for the will, *diyyateqe*. Strack-Billerbeck have a long note explaining the Jewish law on the matter and referring to the Rabbinic sources for examples of its use, and it is sufficient simply

---

[1] Cant. R. i. 2, 4 (Soncino trans.), p. 26.

[2] Ab. vi. 11, and cf. Ab. v. 2, 3.

to refer to their note.[1] It may be of significance in interpreting the difficult New Testament passages, in which there is doubt as to whether the sense of διαθήκη is 'covenant' or 'testament', that the Jews were at this time quite familiar with the concept of testament, and, indeed, had taken over the very Greek term used in the New Testament to describe it.

IV. διαθήκη IN THE SEPTUAGINT

When the LXX translators came to the Hebrew *berith* they almost invariably rendered it by διαθήκη (277 times in all), and conversely *berith* is the only word which διαθήκη translates with any frequency.[2] Clearly the LXX translators regarded διαθήκη as very nearly equivalent in meaning to *berith*.

It is interesting to notice this choice of rendering, for it means that the LXX translators passed over συνθήκη, the usual word for covenant in the sense of 'compact', or 'agreement'. Instead, the word they chose is one which indicates a unilateral arrangement, and thus is well adapted to indicating an arrangement where one partner is dominant and dictates the terms, as in all the cases where God is one of the partners. It is true that the word is used also in the LXX of covenants between men, but this is not a very natural translation, and we must feel that the translators were influenced by the fact that the important covenants in the Old Testament are all covenants which involve God. Having thus sought and found a word which renders *berith* in its typical Old Testament context, they were more or less bound to use it also for those other arrangements which were less typical.

Etymologically διαθήκη carries the notion of a laying-down, a disposition, the preposition with its indication of duality directing attention to a laying down with reference to another. Eventually it came to signify a disposition of property by testament, but before this stage was reached it is quite possible that it meant rather an authoritative disposition in general without regard to whether it took place in a testament or not. If this is so the usage of the LXX

---

[1] Vol. III, pp. 545ff.

[2] The other words represented are *'ahawah* 'brotherhood', *dabhar* 'word', *kathub* 'that which is written', *torah* 'law', each of which occurs once in this connection, and *'edhuth* 'testimony', which is used four times. In addition διατίθεμαι διαθήκην once translates *shlm* (Hiph.).

is explained, for as we have seen, this is the sort of idea which the Hebrew *berith* conveys. In so far, then, as the underlying Hebrew gives us the meaning of διαθήκη, it indicates that the word signified a transaction between two parties in which one party held the decisive position, laid down the conditions of the agreement, and in general imposed his will, the sole function of the other party being to accept or reject what was determined by the dominant partner.

This sense is supported by the words in the LXX which occur in parallel with διαθήκη, such as νόμος, πρόσταγμα, ἐντολαί, δικαιώματα, κρίματα.[1] None of these terms accords with a compact or mutual agreement, but all rather indicate an ordering that is completely unilateral.

V. διαθήκη IN NON-BIBLICAL GREEK

Outside the Septuagint and the New Testament διαθήκη seems to have meant a will or testament almost invariably. Thus for the κοινή we note that MM say: 'In papyri and inscrr. the word means *testament, will* with absolute unanimity, and such frequency that illustration is superfluous', and the article goes on to emphasize this by contrasting the use of συνθήκη which 'is to the last the word for *compact*, just as διαθήκη is always and only the word for will'.

W. S. Ferguson's examination of legal terms in the Macedonian inscriptions leads to a similar conclusion. He says of διαθήκη:

'1. That it is testamentary rather than contractual. It is not a mutual compact to which both parties give assent, mutually contracting to do certain things, but the act of one person giving charges to another, or bestowing property on another, or both of these . . .

'2. The thing enjoined in the διαθήκη is apparently always to be executed after the decease of the testator . . .

'3. When property is bequeathed it may be accompanied by a charge to be fulfilled, and in such a way that the commission must be accepted in order to obtain the property . . .

'4. The usage of the term διαθήκη in the inscriptions is similar to its usage in the Old and the New Testaments in that the

[1] See TWNT, II, p. 129.

initiative is always taken by one person. . . . The one making the
διαθήκη always assumes the right to command, and to withhold
his bequest if the conditions attached to it are not fulfilled'.[1]

F. O. Norton has conducted a thorough examination of the use
of the word from the earliest times until well into the classical
period and, in general, he supports the position reached by the
writers cited above. But while recognizing that διαθήκη generally
signifies a testament, he leaves room for the thought that this is
not its inherent meaning, saying that it refers 'to the arrangements
or dispositions a person makes with reference to his property in
view of death. This specific connotation is probably not necessary,
but the context of the passages in which the word is found indicates that it has such reference in these instances. It is quite probable
that, if we had more instances of its use, we should find it
employed with reference to other things than distribution of
property in view of death'.[2] This is in accordance with what we
would expect from the etymology of the word, but Norton is
able to cite only two passages in support of his contention that the
word sometimes means a compact (Isae. vi. 27; Aristoph. Av.
440), and of these two, the former certainly refers to a testament, Norton's argument being that it is a compact as well as a
will, and that the compact aspect is primary. However, this cannot
be regarded as an impressive example, and we are left with but
one use of διαθήκη in the classical writings to denote a compact,
namely Aristoph. Av. 440. Certainly there can be no doubt about
this one (despite Ramsay's hesitation[3]), partly because such a sense
is demanded by the immediate context ('Not I, by Apollo, unless
they make a covenant [διάθωνται διάθηκην] with me such as that
monkey, the sword-maker, made [διέθετο] with his wife, not to
bite me, etc.'),[4] and partly because a little later the same agreement
is referred to as τὰς σπονδάς.

---

[1] *The Legal Terms Common to the Macedonian Inscriptions and the New Testament*, Chicago, 1913, p. 46.

[2] *A Lexicographical and Historical Study of ΔΙΑΘΗΚΗ*, Chicago, 1908, p. 30.

[3] He says: 'The only exception quoted . . . is not very clear. It contains a joke
founded on some unknown popular story of the ape and the woman (or his
wife)' (*The Expositor*, Fifth Series, VIII, p. 325n).

[4] Cited from Norton, *op. cit.*, p. 37.

However, when full allowance is made for the importance of this reference as an aid to the understanding of the history of διαθήκη, it must be admitted that it is well before New Testament times, and that this one clear example from such early days does little to invalidate the fact that, in the first century A.D., and indeed for centuries before that, the uniform significance of διαθήκη (apart from the noteworthy exception of the LXX) was of a will, a testament.

We should point out, however, that the testament in mind was not exactly the same as a will in our sense of the term. In Greece in early days property seems to have descended automatically to the deceased's children, who performed certain duties in connection with the burial of the deceased, and afterwards indulged in a species of ancestor-cult. This came to be regarded as of very great importance and, accordingly, it was a serious matter for a man to die without male issue. Consequently, when a man had no heir, it was usual for him to adopt a son who would after his death receive his property and see that the appropriate rites were carried out. As Ramsay says: 'the Diatheke was primarily an arrangement for the devolution of religious duties and rights, and not merely a bequeathing of money and property . . .'[1]

The adoption of a son was a decisive step, and was, in fact, irrevocable. If, after an adoption, a natural son was born, the adopted son could not be disowned, but must share the inheritance with the natural son. In this particular matter the adopted son was on a better footing than the natural son, for the latter could be put away. Indeed Ramsay calls attention to a passage where a son who had been put away by his father, then restored to favour, and then disowned again, makes his plea that this second putting away is illegal, for he now has the status of an adopted son.[2]

Ramsay makes this an argument for the irrevocability of the διαθήκη. But while this may have been the case in early days, the evidence adduced by Norton seems to show that, at later times, there was the necessary machinery to enable a testator who had changed his mind, to give effect to his new desires. However, if an

[1] Op. cit., p. 324.

[2] Op. cit., p. 302.

adoption was involved Norton thinks this could not be revoked without the consent of both parties.[1] (All early wills centred on an adoption, but in later times it was possible to bequeath one's property even where no adoption was in question.)

Thus the evidence from profane Greek indicates the possibility that διαθήκη at an early stage in its history denoted any authoritative disposition, but that, whether this were so or not, in later times the word became confined (as far as the extant sources show) to a last will and testament, the only exception being the Septuagint where the postulated earlier use seems to be the usual, probably the only, one.

VI. διαθήκη IN THE NEW TESTAMENT

It is not easy to determine which of the two meanings of διαθήκη is to be understood in the New Testament. Some passages use the word with reference to Old Testament covenants and in such contexts it must be understood in the same sense as in the LXX. On the other hand, there are some passages where the meaning 'will' or 'testament', seems indicated, and the final determination of the word's significance in doubtful places is accordingly very difficult.

a. διαθήκαι of Men
It will be convenient to begin our discussion with a consideration of the passages which appeal to the practice among men, and reason from this to the divine διαθήκη. The first of these is Gal. iii. 15f. where Paul reasons: 'Brethren, I speak after the manner of men: Though it be but a man's διαθήκη, yet when it hath been confirmed, no one maketh it void, or addeth thereto . . . Now this I say: A διαθήκη confirmed beforehand by God, the law, which came four hundred and thirty years after, doth not disannul, so as to make the promise of none effect. For if the inheritance is of the law, it is no more of promise: but God hath granted it to Abraham by promise'. Here there are some considerations which point strongly in the direction of testament as the meaning of διαθήκη. The speaking 'after the manner of men' would naturally indicate that the term is to be understood in the normal way, and as we have seen, the extant literature is clear that that would be in the sense of a will. The unchangeability referred to might be

[1] Op. cit., pp. 63f.

understood (as by Ramsay, *op. cit.*) as a reference to a will involving an adoption, which would be an irrevocable provision. Further, the reference to 'inheritance' in verse 18 would accord well with a testamentary action.

While this looks a formidable body of evidence, it is not irrefutable. The speaking 'after the manner of men' may mean no more than that Paul, having derived his illustrations hitherto from Scripture, now proposes to use one from the affairs of men. Again, even a Greek will involving adoption could be modified later, as we have seen. Then, too, Burton shows that the κληρονομία of verse 18 need not necessarily refer to inheritance in the strict sense of the word, the term being sometimes used to signify 'possession'.[1]

A strong argument that the word means 'covenant' is to be discerned in the fact that the reference to the transaction with Abraham in verse 17 is a reference to the Hebrew *berith*. Thus διαθήκη here must be understood in the same sense as in the LXX. But the whole force of the argument demands that the διαθήκη of verse 15 be of the same type as that in verse 17. This seems a decisive consideration, and accordingly we adopt the view that διαθήκη here denotes 'covenant', rather than 'testament', while admitting the strength of the arguments for the opposite view. But we do so understanding the passage as does Duncan who says: 'it matters little which of the two renderings we adopt, for from a truly spiritual standpoint a "covenant" in which God takes part is as essentially a one-sided proposal as a "will" is.'[2] Further, it seems probable that, while covenant is the essential meaning of διαθήκη here, the apostle is making a play on the other meaning of the word. The death of Christ is not far from his thought.

The other passage which falls to be considered under this heading is Heb. ix. 16f.: 'For where a διαθήκη is, there must of necessity be the death of him that made it. For a διαθήκη is of force where there hath been death: for doth it ever avail while he that made it liveth?' Here, again, it would seem on a first reading as though the meaning is 'testament', and many commentators have adopted this rendering. A big difficulty in the way of accepting this is the

---

[1] *Galatians* (I.C.C.), pp. 185f., 503.

[2] *Galatians* (MNTC), p. 106.

fact that, in this passage, διαθήκη seems to be used in the sense 'covenant' both earlier and later than the verse cited. If it means 'testament' we should have to suppose that the writer began by thinking of the word as conveying the thought 'covenant', changed over to 'testament', and then back again to 'covenant', which seems a most unlikely procedure.

Again, Westcott draws attention to the use of the verb φέρεσθαι: 'It is not said that he who makes the covenant "must die", but that his death must be "brought forward", "presented", "introduced upon the scene", "set in evidence", so to speak'.[1] It is of consequence that we do not simply have it said that the maker of a διαθήκη must die, but Westcott does not seem to give sufficient heed to the value of the various alternatives which he notes. For example Delitzsch argues strongly in favour of the idea that the verb conveys the thought that a will is only valid when the death has become 'a fact of common notoriety', for 'before that is known and established, the testament has no legal force'.[2] The use of φέρεσθαι is curious, but it cannot be said to tell strongly against the meaning 'testament'. The same is true of the ἐπὶ νεκροῖς of verse 17; it is not what we would have expected. But, in view of the second half of the verse with its reference to ὁ διαθέμενος, it cannot be held to be proof that anything other than the death of the testator is in the writer's mind. Carr's remark that 'it cannot be affirmed that a will is only of force on the death of the testator. A will properly drawn up and attested is valid or of force during the testator's lifetime'[3] must be unhesitatingly dismissed, for it is surely obvious that a will remains completely inoperative until the testator's death. That is to say, a Roman will does, though we have already seen that a Greek will may become operative immediately. But there is agreement among the commentators that the *auctor ad Hebraeos* moves in the sphere of Roman law rather than Greek, and that it is the Roman will that is in view here if there is any reference to a will, and the Roman will was inoperative until the testator's death.

---

[1] *Hebrews*, p. 265.

[2] *Hebrews*, II, p. 107.

[3] *The Expositor*, Seventh Series, VII, p. 350.

Carr's further suggestion that βεβαία and ἰσχύει point rather to a covenant than to a will[1] must similarly be dismissed. They apply quite well to a will, and the question must be decided on other grounds.

The crucial point seems to be the necessity for the death of the διαθέμενος if the διαθήκη is to become effectual. Westcott explains this as indicating the necessity of the death of the animal victim in covenant sacrifice, which symbolized the death of the party to the covenant so that he no longer had life or power in the matter. 'The unchangeableness of a covenant is seen in the fact that he who has made it has deprived himself of all further power of movement in this respect: while the ratification by death is still incomplete, while the victim, the representative of him who makes it, still lives, that is, while he who makes it still possesses the full power of action and freedom to change, the covenant is not of force'.[2] It may be noticed in passing that, to get this meaning out of the text, Westcott has had to abandon his idea that the meaning of blood is life rather than death, so that 'the blood of the covenant' would mean something different altogether from other sorts of blood. A stronger objection is that Westcott has put all the emphasis on the unchangeability of the covenant, the death being the indication that now the διαθέμενος has no further liberty in this matter. But the unalterable nature of the agreement is not what the writer to the Hebrews is emphasizing, but its coming into effect. Paul in Galatians was saying 'No one annuls or adds to a διαθήκη', but that is not the thought of this passage, which is, rather, 'A διαθήκη is of force, is effectual, comes into operation, only when a man dies'. On the impossibility of fitting this naturally into the framework of covenant Westcott's interpretation breaks down, and we are left to conclude that the passage here must be held to have its natural meaning. The death of Jesus was a necessary thing, for it is only when a διαθέμενος dies that his διαθήκη comes into force.[3]

[1] *Ibid.*

[2] *Op. cit.*, p. 267.

[3] Moffatt speaks of the author 'playing effectively upon the double sense of the term', and goes on to point out that this illustration of a will 'has its defects, but only when pressed beyond what the writer means to imply' (*Hebrews*, I.C.C., p. 127).

This discussion will have shown the extraordinary difficulty of giving a completely satisfying interpretation of διαθήκη in New Testament times. It may well be that the best interpretation is that which sees in διαθήκη essentially the thought of an authoritative disposition. This could naturally pass over into the thought of a testament, or to the sort of covenant we see in the Old Testament with all the emphasis on what God does, and not upon a two-sided compact, with God and man coming to some sort of agreement. The main point to be kept in mind is that the word denotes a divine action, with man the recipient of blessing; and we have no grounds for thinking that, in New Testament times, the word would have been understood of a compact with two partners agreeing that each should assume certain liabilities and obligations.[1]

b. The Old διαθήκη

The passage in Heb. ix which we have just considered shows clearly that in at least one instance the New Testament uses διαθήκη in the sense of will or testament, and, as some think, this meaning is to be discerned also in the background of the passage in Gal. iii. The question may be asked, therefore, whether this use is not (as might be expected from secular usage) the dominant one in the New Testament. An examination, however, of the fourteen New Testament instances of the use of διαθήκη with reference to Old Testament covenants will show indisputably that the usage of the LXX is to be found in the New Testament also.

This use is undeniable in passages like Heb. viii. 9 where διαθήκη occurs twice in a quotation from Je. xxxi. It is true that Jeremiah is speaking of the new covenant rather than the old, but the point is that διαθήκη is used at this point in Hebrews in exactly the LXX manner as the equivalent of the Hebrew *berith*. The same must be said of the references to the ark of the covenant and to the tables of the covenant (Heb. ix. 4) which clearly point to the Old Testament and are not to be understood of a will.

---

[1] It denotes an action which in its main essentials is unilateral although that is not to deny that there is an aspect in which the people have to accept or reject the διαθήκη. But the word places the stress not so much on this acceptance or rejection as on the authoritative laying down of the provisions of the covenant.

The Sinai covenant seems to be in mind throughout the passage Heb. ix. 15ff., and this becomes obvious when we reach verse 19 with its reference to Moses sprinkling the people with blood. Then in verse 20 'the blood of the covenant which God commanded' is a clear allusion to Ex. xxiv. 8,[1] and it shows that the scene on Sinai was present to the minds of early Christians when they heard the words 'the blood of the covenant'. The change of verb from the covenant which God made (διέθετο) of Ex. xxiv. 8 to the covenant which God commanded (ἐνετείλατο) here should be noted, as it fits in with the general idea of διαθήκη as signifying an authoritative disposition. However we translate the word, and whatever we regard as the primary idea expressed by the Greek term, it is clear that what is denoted is an action in which the sovereignty of God has full sway.

A reference to the covenant at Sinai is to be found also in the phrases 'the first covenant' (Heb. ix. 15; cf. 'the first', with covenant understood, in Heb. viii. 7) and 'the old covenant' (2 Cor. iii. 14). In the latter place Paul speaks of 'the reading of the old covenant', by which unusual turn of phrase he seems to be referring to the records of the old covenant. By this would be meant not only the account of the covenant making, whereby the nation was brought into covenant-relationship with God, but also all the documents which depend on this relationship and expound it. The adjective which he uses is παλαιός, a word which is often used 'of things not merely old, but worn by use'[2] and which gives the expression a flavour different from that which would result were ἀρχαῖος used. Both these phrases it may be noted have an implicit reference to the new covenant, and the same is true of Gal. iv. 24 where the Sinai covenant is contrasted with the new covenant.

In this last passage the plural διαθῆκαι is used, and this is the case also in Rom. ix. 4 and Eph. ii. 12 where Old Testament covenants in general are indicated with no close definition, except

---

[1] This may be of importance in understanding other New Testament passages which speak of blood with reference to the new covenant.

[2] Abbott-Smith, *A Manual Greek Lexicon of the New Testament*, Edinburgh. 1944, *sub* παλαιός.

that both passages regard them as peculiarly the possession of the Jew.[1] The Ephesians verse speaks of 'covenants of promise' (the verse in Romans also includes a reference to the promises) which directs attention to the characteristic emphasis on the divine side which is typical of the arrangements between God and men which the LXX calls διαθῆκαι.

Thus we see that the references in the New Testament to the old covenant establish the use of διαθήκη to indicate 'covenant' rather that 'will', but only in such a manner as to indicate the sort of covenant which is dominated by one partner. This is supported by the reference to the covenant which God made with Abraham, which is explicitly mentioned four times in the New Testament (Lk. i. 72; Acts iii. 25, vii. 8; Gal. iii. 17), and on each occasion it is quite clear that the incident referred to is one which, in the Old Testament, is designated *berith*. But again we notice that the emphasis is on what God has done, for the first passage mentioned equates the διαθήκη with 'the oath which He sware unto Abraham'; the second gives the essence of the διαθήκη as God's promise to Abraham, 'in thy seed shall all the families of the earth be blessed'; the third says God 'gave' the covenant; and the fourth is a critical part of Paul's argument that God's way with man is the way of promise, of free grace, and not a way of law-works of any sort.

Under all the circumstances it is, perhaps, unfortunate that διαθήκη is rendered in English by 'covenant', for this word carries with it associations of compact, of agreement, of conditions mutually determined, which are not to be found in the arrangements under consideration. But it is not easy to suggest a better translation, and in any case the rendering is so well established that it would be darkening counsel to suggest an alteration now. But it is important to bear in mind the limitations of this translation.

To sum up. The passages in the New Testament which refer to the old covenant make it clear that we cannot confine the meaning of διαθήκη in the New Testament to the signification 'will', but they do not shake the thought of almost unilateral action

---

[1] The Rabbinic writings sometimes refer to covenants in the plural. See SB, III, p. 262.

which this latter term connotes. The New Testament is just as firm as the Old in its insistence that any covenant with God is one in which God is supreme and man merely the consenting recipient of God's favours and directions.

(c) The New διαθήκη

Underlying the early Christians' use of the term 'the new covenant' is that same presupposition which led later believers to speak of 'the Old Testament' and 'the New Testament', and which leads us to accept unhesitatingly this division of our Scriptures. It is the conception that in Jesus Christ God has done a new work bringing in a radical alteration in man's relationship to his Maker, and making it possible for man to come to God in a way which is quite impossible apart from Him. Whereas hitherto men had tackled the problem of man's sin by the way of the law, they now found it dealt with in a different way, so that they were free from both the penalty and power of sin. As Paul put it: '. . . what the law could not do, in that it was weak through the flesh, God, sending his own Son in the likeness of sinful flesh and for sin, condemned sin in the flesh: that the ordinance of the law might be fulfilled in us, who walk not after the flesh, but after the Spirit' (Rom. viii. 3–4). This conviction that in Jesus Christ God has acted decisively for man's salvation, thus bringing about an entirely new situation, is the master thought of the Christian faith, and it underlies much of the New Testament. When the writers speak of 'the new covenant', then, what they are doing is taking over a well-known concept (well-known, that is, to Jews and all those familiar with the Jewish Scriptures) to express an important aspect of this great new fact. The very fact that the expression 'the *new* covenant' is used indicates that the *berith* of the old Scriptures is in mind and that the New Testament writers, when they use διαθήκη, are thinking primarily of a disposition of God along the lines of Old Testament models, and not the conception of a will. Nevertheless, in view of the universal use of the word outside the Scriptures and of the place they assigned to the death of Christ in the making of the new covenant, it seems probable that in most cases where διαθήκη occurs there is the secondary thought of a death to be discerned with a corresponding benefit to those who were heirs.

But it must be borne in mind that the New Testament writers conceived of the new covenant as in essential harmony with what was known of the nature of God in earlier days, particularly as He had revealed Himself to the patriarchs. There is an important difference in the ways in which they regard the Sinai covenant and that with Abraham, and we proceed to notice this difference.

(i) *The New Covenant and the Covenant with Abraham.* As we have already seen, the covenant with Abraham is referred to four times in the New Testament, and in three of these places it seems to be regarded as of continuing force, the exception being Acts vii. 8 where 'the covenant of circumcision' is mentioned, though even here it is possible to hold that what is being emphasized is not circumcision, but the election of Abraham as shown in the covenant. But putting this aside we find that in Lk. i. 72f. the essence of the covenant is that 'we being delivered out of the hand of our enemies should serve him without fear, in holiness and righteousness before him all our days', and this overruling of God that His people might serve Him is clearly thought of as continuing. The whole point of the reference here is that in the events which arouse Zachariah's song of praise God is remembering His covenant and acting in accordance with it. The covenant with Abraham is not thought of as one of bondage, but one characterized by God's 'visiting' and 'redeeming' His people, raising up 'a horn of salvation' for them, and 'showing mercy'.

Less poetic, but equally definite, is the reference in the speech of Peter in Acts iii. Here Moses, and then 'all the prophets from Samuel and them that followed after, as many as have spoken', are cited as witnessing to Christ; and then the speaker says: 'Ye are the sons of the prophets, and of the covenant which God made with your fathers, saying unto Abraham, And in thy seed shall all the families of the earth be blessed. Unto you first God, having raised up his Servant, sent him to bless you, in turning away every one of you from your iniquities' (Acts iii. 25, 26). Here again, the Abrahamic covenant is thought of as being of continuing force, and the coming of Christ is seen in the context of the promise made to the patriarch.

So it is with the fourth passage, Gal. iii. 15ff. Here the covenant with Abraham is contrasted with the giving of the law, and the conclusion is: 'A covenant confirmed beforehand by God, the law, which came four hundred and thirty years after, doth not disannul, so as to make the promise of none effect. For if the inheritance is of the law, it is no more of promise: but God hath granted it to Abraham by promise' (Gal. iii. 17f.). These words show that the Abrahamic covenant is thought of as giving us God's permanent way of dealing with men—it is by grace or promise, not by law. The Abrahamic covenant is of permanent validity, whereas the law is temporary, being simply 'added because of transgressions, till the seed should come to whom the promise hath been made' (Gal. iii. 19).[1] Again it was 'our tutor to bring us unto Christ, that we might be justified by faith. But now that faith is come, we are no longer under a tutor' (Gal. iii. 24f.). The whole passage stresses the subordinate place assigned to the law in the purposes of God (cf. also Rom. iii. 20, v. 20, viii. 3, x. 4; Gal. ii. 16, 21, etc.), and the line of argument adopted assumes the permanency of the Abrahamic covenant. Because the covenant with Abraham has been confirmed of God, therefore nothing can be added to it nor can it be annulled, and the law can be interpreted only in the light of this fact.

Nor is this an isolated thought of the apostle. We find it again in Rom. iv where he is arguing that Abraham was saved by faith just as Christians are in later days. The continuity of the Christian revelation with the covenant with Abraham is assumed. The same basic assumption lies behind Jas. ii. 21ff., although there the writer is concerned to establish the necessity for works rather than faith. But the point is that he assumes that the principles that determined Abraham's position in the sight of God are the same as those which determine the Christian's position. Again, while it may be argued that the conception of faith in Heb. xi is not the same as that which we see in other parts of the New Testament, yet here we see the same thought stressed, namely that Abraham was accepted with God in the same way as Christians are.

[1] See the commentaries on this verse (e.g. Lightfoot, Duncan, Burton) for the thought that the law was essentially subordinate to the covenant, its function being only to convict men of sin. Cf. G. O. Griffith: 'The Law, properly understood, is in the service of grace; it is the means used by God to school man in the truth of his own insufficiency, and thus to lead him to righteousness where alone it can be found' (*Op. cit.*, p. 108).

Thus it may be claimed that the New Testament witnesses to a genuine continuity between the Abrahamic covenant and the Christian revelation, what was implicit in the former being revealed in the latter. God's dealings with the patriarch were on the principle of grace, and he received the blessings through faith. It is not otherwise with the Christian; only for him the principle of grace has reached its fulfilment in the life and work of Christ.

(ii) *The New Covenant and the Covenant on Sinai.* We saw when we were dealing with the Sinai covenant that it is possible to discern there the principle of grace, but that there is joined thereto the law, which the people solemnly undertook to obey. Further there are many places in the Old Testament where the prophets castigate the nation for failing to keep the covenant, which, in consequence, has become null and void. It is this legal aspect of the Sinai covenant on which the New Testament writers fasten their attention, so that it was just as natural for them to regard the Christian way as the antithesis of the Sinai covenant as it was for them to see in it the continuation and fulfilment of the Abrahamic covenant. In particular, they see in the Christian way a better way than that of Sinai, and a fulfilment of that which Sinai fore-shadowed but could not perform, namely the remission of sin. We deal with these points in order.

1. The *auctor ad Hebraeos* explicitly speaks of the new as a 'better covenant' (Heb. vii. 22, viii. 6) and goes on to point out that 'if that first had been faultless, then would no place have been sought for a second' (Heb. viii. 7) and he proceeds to quote Jeremiah's prophecy of the new covenant, significantly introducing it with the words, 'For finding fault with them, he saith' (Heb. viii. 8). He brings this section to a close by saying: 'In that he saith, A new covenant, he hath made the first old. But that which is becoming old and waxeth aged is nigh unto vanishing away' (Heb. viii. 13). There can be no question but that he conceived of the old covenant as having served its purpose[1] and of having now passed into

---

[1] Cf. F. C. N. Hicks: 'For the Old Testament—or, to speak more correctly, the whole pre-Christian experience of the chosen people—does not solve the problem of life. Its function is to discover it and to state it' (*The Fullness of Sacrifice*, London, 1946, p. 117).

disuse, being replaced by the new relationship made possible by
the work of Jesus Christ; and he proceeds to enlarge upon this in
chapter nine.

Although Paul does not use the category of covenant as fully as
does the writer to the Hebrews, he yet has essentially the same
thought in such a passage as 2 Cor. iii. 6ff. where he speaks of
'ministers of a new covenant; not of the letter, but of the spirit';
and he goes on to point out that 'the letter killeth, but the spirit
giveth life', and to contrast 'the ministration of condemnation'
with 'the ministration of righteousness'. It is clear that here again
we have the old way contrasted with the new, and that the new is
thought of as immeasurably superior to the old. It is one of Paul's
leading ideas that before Christ men struggled to serve God by the
way of the law, but that now it is the way of grace that has been
revealed. Thus in Galatians iii he argues vehemently that the way
of approach to God is the way of promise or grace; definitely it is
not the way of law. It is true that in this chapter and in others he
reasons that Abraham received the blessing, but he presses home
his point that he did so because of his faith, and this becomes
another point in favour of his thesis that not law but grace is the
way. His thought is that God has always accepted men by grace,
and the way of approach by law was never valid. The law he
regards as of divine origin, but it was limited in scope being but a
schoolmaster to bring men to Christ, so that the covenant associated with the giving of the law was immeasurably less than the
new covenant which makes it abundantly plain that the way is by
grace and through faith. There can be no doubt that he would
have accepted the thought of Heb. ix. 15 that the death of Christ
availed for the transgressions committed under the first covenant,
for he is positive that the one way of putting away sin is through
the work of Jesus Christ. It is clear that for Paul, as for the writer to
the Hebrews and, indeed, for all the New Testament writers, the
new way transforms everything; it is infinitely better than the old
way.

Wherein does the superiority of the new consist? Basically
because of the truth expressed in Paul's words 'the letter killeth,
but the spirit giveth life' (2 Cor. iii. 6). This saying recalls the
words of the Lord 'I came that they may have life, and may have
it abundantly' (Jn. x. 10). Indeed, it is characteristic of the New

Testament writers that they stress the quality of the life that is possible for men now that Jesus has come and has wrought His great work of atonement. It is not that they despise the old covenant; on the contrary they regard it as of divine origin and appointment. But it was essentially preparatory and preliminary, and they looked to the fulfilment of what it foreshadowed in the work of Christ. Thus the writer to the Hebrews assigns a subordinate place to the Jewish sacrifices: 'In those sacrifices there is a remembrance made of sins year by year. For it is impossible that the blood of bulls and goats should take away sins' (Heb. x. 3f.). But it is of the very essence of his argument that what the blood of bulls and goats could not do, the blood of Christ both could and did do.

2. This brings us to the point that the new covenant is regarded as essentially an arrangement having regard to the forgiveness of sin. This contrasts with the covenant of Exodus xxiv where the people readily acquiesce in the obligation to carry out the commandments of God. Through the years such obedience was seen to be impossible as generation after generation failed to live up to the standard set before them. It is significant that, when we come to Jeremiah's great prophecy of the new covenant, it includes the provision 'I will put my law in their inward parts, and in their heart will I write it; . . . I will forgive their iniquity, and their sin will I remember no more' (Je. xxxi. 33f.). This aspect of the new covenant comes prominently before us in the New Testament passages. Thus in Heb. viii. 8f., where the passage from Jeremiah is quoted and applied to the Christian fulfilment, the words of the prophet are fully noted right down to the forgiveness of sin, and it is at this point that the writer speaks of the new covenant replacing the old which is 'nigh unto vanishing away'. This connection is even more plain a little later in the Epistle, when the writer again refers to the passage in Jeremiah. This time his quotation is much shorter and he picks out only the passages important for his argument, thus: 'This is the covenant that I will make with them after those days, saith the Lord; I will put my laws on their heart, and upon their mind also will I write them; then saith he, And their sins and their iniquities will I remember

no more' (Heb. x. 16f.). Admittedly the 'then saith he' is an explanatory gloss of the translator, but it truly expresses the mind of the author, and it is significant that he couples the reference to forgiveness with that to the new covenant, though they are separated by several verses in the original. Obviously forgiveness was to him the essential part of the new covenant.[1] It could easily be demonstrated from the Epistle that the author found a large place for forgiveness in his total view of things Christian. What the above citations show is that not only is this the case, but that this forgiveness was present to his mind *when he used the expression, 'the new covenant'.* The element of grace, which, while present in the old covenant, was obscured by the necessity for keeping the law, he sees stressed in the new covenant; for it is essentially a covenant based upon divine forgiveness of sin.

We see the same tendency towards associating the new covenant with forgiveness of sin in St. Paul's only reference to the new covenant having been foretold. Thus he quotes Isaiah as follows: 'There shall come out of Zion the Deliverer; he shall turn away ungodliness from Jacob: and this is my covenant unto them, when I shall take away their sins' (Rom. xi. 26f.). There is no particular difficulty about the first part of this quotation which is a rather free citation of the LXX of Is. lix. 20. But the words about forgiveness of sin are not to be found in this passage; they come from Is. xxvii. 9. Here we see at work, and in a more striking form, the same process we have already noted in Hebrews. Paul is writing about the covenant, and as he wishes to express its essence, he adds to his citation from Is. lix. 20 other words, separated in the original by many chapters, but which bring out the central truth expressed by the new covenant.

Thus, each time the New Testament refers to the new covenant as having been prophesied it does so linking an explicit reference to forgiveness of sin with the new covenant. This happens also in a number of passages where prophecy is not in question. Thus in Heb. ix. 15 we have the interesting expression, 'And for this

---

[1] Cf. Moffatt on Heb. viii. 8: 'The real interest of the writer in the Jeremianic oracle is shown when he returns to it in x. 16-18; what arrests him is the promise of a free, full pardon at the close'.

cause he is the mediator of a new covenant, that a death having taken place for the redemption of the transgressions that were under the first covenant', where the death that inaugurates the new covenant is seen as providing the way of forgiveness, even for those transgressions committed under the first covenant. The obvious inference is that such sins could not really be forgiven under the provisions of the first covenant, and that therefore the new covenant was an absolute necessity. Probably it is this truth that is in mind also when the same writer says that Jesus is 'the mediator of a better covenant, which hath been enacted upon better promises' (Heb. viii. 6), the better promises being those concerned with forgiveness and man's reconciliation with God, as is seen from the following section.

This thought is not so prominent, but nevertheless it seems to be in the background, in two Pauline references. Thus, when Paul speaks of the two covenants, contrasting the Jerusalem that now is with the Jerusalem that is above, the aspect that he stresses is that of the freedom that accrues to those in the new covenant. He says of the present Jerusalem that 'she is in bondage with her children' (Gal. iv. 25), whereas 'the Jerusalem that is above is free'. It seems clear that one aspect in the freedom that is spoken of is freedom from the power of sin, that is the freedom that comes to the believer because Christ has put away his sin. It is not otherwise with the passage in which Paul speaks of himself as a minister of a new covenant and proceeds to contrast 'the ministration of condemnation' with 'the ministration of righteousness'. For surely he means here that, under the old covenant, the outcome must be condemnation; whereas, under the new, man's sin is put away so that he stands righteous.

This aspect of the new covenant seems also to be indicated by those passages which refer to the 'blood of the covenant', for it is by the shedding of Jesus' blood that sin is put away and the covenant established. There seems to be a linking of the two ideas, and this comes to the surface sometimes as in Mt. xxvi. 28: 'This is my blood of the covenant, which is shed for many unto remission of sins'. Most commentators regard 'unto remission of sins' as a gloss; but even so the expression shows what covenant blood meant to a very early Christian.[1] The Markan parallel lacks the reference to the forgiveness of sins, but it speaks of the blood being shed for many; and the Lukan passage (which is usually rejected on textual grounds, though its genuineness is accepted, as for example by Vos in HDCG) runs: 'This cup is the new covenant in my blood, even that which is poured out for you', so that it, too, stresses the place of the shedding of Christ's blood. While this does not demand for its interpretation that we understand the passage as referring to the remission of sins, at the very least it is quite consonant with such an understanding, and the same may be said of the other passages where 'the blood of the covenant' is spoken of.

This is quite in accordance with what we saw in our treatment of the covenant of Exodus xxiv, and in particular of the significance of 'The blood of the covenant' in that passage. There we saw reason for thinking that the expression symbolized both expiation and consecration, as the people were cleansed for their new relationship to God. So, in the new covenant, the blood shed was a means of purifying the people by providing for the remission of their sins, and of consecrating them to their new relationship to God. If, as seems probable, we are to see in the New Testament references to 'the blood of the covenant' allusions to Ex. xxiv. 8, then we must see in them also references to an expiatory and consecratory death, whereby men are brought into a new relationship with God.

It is, of course, just possible that the New Testament references to 'the blood of the covenant' point back to Zc. ix. 11, rather than to Ex. xxiv. 8, and Vincent Taylor cites Joachim Jeremias as an exegete who adopts this interpretation.[2] Twice in the Rabbinic

---

[1] On this verse Allen comments: 'Mt., by adding εἰς ἄφεσιν ἁμαρτιῶν shows that he understood the covenant to be a covenant between God and the many by which remission of sins was secured to them' (I.C.C., p. 276). More apposite for our present purpose is the comment of McNeile who sees in 'This is my blood of the covenant' a reference to the peace-offering, and in 'unto remission of sins' a reference to the sin offering, and adds, 'But the latter is presupposed in the former, even if Jesus did not say "for the remission of sins"' (Comm. *in loc*). That is, he sees the thought of remission in the very idea of the new covenant.

[2] *Jesus and His Sacrifice*, London, 1939, pp. 138f. R. Mackintosh (*Historic Theories of Atonement*, Toronto, 1920, pp. 54f.) also accepts this point of view.

literature the blood of the Passover victim is spoken of as 'covenant-blood', Zc. ix. 11 being interpreted of the deliverance of Israel from Egypt; and Jeremias thinks that Jesus (who had this chapter of Zechariah in mind during His last days as we see from Mt. xxi. 5) was comparing His blood to that of the Passover lamb at the departure from Egypt. Jeremias thinks that Jesus is describing 'His death as an atoning death which establishes the new and eternal communion of a humanity cleansed from sin with its God—the communion of the Kingdom of God'. We would agree with Dr. Taylor that this is not as probable as a reference to Ex. xxiv. 8, but as the words last quoted show, even if Jeremias' view be accepted, the significance of the covenant-blood is much the same. It still remains true that it is the means of cleansing and that it brings men into communion with God.

3. The rite described in Exodus xxiv had the effect of bringing the people into such a relationship with God that they could be called a holy people, and this aspect can be paralleled with regard to the new covenant. Thus Heb. x. 29 speaks of 'the blood of the covenant, wherewith he was sanctified', and Heb. xii. 24 of coming to 'Jesus the mediator of a new covenant, and to the blood of sprinkling that speaketh better than that of Abel' where the reference to 'blood of sprinkling' seems to point to the sprinkling of the people recorded in Exodus xxiv whereby they were consecrated to their new relationship to God and symbolically purified.[1] We have another reference to sprinkling in 1 Pet. i. 2, and here again it would seem that we are to see a reference to the covenant of Exodus xxiv for, as Hort points out,[2] there are only three examples of people being sprinkled with blood in the Old Testament, and there is no reason to see in this passage an allusion to either of the others. The writer is thus directing the attention of his readers to the fact that Christians are brought into a new covenant with God, and that they have been sprinkled with blood as the means of admission thereto. The significance of this is, if we may again cite Hort, 'the sprinkling presupposed a shedding;

---

[1] Cf. Delitzsch: 'It is common to the blood-sprinkling under both testaments that it is the medium whereby the apprehension of the promises proper to either covenant is realized' (*Hebrews*, II, p. 354).

[2] *The First Epistle of Peter*, London, 1898, p. 23.

the consecration of the New Covenant presupposed the antecedent sacrifice of the Cross'.[1] The fact that in this context the writer speaks of obedience gives another point of contact with the Old Testament passage, for there the people agreed to obey the commandments of Yahweh. Though the men of the new covenant rely on the work of Christ for their acceptance, and not on any deeds of their own, yet true faith brings forth in their lives the fruit of godly living. These passages indicating the sanctifying aspect of the new covenant bring this out.

But the passages cited seem to teach more than that a high ethical standard is set before Christians. There seems to be the thought that there is a power given them to enable them to live the sort of lives they should. The quotation from Jeremiah xxxi in Heb. viii. 8ff. includes the passage: 'For this is the covenant that I will make with the house of Israel after those days, saith the Lord; I will put my laws into their mind, and on their heart also will I write them'; and this activity within the people of the new covenant the early Christians found fulfilled in the activity of the Holy Spirit in their hearts. At any rate the empowering of the Holy Spirit of God is an integral feature of the new covenant, so that, while the standards are not relaxed one whit, the indwelling Spirit enables those in the new covenant to have a continual victory over the forces of evil.

4. A further aspect of New Testament teaching on the new covenant is that which draws attention to the finality of the new arrangement. This might be held to be implied in the fact that the new covenant is based on forgiveness of sins, and of course its finality is directly prophesied in Je. xxxi. 34 with its 'their sin will I remember *no more*'. In the New Testament it comes to expression in such a passage as Heb. xiii. 20 in the benediction which speaks of 'the blood of the eternal covenant', the adjective reminding us that this covenant passes not away. Probably we are to deduce the same from the reference in Rev. xi. 19 to the ark of the covenant in heaven. The allusion is rather mysterious, but it seems to indicate that there is heavenly warrant for thinking that God's new covenant is permanent.

[1] *Op. cit.*, p. 24.

VII. CONCLUSION

There does not seem to be any necessary connection between covenant and substitution, unless the death of the victim, which formed a necessary part of the covenant-making process, is regarded as the symbolical death of the partners. This is possible, and, as we have seen, is adopted, for example, by Westcott. But we accept as more probable the idea that the death of the victim is a symbolic calling down of a curse on the one who breaks the covenant. Regarded in this way a covenant is a very solemn agreement between two partners which involves obligations and blessings, though in the case of any given covenant these may be one-sided. But there is no reason for associating substitution with such a covenant any more than with any other form of compact.

But though, in general, covenant may not be held to involve a process of substitution, it is quite possible that any given covenant may include a substitutionary aspect. Thus a number of commentators think there is a process of substitution involved in the incident related in Exodus xxiv either from the point of view of the victim being thought of as a substitute for the partners in the blood-brotherhood or as an atoning sacrifice substituting for the sinners.

When we turn to the New Testament we notice that there is a necessary connection between the death of Christ and the establishing of the covenant. Into his discussion of the new covenant the writer of the Epistle to the Hebrews inserts 'for where a διαθήκη is, there must of necessity be the death of him that made it', and this statement seems to be in accord with the general line of New Testament teaching on the subject. Although it does not often come to the surface, yet it seems to be understood by all that there was a necessity in the death of Christ; had He not died there would have been, there could have been, no new covenant. This is expressed at least in part by the use of διαθήκη to denote the new covenant for, as we have seen, the word was in general use for a will, and it would normally conjure up thoughts of death in men's minds. Even when it is the thought of covenant rather than will that is in mind the other meaning of the word must have been present to give the expression an unusual flavour. 'A Hellenist like the *auctor ad Hebraeos*, or even a Jew like Paul, with Greek language in the very fibre of his thought, could never have used δ. for *covenant* without the slightest consciousness of its ordinary and contemporary meaning'.[1]

This is implied, too, in the passages which associate forgiveness with the covenant. As we have seen this is a common New Testament conception; and it is also common in the New Testament that the death of Christ is associated with our forgiveness. It will hardly be seriously disputed that the New Testament writers rightly or wrongly conceived of the death of Christ as necessary to the forgiveness of sin, so that where they speak of this forgiveness as an essential element in the new covenant they clearly make the death of the Lord integral to the process, and not merely something incidental.

The same thing follows from the fact that the new covenant is modelled on that of Exodus xxiv. Whatever may be said about covenants in general it cannot be denied that the blood of the victim was necessary in that rite; and if the new covenant is derived from the old, it may well be argued that the death of Christ is a necessary part of the process accordingly. The same, too, would follow from the repeated references to 'the blood of the covenant' for, as we shall see in the next chapter, blood in the Scripture must be understood of the infliction of death. The fact that the blood of the covenant is met with on several occasions shows that it was not regarded as a non-essential but as a very important part of the process.

If we hold to the view that the essence of sacrifice was seen in vicarious punishment in New Testament times (as Paterson in HDB; A. E. Garvie in *The Christian Certainty Amid the Modern Perplexity*, p. 79; H. Maldwyn Hughes, *What is the Atonement?* p. 58), then such considerations as these will impel us to believe that the establishment of the new covenant required the death of Him that established it as a substitute for the death of sinners. But this aspect is not stressed in the covenant terminology, for there the dominant idea is the new relationship between God and those who become the people of God.

Thus we may say that the use of the term covenant to describe the work of Christ reminds us that because of His death there has

---

[1] MM sub διαθήκη.

come into being the people of God, bound to Him by especially close ties. Looking backward we can say that this emphasizes forgiveness, for only those who are cleansed from sin may fittingly be termed God's people, and this explains the stress we have seen laid on forgiveness in connection with covenant. Looking forward we can say that it emphasizes newness of living for God's people must be *God's* people.

ADDITIONAL NOTE: COVENANT AND MEDIATION

It will be convenient to add here a few words about the subject of mediation, since Jesus is said to have been 'the mediator' of a new or better covenant three times, and 'the surety' for it once.[1]

If we may begin with this latter term, the Greek word used is ἔγγυος, which seems to be derived from an old word for 'hand' and thus signifies 'in the hand'. It conveys the idea then of guarantee, for what is in the hand is assured. The word according to MM is common in legal documents in the sense of surety, guarantor. When we read, then, that Jesus has become 'the surety of a better covenant' (Heb. vii. 22) we are confronted with the idea that Jesus guarantees the new relationship; He has brought it about by His own action, and now nothing less than His Person assures us that the new relationship is valid.

The other term, μεσίτης, signifies etymologically 'one who stands in the midst', and it is used of an arbitrator or of a peacemaker. Oepke distinguishes three senses: '1. The neutral, or trusted person (arbitrator or peace-negotiator), 2. The mediator in a general spatial sense, 3. The reconciler, negotiator in the sense of the restoration of a relationship which otherwise would not be in existence'.[2] He finds the first of these meanings in the Epistle to the Hebrews and the third in other parts of the New Testament, while the second is lacking in these writings. MM rather similarly find the word used in the papyri often for arbiter, also for intermediary and for surety.

[1] The idea of mediation is much more widespread than its mention in set terms. Ryder Smith says it 'pervades the New Testament' (*The Bible Doctrine of Salvation*, London, 1941, p. 220).

[2] TWNT, IV, pp. 603f.

Of the New Testament occurrences of the term, those in Gal.
iii. 19f. are of some importance as showing what was understood
by the term, although they do not immediately concern us here
because they do not refer to the new covenant. Paul says the law
'was ordained through angels by the hand of a mediator. Now a
mediator is not of one; but God is one'. The first mediator is
clearly Moses and this is of help as it enables us to see that the sort
of activity engaged in by this patriarch at the time of the establishing of the first covenant is to be thought of as mediatorship.
Then comes the principle 'a mediator is not of one', which is to
say that the very presence of a mediator implies the existence of
two parties; there could be no mediator if only one party were
concerned. In Westcott's words: 'A covenant generally, and
obviously a covenant between God and man, requires a mediator,
one who standing between the contracting parties shall bring
them duly into fellowship.'[1]

In the Epistle to the Hebrews there are three passages which fall
to be considered: 'But now hath he obtained a ministry the more
excellent, by how much also he is the mediator of a better covenant, which hath been enacted upon better promises' (Heb. viii. 6);
'And for this cause he is the mediator of a new covenant, that a
death having taken place for the redemption of the transgressions
that were under the first covenant, they that have been called may
receive the promise of the eternal inheritance' (Heb. ix. 15); (ye
are come) 'to Jesus the mediator of a new covenant, and to the
blood of sprinkling that speaketh better than Abel' (Heb. xii. 24).
All three passages speak of the blessings that accrue to those in the
new covenant, and the latter two explicitly mention the death of
the Lord, by which the covenant was brought about. The media-
torial activity seems to consist in that death which established the
covenant and thus brought God and man together. Moffatt thinks
that μεσίτης in these passages 'is practically a synonym for
ἔγγυος',[2] but this hardly seems warranted. It is better (with
Westcott) to regard each word as retaining its own meaning, the
establishing of the covenant being in mind in these passages and
the guaranteeing of it in Heb. vii. 22.

[1] *Hebrews*, p. 220.

[2] *Hebrews* (I.C.C.), p. 107.

The idea of mediation then, brings us the two thoughts that the new covenant is one expressly guaranteed by Christ Himself, and that it is His activity which establishes the covenant. Both thoughts drive us back to the characteristic biblical position that our salvation is all of God, for it is all of Christ.

'For there is one God, one mediator also between God and men, himself man, Christ Jesus, who gave himself a ransom for all' (1 Tim. ii. 5f.).

CHAPTER III

THE BLOOD

THE meaning of the word 'blood' in Scripture, especially with
reference to the blood of the sacrifices in the Old Testament
and to the blood of Christ in the New, has been the subject of some
discussion, and the writings of Milligan, Westcott, Hicks, and
Vincent Taylor, to name but a few, have urged the opinion that
by 'the blood' life is meant rather than death; so that the essential
thing in sacrifice is the offering up of life. This view has been
opposed by such scholars as Denney, Moffatt, Armitage
Robinson, and more recently, Behm (Art. αἷμα in TWNT) and
F. J. Taylor (Art. 'Blood' in *A Theological Word Book of the Bible*).[1]
There seems room for an inquiry into the biblical use of the term.

I. 'BLOOD' IN THE OLD TESTAMENT

a. Classification of Passages
The word *dam* is used in the Hebrew Bible 362 times with various
shades of meaning, and the occurrences may be grouped as follows:

(i) *Death with violence of some kind:* 203 examples.

(1) Generally: 165 examples. Here I class passages like 'Whoso
sheddeth man's blood, by man shall his blood be shed' (Gn. ix. 6);
'the avenger of blood' (Nu. xxxv. 19, etc.); 'he that maketh
inquisition for blood remembereth them' (Ps. ix. 12).

(2) In the phrase 'innocent blood': 21 examples. 'Thou shalt
put away the innocent blood from Israel' (Dt. xix. 13).

(3) One's blood being on oneself: 12 examples. 'For every
one that curseth his father or his mother shall surely be put to
death . . . his blood shall be upon him' (Lv. xx. 9).

(4) Death of animals: 5 examples. 'What man soever there
be of the house of Israel, that killeth an ox, or lamb, or goat . . .
and hath not brought it unto the door of the tent of meeting, to

---

[1] See additional note on pp. 122ff. for some important statements.

offer it as an oblation unto the Lord . . . blood shall be imputed unto that man; he hath shed blood' (Lv. xvii. 3f.).

(ii) Connecting life with blood: 7 examples.

'For as to the life of all flesh, the blood thereof is all one with the life thereof' (Lv. xvii. 14).

(iii) Eating meat with blood: 17 examples.

(1) The practice prohibited: 12 examples. 'Ye shall eat neither fat nor blood' (Lv. iii. 17).

(2) The practice occurring: 5 examples. 'The people did eat them with the blood' (1 Sa. xiv. 32). This group is closely connected with the previous as Lv. xvii. 11, 14 will show.

(iv) Sacrificial blood: 103 examples.[1]

(1) Generally: 94 examples. 'Thou shalt not offer the blood of my sacrifice with leavened bread' (Ex. xxiii. 18).

(2) The institution of the Passover: 6 examples.

(3) Heathen sacrifices: 3 examples.

(v) Other uses: 32 examples.

(1) Turning the Nile into blood: 8 examples.

(2) Processes of birth, etc.: 12 examples.

(3) Bleeding: 3 examples.

(4) Colour: 3 examples.

(5) Of grapes: 2 examples.

(6) 'A bridegroom of blood': 2 examples.

(7) Metaphorical: two examples. 'Shall I drink the blood of the men that went in jeopardy of their lives?' (2 Sam. xxiii. 17).

From these figures it is clear that the commonest use of *dam* is to denote death by violence, and, in particular, that this use is found about twice as often as that to denote the blood of sacrifice. There is a difference also in distribution, for the blood of the sacrifices is often mentioned in Leviticus and Exodus (the actual figures are fifty-nine for Leviticus and nineteen for Exodus), but rarely elsewhere, there being only twenty-five references to sacrificial blood in all the rest of the Old Testament. By contrast the use of blood to denote violent death is not specially located in

---

[1] It may well be that after examination it will appear that the meaning of sacrificial blood is essentially that of one of the other groups, but for the present it seems best to leave it as a separate group.

any part of the Old Testament, and is found almost throughout. As far as it goes, then, the statistical evidence seems to indicate that the association most likely to be conjured up when the Hebrews heard the word 'blood' used was that of violent death.

b. The Connection between Blood and Life

Those who think that 'the blood' means essentially 'the life' pay much attention to Lv. xvii. 11, 'For the life of the flesh is in the blood: and I have given it to you upon the altar to make atonement for your souls: for it is the blood that maketh atonement by reason of the life', and to Gn. ix. 4, Dt. xii. 23, which give the thought that 'the blood is the life'. They also draw attention to the prohibition of eating flesh with the blood yet in it (Lv. iii. 17, vii. 26f., xvii. 10, 12, 14, etc.), the refusal of David to 'drink the blood of the men that went in jeopardy of their lives' (2 Sa. xxiii. 17), the parallel statements that Yahweh will require 'your blood, the blood of your lives' and 'the life of man' (Gn. ix. 5), and the psalmist's parallel use of 'soul' and 'blood' (Ps. lxxii. 14). This represents a formidable body of evidence and indicates that among the Hebrews there was a recognized close connection between life and blood.

But does it indicate more? Many think it does; for example, Vincent Taylor says: 'The victim is slain in order that its life, in the form of blood, may be released . . . the aim is to make it possible for life to be presented as an offering to the Deity. More and more students of comparative religion, and of Old Testament worship in particular, are insisting that the bestowal of life is the fundamental idea in sacrificial worship'.[1] On this view the slaughter of the animal is necessary, but only because there is no other way of obtaining the blood, the life, and the death plays no real part in the sacrifice.

It is difficult to see how such a view can be substantiated. It goes beyond the words of the passages cited, for there is none which speaks of the blood as indicating life in distinction from death. Some of the passages adduced lend no real support to the idea when we look into them. Thus, while it is true that in Gn. ix. 5 'your blood, the blood of your lives' is used in the same fashion as 'the life of man', yet as soon as we ask what the passage means we

---

[1] *Jesus and His Sacrifice*, London, 1939, pp. 54f.

see that death is signified rather than life. When Yahweh says He
will require the life or the blood of man, He is not asking men to
produce life or hand it back to Him: He is saying that men will be
held responsible for destroying life. It is not otherwise with the
parallelism of 'soul' and 'blood' in Ps. lxxii. 14. What is meant by
'precious shall their blood be in his sight' is made clear by the
very similar statement of Ps. cxvi. 15, 'Precious in the sight of the
Lord is the death of his saints', so that redeeming the soul in the
first half of the verse is an expression meaning 'to deliver from
death' (cf. Ps. cxvi. 8). Similarly David's refusal to 'drink the
blood of the men that went in jeopardy of their lives' is a metaphorical statement and must be understood so. David certainly did
not mean that he would literally be partaking of either the blood
or the lives of the men, and the statement must not be tortured
into giving an unreal meaning. It is a defect of the view we are
considering that it insists on taking very literally certain statements about blood, when there is abundant evidence that the
word was used continually in a variety of metaphorical senses.
Thus we read of 'innocent blood', and there are many expressions
like 'his blood be on his own head' which make nonsense if we try
to take them in a literal sense. So it is when we read: 'Cursed be he
that taketh reward to slay an innocent person (lit. the blood of the
innocent)' (Dt. xxvii. 25), for it is manifestly impossible to limit
the application of the words to cases in which blood literally
flows, whilst exempting murders contrived without actual spilling
of blood. Again, A. M. Stibbs draws attention to another figurative use of 'vivid word pictures involving "blood" . . . especially
to indicate people's connection with someone's death',[1] and he
cites Judah's saying concerning Joseph, 'What profit is it if we slay
our brother, and conceal his blood?' (Gn. xxxvii. 26), the
description of Joab as one who 'shed the blood of war in peace, and
put the blood of war upon his girdle . . . and in his shoes' (1 Ki.
ii. 5), and the psalmist's idea of the vengeance of the righteous
when 'he shall wash his feet in the blood of the wicked' (Ps. lviii.
10). Such examples could be multiplied, and in the face of them it
is difficult to insist that passages like Lv. xvii. 11 mean that life is
literally in the blood.

[1] *The Meaning of the Word 'Blood' in Scripture*, London, 1947, pp. 10f.

Further, it may not be without significance that *nephesh* which is translated 'life' in Lv. xvii. 11 is not coterminous with the English 'life' and can mean something very like 'life yielded up in death'. I am not thinking of passages which refer to 'taking away', 'losing', 'destroying', 'giving up' or 'devouring' life, or to 'putting one's life in one's hand' or of the life 'departing'. Nor even am I thinking of the fact that a not uncommon way of referring to slaying is to speak of 'smiting the *nephesh*' (Gn. xxxvii. 21; Nu. xxxv. 11; Je. xl. 14, etc.), or that those who desire to murder someone are usually said to 'seek his *nephesh*', an expression which occurs thirty times (e.g. Ex. iv. 19; Ps. xxxv. 4) and which is reinforced by others which speak of 'lying in wait for the *nephesh*', 'laying a snare for the *nephesh*', etc. (1 Sa. xxviii. 9; Pr. i. 18) or of the passages which refer to 'slaying the *nephesh*' or the *nephesh* 'dying' (Nu. xxxi. 19; Ezk. xiii. 19, xviii. 4), although there may be significance in the fact that the word is used in such a variety of ways with regard to death. But more important for our present purpose are passages where *nephesh* plainly points to death. Thus the sailors, about to cast Jonah into the sea, pray 'let us not perish for this man's *nephesh*' (Jon. i. 14) where it is plainly his death and not his life they have in mind. It is not otherwise with a number of passages which speak of 'life for life' as the punishment for murder, for example, 'Deliver him that smote his brother, that we may kill him for the *nephesh* of his brother whom he slew' (2 Sa. xiv. 7).[1] Then there are passages wherein *nephesh* is translated by 'dead' or a similar term, as 'Ye shall not make any cuttings in your flesh for the dead (*lanephesh*)' (Lv. xix. 28, and cf. Lv. xxi. 1, xxii. 4; Nu. v. 2, vi. 11, ix. 6, 7, 10; Hg. ii. 13, and, with the addition of *meth*, Lv. xxi. 11; Nu. vi. 6, xix. 11, 13). The expression 'blood of the life (lives)' is found twice (Pr. xxviii. 17; Je. ii. 34) and both times it signifies violent death. From all this it is clear that the association of *nephesh* with *dam* in Lv. xvii. 11, etc., cannot be held to prove that life is thought of as still existent after the blood has been poured forth. This use of both *nephesh* and *dam* in other contexts makes it more probable that the meaning here is of

---

[1] Cf. Ex. xxi. 23; Lv. xxiv. 18; Dt. xix. 21, and passages where the letting go of a prisoner is to be punished by the execution of the guard responsible, 1 Ki. xx. 39, 42; 2 Ki. x. 24.

life given up in death.[1] This is supported by the fact that it is 'the life *of the flesh*' that is said to be in the blood, and it is precisely this life which ceases to exist when the blood is poured out. For the understanding of sacrifice there is an important use of *nephesh* in Is. liii. 10ff. where the offering of the *nephesh* is spoken of in sacrificial terms (it is an *'asham*, a guilt offering). But in verse 12 we have this offering of *nephesh* described as 'he poured out his *nephesh* unto death'.

Again, to speak of the life as in some way existent in the blood subsequent to the slaughter of the animal is to ignore the Hebrew stress on the connection of life with the body. So far were the Hebrews from thinking of an immaterial principle of life that they associated life in the age to come not with the immortality of the soul, but with the resurrection of the body. If they found difficulty in thinking of human life persisting after the death of the body, it is most unlikely that they would think of the life of an animal as persisting after slaughter. Indeed, in the case of most of the sacrifices there is explicit mention of the animal being killed before the blood is referred to. To take an example at random: it is very difficult to believe that the writer had life in mind when he said, with reference to the cleansing of a leprous house, the priest 'shall . . . dip (certain things) in the blood of the slain bird' (Lv. xiv. 51), for the bird is expressly said to be 'slain'. We seem far from the extremely practical Hebrew turn of mind when we read of 'soul-substance' (with Oesterley and E. O. James), or of the term blood suggesting 'the thought of life, dedicated, offered, transformed, and open to our spiritual appropriation'.[2] It is much more likely that Stibbs is correct when he sums up as follows: 'Blood shed stands, therefore, not for the release of life from the burden of the flesh, but for the bringing to an end of life in the flesh. It is a witness to physical death, not an evidence of spiritual survival.'[3]

[1] Cf. Lods' explanation of the verse: 'There is a ransom, a redemption, a death by proxy' (*The Prophets and the Rise of Judaism*, London, 1937, p. 294).

[2] Vincent Taylor, *The Atonement in New Testament Teaching*, London, 1946, p. 198. It is largely his view of the meaning of blood which leads him to say 'those scholars are justified who insist that the most significant conception in sacrifice is that of life offered to God' (*Jesus and His Sacrifice*, London, 1939, p. 59). But he frankly admits 'It would be folly to pretend that this conception of sacrifice is taught in the Old Testament or was a theme of Rabbinical teaching' (*Ibid.*).

[3] *Op. cit.*, p. 12.

c. The Problem of Atonement

Examination of the passages treating of atonement is relevant to our present inquiry, for if they show that atonement is generally linked with life, then, in view of Lv. xvii. 11, they will support the idea that life and blood are much the same thing, and further, they will strengthen the hands of those who feel that the essential thing in sacrifice is the offering of life. But if, on the other hand, we find that atonement is linked with death they will form evidence against both these conclusions.

Atonement seems to be connected with the blood in the manner of Lv. xvii. 11 eleven times outside that verse, some of the passages being so specific as to leave us in no doubt as to the atoning efficacy of blood, as, for example, when we read of the bullock and goat 'whose blood was brought in to make atonement in the holy place' (Lv. xvi. 27), or the direction that 'with the blood of the sin offering of atonement once in the year shall he make atonement for it' (Ex. xxx. 10). But before we conclude that such passages mean that atonement is made by offering of life we must set beside them another verse in which blood is said to atone, namely, Nu. xxxv. 33, 'for blood, it polluteth the land: and no atonement can be made for the land for the blood that is shed therein, but by the blood of him that shed it'. Here we have explicit mention of atonement by blood, but it is certainly the execution of the murderer that is spoken of and not any presentation of his life before God. The importance of this verse as a commentary on Lv. xvii. 11 is not always realized. The Leviticus passage is ambiguous, for the reference to blood could be understood as signifying the presentation of life, or, equally naturally, as indicating the infliction of death, and the same may be said about nearly all the other passages which connect blood and atonement. This enhances the importance of Nu. xxxv. 33, for in this verse there is no ambiguity—the blood which atones is that which flows when the death penalty is inflicted on the criminal. It is true that this is not a sacrifice in the strict meaning of the term, and therefore some will doubt the validity of its application to the sacrificial scene. But consider that in both cases it is expiation of sin that is in question, in both cases the means is blood, in both cases the action is directed towards God, and in both cases atonement is said to be secured. Under these circumstances it is difficult to deny the relevance of the passage.

In addition to this passage there are twenty-two others where atonement is effected by means other than the cultus, which are relevant as showing that atonement and the offering of life were not inseparably connected in Hebrew thought. Of these, four are particularly significant, namely, those in which Moses says he will try to make atonement for the sin of the people and makes his attempt by asking God to blot him out of the book which He has written (Ex. xxxii. 30–32), Phinehas is said to have made atonement by killing Zimri and Cozbi (Nu. xxv. 13), David makes atonement by delivering up seven descendants of Saul to be hanged by the Gibeonites (2 Sa. xxi. 3f.), and the heifer is slain to avert punishment when murder has been committed by a person unknown (Dt. xxi. 1–9). In each of these passages there is atonement made or contemplated, and in none of them can it fairly be argued that what is meant is the presentation of life to God. In each case it is the termination of life, the infliction of death that atones; and so far from any symbol of life being presented to God, the descendants of Saul were hanged, and the heifer killed by having its neck broken. This last passage is remarkable in that in verses 7–9 blood is mentioned four times and the verb *kipper* occurs twice, yet atonement is not connected with blood at all.

Turning now to those passages where atonement is connected with the cultus, the usual way is to speak quite generally of the whole sacrifice, as when we read 'he shall prepare the sin offering, and the meal offering, and the burnt offering, and the peace offerings, to make atonement for the house of Israel' (Ezk. xlv. 17). Thirty-eight times in all atonement is referred to in this way, and though probably it would not be wise to build too much on this, yet the general impression from them all is that it is the whole offering, rather than the presentation of the blood that is thought of as effecting atonement. This impression is strengthened by the fact that sometimes the mention of atonement is attached to a point in the ritual other than the manipulation of the blood. Thus it is mentioned in connection with the laying of hands on the head of the beast (Lv. i. 4),[1] or with the burning of the fat

---

[1] Similarly in the Mishna we find mention of atonement in the confession while hands are laid on the head of the animal (Yom. iii. 8, iv. 2, vi. 2).

(Lv. iv. 26).[1] These turns of expression are natural enough if it is the whole offering which atones, but they represent a strange way of speaking if the essence of it all is the offering of life contained in the blood.

Then there are passages in which atonement is mentioned in connection with rites prescribed by the cultus, but where the blood seems definitely to be excluded. Thus Aaron and his sons are instructed that 'they shall eat those things wherewith atonement was made' (Ex. xxix. 33), where, since the reference is to a carcass from which the blood has been drained, neither blood nor life can possibly be meant. Similar is the passage in which Moses rebukes the sons of Aaron, asking: 'Wherefore have ye not eaten the sin offering in the place of the sanctuary, seeing it is most holy, and he hath given it you to bear the iniquity of the congregation, to make atonement for them before the Lord?' (Lv. x. 17). In neither of these examples does it seem possible to maintain that the essence of atonement is through offering of life. On the contrary, in both cases the death of the animal seems to be regarded as a necessity in the making of atonement.

In this connection attention should be drawn to certain passages in which the slaughter of nations is likened to sacrifice. Thus Jeremiah speaks of the destruction of the mighty men of Egypt and her allies and proceeds: 'And the sword shall devour and be satiate, and shall drink its fill of their blood: for the Lord, the Lord of hosts, hath a sacrifice in the north country' (Je. xlvi. 10). So also Zp. i. 7, 'for the Lord hath prepared a sacrifice, he hath sanctified his guests'. If the essence of sacrifice is the presentation of life before God such passages are completely inexplicable, and they only receive adequate explanation when we hold that sacrifice is inherently the destruction of the victims.

---

[1] In view of this association of atonement with the fat it is worth noticing that a very important place is assigned to the fat throughout the sacrifices, so that this association with atonement is not surprising. Thus it is explicitly said that 'all the fat is the Lord's' (Lv. iii. 16), and there is a prohibition of eating the fat in exactly the same terms as that of partaking of the blood (see Lv. iii. 17). Similarly the fat and the blood are closely associated with one another in Isaiah's denunciation (see Is. i. 11 and cf. Is. xxxiv. 6). If the manipulation of blood and the final pouring of it at the base of the altar are essentials of sacrifice, no less so is the burning of the fat on the altar. Again, in David's lamentation over Saul and Jonathan (2 Sa. i. 22) fat is clearly just as much a symbol of life (or death) as is blood.

In other places atonement is connected with such ceremonies as the pouring of oil on the head of the cleansed leper (Lv. xiv. 18, 29), the offering of incense (Nu. xvi. 46), the scapegoat (Lv. xvi. 10), and there are others. But these do not seem to forward our inquiry so we pass over them, merely noting that in each case the removal of the particular thing sacrificed from the possession of the offerer seems indicated.[1] In the case of the animal offerings this is almost invariably by death.

Attention should also be drawn to the Passover ritual. In the original Passover, although there is no mention of atonement, there is mention of the blood as a means of averting destruction. 'And the blood shall be to you for a token upon the houses where ye are: and when I see the blood, I will pass over you, and there shall no plague be upon you to destroy you, when I smite the land of Egypt' (Ex. xii. 13). It is impossible to understand from the splashing of blood on the lintel and doorposts that a life is being presented to anyone: the obvious symbolism is that a death has taken place, and this death substitutes for the death of the firstborn.

We conclude, then, that the evidence afforded by the use of the term *dam* in the Old Testament indicates that it signifies life violently taken rather than the continued presence of life available for some new function, in short, death rather than life, and that this is supported by the references to atonement.

II. 'BLOOD' IN THE NEW TESTAMENT

The word αἷμα is found in all ninety-eight times in the New Testament, sometimes simply of blood without any implication of life or death or the like. Thus five times we meet the expression 'flesh and blood', there are four references to the woman with the issue of blood, and there is the unusual expression 'born not of bloods' in Jn. i. 13. Altogether such passages account for twenty-four occurrences of the word.

---

[1] Hubert and Mauss in their important examination of the concept of sacrifice concluded that the essential thing is the destruction of the victim, at least as regards possession by the worshipper. See *L'Année Sociologique*, 1897–8, pp. 71, 76f., 133, etc. Eugène Masure finds the essence of sacrifice in 'a religious transfer of property' (*The Christian Sacrifice*, London, 1944, p. 34).

Twenty-five times the word indicates violent death, this being the largest group, as we have already seen to be the case in the Old Testament. A good example is the statement of St. Paul, 'when the blood of Stephen thy witness was shed, I also was standing by' (Acts xxii. 20), for as that death was by stoning there is no emphasis on the literal outpouring of blood. The expression stands simply for violent death. So is it with the query of the martyrs in the Apocalypse, 'How long, O Master, the holy and true, dost thou not judge and avenge our blood on them that dwell on the earth?' (Rev. vi. 10). It makes nonsense of this passage to insist that there is any emphasis on a literal shedding of blood. The people in question are those 'that had been slain for the word of God, and for the testimony which they held' (Rev. vi. 9), quite irrespective of how they met their death. Very important in this group are the references to 'the blood of Abel' and the 'blood of Zachariah' (Lk. xi. 51), for they form parallels to 'the blood of Christ', and both of them plainly signify death and not any offering of life.

A usage which is probably derived from this is that in which 'blood' signifies spiritual, rather than physical, death, as when St. Paul says to the Jews opposing him: 'Your blood be upon your own heads; I am clean: from henceforth I will go unto the Gentiles' (Acts xviii. 6; and see Acts xx. 26).

Twelve times we come across references to the blood of animal sacrifices, all of them in Hebrews; but with one exception they tell us little about the way sacrifice was regarded, being allusions to what was actually done without any attempt to explain why it was done. The only possible exception is Heb. ix. 13 where 'the blood of goats and bulls' is linked with 'the ashes of a heifer', and since the latter undoubtedly points to death it may be held that the former does also, or at the very least that it is congruous with it.

The remaining passages all refer in one way or another to the blood of Christ, and on a number of occasions the reference seems plainly to His death, without any necessary implication of sacrifice. Thus in Rom. v. 9 we are said to be 'justified by his blood' and 'saved from the wrath through him'. This is parallel to 'reconciled . . . through the death of his Son' and 'saved by his life' in the next verse, while it follows references to dying in each of the three preceding verses. It does not seem possible to resist the conclusion that 'his blood' here refers to the death of the Lord. It is not otherwise with 'the blood of his cross' (Col. i. 20), for a cross has no place in the sacrificial system, and stands only for a particularly unpleasant death. There seems no reason for interpreting Eph. ii. 13 in any other way, especially since here 'made nigh in the blood of Christ' seems to give much the same thought as 'might reconcile them both in one body unto God through the cross' (verse 16). Very clear is the word of the high priest to the apostles, 'ye have filled Jerusalem with your teaching, and intend to bring this man's blood upon us' (Acts v. 28), where the reference is plainly to the death of Christ, this time with the added thought of responsibility for that death. The death is meant also in 1 Jn. v. 6, where Jesus is said to have come 'by water and blood'; of which passage even Westcott, who holds strongly to the thought that blood signifies release of life, can say: 'There can be no doubt that the Death upon the Cross satisfies the conception of "coming by blood" '.[1] Probably we should include in this group also two passages in the Apocalypse, i.e. those which refer to Him 'that loosed us from our sins by his blood' (Rev. i. 5), and to His vesture, 'a garment sprinkled with (or dipped in) blood' (Rev. xix. 13), though perhaps some would prefer to include them among passages referring to sacrifice.

There is an interesting passage where the blood cannot be interpreted as a reference to sacrifice, namely that referring to the drinking of Christ's blood (Jn. vi. 53ff.), for there is no place in the Hebrew sacrificial system for drinking blood. To understand this passage as signifying a participation in the life of Christ is to assume the point at issue, for it certainly does not prove it. Indeed, the indications are the other way, for the mention of blood and flesh in separation points to death rather than life,[2] and, moreover, we cannot overlook the fact that drinking the blood is coupled with eating the flesh. There is no reason for thinking that the two

[1] Comm. *in loc.*

[2] Bernard says that the use of the expression πίνειν τὸ αἷμα in Jn. vi. 53 'as distinct from φαγεῖν τὴν σάρκα, indicates that the Flesh and Blood have been separated, and thus it suggests death, even more definitely than φαγεῖν τὴν σάρκα does' (I.C.C. *in loc.*). Westcott also sees in the separation indication of violent death (Comm. *in loc.*).

expressions give essentially dissimilar ideas, and it is very difficult to understand the latter expression of participation in the life. Even if we do, we have destroyed the case for thinking that the life is in the blood; it would then be also in the flesh. Plainly the passage points to the death of Christ.[1] Perhaps we should also notice 1 Cor. x. 16, xi. 27 here, for although neither of them speaks explicitly of drinking the blood, they are passages of the same type. All things considered, it would seem that the passages noticed in this paragraph are satisfactorily interpreted only if the blood of Christ be taken as pointing us to His death.

A further group refers to the blood of Christ as the price of our redemption (Acts xx. 28; Eph. i. 7, etc.). This group seems to point to the blood as meaning death, but no stress is laid upon the passages which comprise it, because it would be possible to interpret them of the offering of life, if that could be substantiated from elsewhere.

The remaining passages seem to point to sacrificial blood. Six times there is reference to covenant blood, which calls for no comment to show the sacrificial reference; in Rom. iii. 25 God is said to have set forth Christ as ἱλαστήριον ... ἐν τῷ αὐτοῦ αἵματι, where the word ἱλαστήριον points us to the sacrifices.[2] In Hebrews ix the whole context with its mention of the blood of sacrificial victims shows that verses 12 and 14 carry a reference to the sacrificial system when they speak of the blood of Christ, and the same is true of x. 19. The unusual phrase 'blood of sprinkling' (Heb. xii. 24) points to a sacrificial action, and the context shows that in Heb. xiii. 12 the sin offering is in mind. The sprinkling of the blood in 1 Pet. i. 2 again indicates a sacrificial action, while the blood 'as of a lamb without blemish and without spot' (1 Pet. i. 19) is clearly sacrificial blood, and the same is probably true of 'the blood of the Lamb' in Rev. vii. 14, xii. 11. Finally, the thought of cleansing associated with the blood in 1 Jn. i. 7 seems to be an allusion to sacrifice.

[1] It may be noted that both expressions are found in a metaphorical sense in the Old Testament, namely Ps. xxvii. 2; 2 Sa. xxiii. 17.

[2] Cf. Sanday and Headlam: 'It is impossible to get rid from this passage of the double idea (1) of a sacrifice (2) of a sacrifice which is propitiatory' (*Romans*, I.C.C., p. 91).

When we were dealing with sacrifice in the Old Testament we saw reason for thinking that the infliction of death rather than the release of life was the dominant thought, and there is nothing in these passages concerning the death of Christ viewed as a sacrifice to disturb that conclusion. There is nothing in the context of any of these passages which shows that the writer was thinking of the offering of life when he spoke of Christ's death in sacrificial terms, and each one of them yields a natural interpretation when we think of the blood as signifying death.

One or two of the sacrificial passages strengthen our impression that the blood means death. Thus in Heb. ix. 14f. we read: 'How much more shall the blood of Christ . . . cleanse your conscience from dead works to serve the living God? And for this cause he is the mediator of a new covenant, that a death having taken place . . .', where it is hard to envisage a reason for interpreting 'the blood' in a sense other than that given by the words which follow: 'a death having taken place'.

If anything the connection between blood and death is even plainer in Heb. xii. 24 where we read of coming 'to Jesus the mediator of a new covenant, and to the blood of sprinkling that speaketh better than (that of) Abel'. Whether we include the words in parentheses or not, the contrast is between the blood of Abel and the blood of Jesus.[1] There can be no doubt that the blood of Abel is a metaphorical way of referring to the death of that patriarch, and it is unnatural accordingly to interpret the blood of Jesus as signifying anything other than His death. Yet the reference to sprinkling shows that the thought of sacrifice is in the writer's mind, so that for him the blood of sacrifice seems to have pointed to death.

Again, we read in Heb. xiii. 11f.: 'For the bodies of those beasts, whose blood is brought into the holy place by the high priest as an offering for sin, are burned without the camp. Wherefore Jesus also, that he might sanctify the people through his own blood, suffered without the gate.' Here the comparison is made between the sin offering and the blood of Jesus, but the point that

---

[1] I regard the view that 'that of Abel' refers to the blood of Abel's sacrifice as untenable, on the ground that the reference to the blood speaking marks the passage as an allusion to Gn. iv. 10. There is no suggestion in Gn. iv of the blood of Abel's sacrifice speaking.

is singled out for notice in the Levitical sacrifice is not the presentation of the blood (though that, too, is important to this writer as we see from his previous references to it), but the burning of the carcass outside the camp, a part of the sacrifice which can point only to the death of the animal, and certainly not to any presentation of life. Again, we see that the sacrificial allusion indicates the death of Jesus.

Thus it seems tolerably certain that in both the Old and New Testaments the blood signifies essentially the death. It is freely admitted that there are some passages in which it is possible to interpret the blood as signifying life, but even these yield a better sense (and one which is consistent with the wider biblical usage) if understood to mean 'life given up in death'. In particular, there seems no reason for disputing the dictum of J. Behm: ' "Blood of Christ" is like "cross", only another, clearer expression for the death of Christ in its salvation meaning'.[1]

ADDITIONAL NOTE ON THE MEANING
OF THE WORD 'BLOOD'

A. M. Stibbs, in his monograph *The Meaning of the Word 'Blood' in Scripture* (London, 1947), gathers passages supporting the first-mentioned view (see p. 110) from the writings of Nathaniel Micklem, C. H. Dodd, O. C. Quick, F. C. N. Hicks, P. T. Forsyth, B. F. Westcott, and Sanday and Headlam (pp. 5ff.). The list could easily be extended. The idea is specially prominent in Trumbull's *The Blood Covenant* (London, 1887), where statements like 'not merely that the blood is *essential* to life, but that in a peculiar sense, it *is* life' (p. 38) abound. Something very like this appears as early as H. Bushnell, who says: 'Not that the life thus offered, the life made sacred and mysterious by such associations gathered to it, carries effect by ceasing to live, that is, by death symbolized in the sprinkling of it. No, it gets its effect as being life, the sacred, mystic new-creating touch of life' (*The Vicarious Sacrifice*, 1866, p. 401). 'It is not death, but life, that is in it' (*Ibid.*,

[1] TWNT, I, p. 173.

p. 434). He has similar statements in *Forgiveness and Law* (1874), but he does not make this view central to his understanding of the atonement.

Against all such views are writers like Moffatt who says: 'Semitic scholars warn us against finding in these words (Lv. xvii. 11) either the popular idea of the substitution of the victim for the sinner, or even the theory that the essential thing in sacrifice is the offering of a life to God' (*Hebrews*, I.C.C., p. xlii).

Denney is very forthright in his opposition and speaks of 'the strange caprice which fascinated Westcott' in distinguishing in the blood of Christ '(i) His death, and (ii) His life; or (i) His blood shed, and (ii) His blood offered; or (i) His life laid down, and (ii) His life liberated and made available for men . . . I venture to say that a more groundless fancy never haunted and troubled the interpretation of any part of Scripture than that which is introduced by this distinction into the Epistle to the Hebrews and the First Epistle of John . . . there is no meaning in saying that by His death His life, as something other than His death, is "liberated" and "made available" for men. On the contrary, what makes His risen life significant and a saving power for sinners is neither more nor less than this, that His death is in it.'[1]

Armitage Robinson's comment is 'To the Jewish mind "blood" was not merely—nor even chiefly—the life-current flowing in the veins of the living: it was especially the life poured out in death; and yet more particularly in its religious aspect it was the symbol of sacrificial death' (*Ephesians*, p. 29). Similarly Frederic Platt refuses to endorse Westcott's distinction between 'a life given' and 'a life liberated and made available for men' (HDAC, I, p. 121), while G. F. Moore deprecates the idea that 'the offering of a *life* to God is the essential thing in sacrifice', pointing out that 'no such theory appears in later Jewish thought' (*Enc. Bib.*, IV, col. 4221 and note). More recently F. J. Taylor has written: 'It is hardly likely that blood could signify life released . . . for early Hebrew thought had no adequate conception of a spiritual survival after death' (TWBB, p. 33), though C. R. North in the same volume (Art. 'Sacrifice') accepts the view that the blood signifies the life. J. Behm equates the death of Christ with 'the

---

[1] *The Death of Christ*, London, 1950, pp. 149f.

Blood' (TWNT, II, p. 136), and reaches a similar conclusion in his treatment of αἷμα (TWNT, I, p. 173). So C. Ryder Smith on Heb. x. 19 says: 'As elsewhere in the New Testament, the Christian emphasis *under the great symbol* is not on life, but on death' (*The Bible Doctrine of Salvation*, London, 1941), and cf. J. S. Stewart, *A Man in Christ*, London, 1947, p. 237, F. W. Dillistone, *The Significance of the Cross*, London, 1946, p. 68, G. O. Griffith, *St. Paul's Gospel to the Romans*, Oxford, 1949, p. 17.

CHAPTER IV

PROPITIATION (1)

I. INTRODUCTION

WE MEET the verb ἱλάσκομαι 'to propitiate' twice in the New
Testament, namely in the prayer of the publican 'O God, be
propitiated for me, the sinner' (Lk. xviii. 13), and in the statement
in Hebrews that Jesus was a High Priest 'to make propitiation for
the sins of the people' (Heb. ii. 17). The noun ἱλασμός, 'propitiation', is found in the expression 'propitiation for our sins' which
occurs twice in the First Epistle of St. John (1 Jn. ii. 2, iv. 10), while
in Rom. iii. 25 God is said to have set forth Christ as ἱλαστήριον
through faith 'in his blood' and the same word occurs in Heb. ix. 5
where it means 'the mercy-seat'. Then there is the adjective ἵλεως,
which we find in the idiomatic expression 'Be it far from thee' in
Mt. xvi. 22, and also in the quotation from Je. xxxi. 34, in Heb. viii.
12, 'I will be propitious with reference to their sins'.

This is not a large number of passages, and some even of these,
such as Mt. xvi. 22 and Heb. ix. 5, do not refer to the atonement,
while Lk. xviii. 13 and Heb. viii. 12, though they may teach us
something about the way God and man are reconciled, were not
originally spoken with specific reference to Calvary. We are left,
then, with but four undisputed references. But we should not, on
that account, dismiss the concept as unimportant, for the idea is
often present where this particular terminology is absent, as for
example in passages dealing with the wrath of God. So persuasive
is this line of reasoning that S. R. Driver can regard propitiation
as one of the three main categories used in the New Testament to
interpret the death of Christ.[1]

ἵλεως is cognate with ἱλαρός, giving the original meaning of
'joyous', 'gay'. Thus Büchsel draws attention to the statement in
Plato that wine ποιεῖ . . . ἵλεων, and to the frequent conjunction
with εὐμενής.[2] From this is derived the verb ἱλάσκομαι with the

---

[1] HDB, IV, p. 132.　　　　　　　　　[2] TWNT, III, p. 330.

significance 'to make joyous or gracious', and hence, 'to appease, propitiate'. This became the characteristic meaning of the verb and governed the usage of the related words, so that the whole word group came to have a propitiatory significance. The noun ἱλασμός then conveyed the idea 'that which makes propitiation', and the adjective ἱλαστήριος meant 'propitiatory'. Other words from this root occur, but apart from ἐξιλάσκομαι, which is found frequently in the LXX, none of them greatly concerns us.

II. THE ἱλάσκομαι WORD GROUP IN NON-BIBLICAL GREEK

There is considerable agreement that this word group denotes 'propitiation', 'appeasement', etc., in pagan usage. This point of view was put strongly by Smeaton when he said of ἱλασμός: 'The uniform acceptation of the word in classical Greek, when applied to the Deity, is the means of appeasing God, or of averting His anger; and not a single instance to the contrary occurs in the whole Greek literature'.[1] Since his day our knowledge, particularly of Hellenistic Greek, has increased immensely, but Moulton and Milligan assure us that in Hellenistic as in classical Greek the word group refers to placating, their comment being that ἱλάσκομαι means ' "render propitious to oneself" c. acc. of the person, as in classical Greek',[2] and they go on to note 'a similar use of the compound ἐξιλάσκομαι, which extends to the LXX'.

Many similar citations could be made, but this would be superfluous, as the point is hardly disputed. Whatever may be the biblical usage there can be no doubt as to the prevailing use in all non-biblical writings. But we go on to notice that the pagan use is said to be not quite unvarying. Thus Dodd says: 'In classical Greek and in the *Koine* ἱλάσκεσθαι, ἐξιλάσκεσθαι, have regularly the meaning "placate", "propitiate", with a personal object. As a secondary meaning ἐξιλάσκεσθαι also bears the sense "expiate", with an impersonal object'.[3] In similar vein is Büchsel's statement that 'It would be difficult to imagine that ἐξιλάσκομαι would be chosen as translation of *kipper* if it hitherto had only signified

---

[1] *The Apostles' Doctrine of the Atonement*, Edinburgh, 1870, p. 455

[2] MM *sub* ἱλάσκομαι.

[3] JTS, XXXII, (July 1931), p. 352. His article is reprinted without substantial alteration in *The Bible and the Greeks*.

make gracious. Therefore it is easily conjectured that ἐξιλάσκομαι and ἱλάσκομαι acquired the meaning, *expiate, atone*'.[1] In another section the same writer discusses the relationship of ἱλασμός and καθαρμός in Greek writers and thinks there was a movement away from the cruder ideas of propitiation held in earlier times, so that he can speak of 'an ethical activity or disposition' and proceed: 'The thought of the jealousy of the Godhead is expressly abjured by Plato'.[2] This process was variable, however, and he admits that 'bloody atonement-rites, etc.', were brought in from the East, and concludes: 'The fear of the Godhead and its judgment was by no means extinct'.[3]

What are we to say of all this? It is noteworthy that Büchsel uses very guarded language, and that he gives it as his opinion from the general trend rather than from specific passages. In fact he does not refer to any such, and, from the point of view of the study of ἱλάσκομαι, etc., this is important. Even a man who thinks from the general trend of Greek thought that men were moving away from early, crude ideas can find no instance wherein ἱλάσκομαι, etc., reflect this trend. It is difficult to resist the conclusion that, while the general trend Büchsel speaks of may have been in evidence, yet the word group under consideration was not used to express it. In other words, while men may have been modifying their ideas about the nature of the gods, when they used ἱλάσκομαι, etc., it was to convey the older thought of propitiation rather than some later development. Failing specific examples of the newer meaning such must be held to be the usage.

Dodd urges two passages in favour of the meaning 'expiation', namely Plat. Legg., 862 c and the Men Tyrannus inscription. The former passage reads τὸ ἀποίνοις ἐξιλασθὲν τοῖς δρῶσιν καὶ πάσχουσιν ἑκάστας τῶν βλάψεων ἐκ διαφορᾶς εἰς φιλίαν ἀεὶ πειρατέον καθιστάναι τοῖς νόμοις. The writer is saying that the legislator must endeavour to restore good relations by payment of indemnity for injuries, and the question at issue is whether τὸ ἀποίνοις ἐξιλασθέν refers to expiation of a crime or to appeasement of a person. The context seems to put it beyond doubt that a person is

[1] *Op. cit.*, p. 316.
[2] *Op. cit.*, p. 312.
[3] *Op. cit.*, p. 312.

indicated.[1] The passage could, perhaps, be interpreted of an expiation; but the most natural exegesis sees in it the acceptance by the wronged party of a compensatory payment, by virtue of which his anger against the one who has injured him is soothed. Büchsel sums up the possibilities well when he comments '. . . one could understand ἐξιλασθέν as expiated in so far as the lawbreaker has become guiltless by means of the compensation which he has paid the wronged person; but better it is (understood) as: comprehended as appeased, in so far as the wronged person is brought by the account-settling compensation to the abandoning of his wrath against the offender, so that the two can come to a state of friendship with one another'.[2] It seems impossible, then, to maintain that ἐξιλασθέν here clearly means 'expiate'; the most that can be said is that such an interpretation is not altogether excluded.

The Men Tyrannus inscription gives stronger support to the upholders of the expiation theory inasmuch as sin is the object of the verb, the relevant part of the inscription reading, ἁμαρτίαν ὀφειλέτω Μηνὶ Τυράννῳ ἣν οὐ μὴ δύνηται ἐξειλάσασθαι. This accusative of the sin is unique outside biblical writers, which leads us to the conclusion that it is most probably an accusative of general reference.[3] In view of the otherwise unvarying usage of pagan writers it is probably best to take the passage as meaning that the man who sins in the specified way commits a sin in respect of which he will not be able to make propitiation. Such seems to be the way in which Moulton-Milligan[4] understand it, though Büchsel joins Dodd in giving the verb here the meaning 'expiate'.[5] In any case the date of the inscription makes it impossible to think that any usage reflected therein could have affected the New Testament writers.

The most, then, that can be said in favour of the view that these words may contain an expiatory meaning is that two passages (one of them later than the Bible) could well be interpreted in this

---

[1] Cf. Büchsel: 'It follows from the preceding parallel part that by the ἐξιλασθέν a person, not a thing, is meant' (*Op. cit.*, p. 317, n. 75).

[2] *Ibid.*

[3] See below, pp. 175ff., for similar accusatives.

[4] *Op. cit.*

[5] *Op. cit.*

way. But neither of them demands such an interpretation and, in view of the otherwise consistent usage of the sources, we must draw the conclusion that, when a first century Greek heard the words of this group, there would be aroused in his mind thoughts of propitiation.

III. THE WRATH OF GOD IN THE OLD TESTAMENT

It has for long been recognized that the use of the ἱλάσκομαι word group in the LXX is not the same as that in profane sources. Westcott, for example, has made much of this difference. In recent years none has done more than Prof. C. H. Dodd to demonstrate both the fact and the significance of this difference, and he roundly denies that we should understand the word group of 'propitiation' at all, affirming that 'expiation' is the meaning. Thus he says of Rom. iii. 25: 'the meaning conveyed (in accordance with LXX usage, which is constantly determinative for Paul), is that of expiation, not that of propitiation. Most translators and commentators are wrong'.[1] Or again: 'The Johannine usage thus falls into line with biblical usage in general. The common rendering "propitiation" is illegitimate here as elsewhere'.[2]

These are important conclusions and they are being increasingly accepted, for it is a relief to know that we have solid grounds for our conviction that the God of the Bible is not a Being who can be propitiated after the fashion of a pagan deity. That this point has been conclusively demonstrated seems certain. The Bible writers have nothing to do with pagan conceptions of a capricious and vindictive deity, inflicting arbitrary punishments on offending worshippers, who must then bribe him back to a good mood by the appropriate offerings. Dodd's important work makes this abundantly clear.

However, when we have rendered our full tribute to the work of this great scholar we must ask to be forgiven for wondering whether the last word has yet been said. We readily agree that pagan ideas of wrath and propitiation are absent from the biblical view of God, but Dodd seems to say that all ideas of wrath and propitiation are absent from it. We have already noted his

[1] *Op. cit.*, p. 360.
[2] *Ibid.*

rejection of the idea of propitiation; but in his commentary on Romans he seems to go further and says that the wrath of God is 'an archaic phrase' suiting 'a thoroughly archaic idea'.[1] To many the wrath of God seems too well rooted in both Old and New Testaments to be relegated to the status of an archaism. Other questions suggest themselves, such as, 'If the LXX translators and the New Testament writers did not mean propitiation, why did they choose to use words which signify propitiation and are saturated with propitiatory associations?'[2] Such a procedure, one would think, is the surest way of being misunderstood; and, if Dodd is right, their choice of words has, in fact, caused them to be misunderstood right up to our own day.

The wrath of God is often confused with that irrational passion we so frequently find in man and which was commonly ascribed to heathen deities. One wonders whether it might not be preferable to understand it in some more worthy fashion and in this way give meaning to a great deal of scriptural teaching. Thus Dr. Maldwyn Hughes says: 'Let it be granted that anger is not an ideal word for our purpose, and that we use it only, as Augustine would say, "in order that we may not keep silent." Our concern is with facts not with words. The fact which we have to face is that in the nature of things there must be an eternal recoil against the unholy on the part of the all-holy God'.[3] If we can understand the wrath of God in some such fashion as this there seems no insuperable objection to our thinking of that wrath as a reality to be reckoned with, and to seeing propitiation as the means of averting

[1] *Romans*, MNTC, pp. 20f.

[2] Cf. R. W. Dale on the Jewish use of the term: 'Not a solitary instance can be alleged in which to propitiate, or any of its derivatives, when used in relation to the restoration of kindly relations between man and man, denotes that by which a change is produced in the disposition of a person who has committed an offence; it always refers to that which changes the disposition of the person who has been offended; and when used in relation to offences against the Divine law, it always describes the means by which the sin was supposed to be covered in order that the Divine forgiveness might be secured' (*The Atonement*, London, 1902, pp. 162f.). James Denney has a remark which is worthy of note, 'The characteristic words of religion cannot be applied in new ways at will. Now the idea of ἱλασμός or propitiation is not an insulated idea. . . . It is part of a system of ideas' (*The Death of Christ*, London, 1950, p. 150).

[3] *What is the Atonement?* London, n.d., pp. 54f.

that wrath from the sinner, who, unless this can be done, finds himself in evil case. In the following sections it will be our aim to show that this is indeed the position, that the Old Testament writers were sure of a wrath of God extended towards all sin, but that God had made provision whereby sinners might escape this wrath, and that this averting of wrath is in mind when the LXX translators find occasion to use ἱλάσκομαι and kindred words.

To the men of the Old Testament the wrath of God is both very real and very serious. God is not thought of as capriciously angry (like the deities of the heathen), but, because He is a moral Being, His anger is directed towards wrongdoing in any shape or form. Once roused, this anger is not easily assuaged, and dire consequences may follow. But it is only fair to add that the Old Testament consistently regards God as a God of mercy, so that, though men may and do sin and thus draw down upon themselves the consequences of His wrath, yet God delights not in the death of the sinner, and He provides ways in which the consequences of sin may be averted.

There are more than twenty words used to express the wrath conception as it applies to Yahweh (in addition to a number of other words which occur only with reference to human anger). These are used so frequently that there are over 580 occurrences to be taken into consideration. This constitutes such a formidable body of evidence, that we cannot hope to deal with it fully, and can only indicate in general terms the result of detailed examination.

There is a consistency about the wrath of God in the Old Testament. It is no capricious passion, but the stern reaction of the divine nature to evil in man. It is aroused only and inevitably by sin, which may be thought of in general terms (Jb. xxi. 20; Je. xxi. 12; Ezk. xxiv. 13), or may be categorized more exactly as the shedding of blood (Ezk. xvi. 38, xxiv. 8), adultery (Ezk. xxiii. 25), violence (Ezk. viii. 18), covetousness (Je. vi. 11), revenge (Ezk. xxv. 17), afflicting widows and orphans (Ex. xxii. 23f.), taking brethren captive (2 Ch. xxviii. 11–13), etc. Wrath comes upon Israel because of the evil of Jeroboam as repeated by Jehoahaz (2 Ki. xiii. 3), and because of the evil of Manasseh (2 Ki. xxiii. 26), while Moses feared that the desire of the two and a half tribes not to pass over Jordan would have a similar effect (Nu. xxxii. 14).

Profaning the sabbath arouses wrath (Ne. xiii. 18), which comes also upon men who 'have not told the truth about' God (Jb. xlii. 7, Moffatt), and Gideon feared that his repeated testing of the Lord would also cause God's anger (Jdg. vi. 39).

Perhaps we are able to see something of the root causes of the divine anger in such passages as 'anger also went up against Israel; Because they believed not in God, and trusted not in his salvation' (Ps. lxxviii. 21f.), or those linking rebellion with the divine wrath such as 'We have transgressed and have rebelled; thou hast not pardoned. Thou hast covered with anger and pursued us' (La. iii. 42f.), or 'It will be, seeing that ye rebel today against the Lord, that tomorrow he will be wroth with the whole congregation of Israel' (Jos. xxii. 18). It is in line with this that the sin above all sins which is said in the Old Testament to arouse God's wrath is the sin of idolatry. This may be asserted in general terms (Dt. vi. 14f.; Jos. xxiii. 16, etc.), or in connection with specific acts of idolatry such as the worship of the golden calf (Ex. xxxii. 10f.), or the iniquity of Baal-peor (Nu. xxv. 3), or practices associated with idolatry (Is. lxvi. 15–17). Sometimes the accusation is accompanied by that of forsaking Jehovah (Dt. xxix. 25ff.; 2 Ki. xxii. 17), while, in Ezr. ix. 14, breaking God's commandments and making affinity with the heathen are mentioned.

From these and many other examples it is clear that in the Old Testament the anger of God may be expected to be visited upon the perpetrator of any sin. God made men for Himself, that they should be His people, and that they should live in accordance with His commandments. When they failed to do so they inevitably aroused His settled opposition, His wrath.

The effects of this wrath, the happenings which show that the Lord *is* angry, are such things as affliction in general (Ps. lxxxviii. 7), or specific evils such as pestilence (Ezk. xiv. 19), 'the cup of staggering' (Is. li. 22), slaughter (Ezk. ix. 8), destruction (Ezk. v. 15), execration, reproach, etc. (Je. xlii. 18), being delivered up to the enemy (2 Ch. xxviii. 9), the destruction of Jerusalem (La. iv. 11), desolation (Is. xiii. 9; Je. iv. 26), drought (Dt. xi. 17), plague (2 Sa. xxiv. 1ff.), leprosy (Nu. xii. 9), and above all, the exile (2 Ki. xxiii. 26; Is. xlii. 25; Ezk. xix. 12, etc.). There are other effects also, and it is clear from the whole picture that almost any disaster could be interpreted as a sign of the divine wrath.

Sometimes the ascription of such disasters to the activity of the wrath of God is taken to indicate that this wrath denotes nothing more than an impersonal retribution, as for example by C. H. Dodd who says that the work of the prophets is such that ' "the wrath of God" is taken out of the sphere of the purely mysterious, and brought into the sphere of cause and effect: sin is the cause, disaster the effect . . . in speaking of wrath and judgment the prophets and psalmists have their minds mainly on events, actual or expected, conceived as the inevitable results of sin; and when they speak of mercy they are thinking mainly of the personal relation between God and His people. Wrath is the effect of human sin; mercy is not the effect of human goodness, but is inherent in the character of God.'[1]

But this hardly seems to fit the facts. In the first place the prophets had a strongly developed view of the sovereignty of God. Nothing that men can do escapes Him, and nothing, it would seem, can be done without Him, for 'the most High ruleth in the kingdom of men' (Dn. iv. 17). The punishment consequent on sin is just as much due to God as is the forgiveness which remits such punishment, for God is in all of life. 'Shall evil befall a city, and the Lord hath not done it?' (Am. iii. 6) is the incredulous query of one of the prophets, and the same man emphasizes that it is the Lord who 'bringeth sudden destruction upon the strong' (Am. v. 9). We read similarly in Is. xlv. 6f.: 'I am the Lord, and there is none else. I form the light, and create darkness; I make peace, and create evil; I am the Lord, that doeth all these things'. There is hardly point in continuing the list, for throughout the Old Testament it is assumed that God is active throughout His creation, and that His hand is to be discerned in the chastisements which come upon men.

Then the prophets and the psalmists use the most strongly personal terms when they speak of the anger of the Lord. What else are we to make of passages like the following? 'Now will I shortly pour out my fury upon thee, and accomplish mine anger against thee . . . And mine eye shall not spare, neither will I have pity . . . and ye shall know that I the Lord do smite' (Ezk. vii. 8f.). Or 'The anger of the Lord shall not return, until he have executed,

[1] *Romans*, MNTC, p. 22.

and till he have performed the intents of his heart' (Je. xxiii. 20). Or 'Behold, the name of the Lord cometh from far, burning with his anger, and in thick rising smoke: his lips are full of indignation, and his tongue is as a devouring fire: and his breath is as an overflowing stream, that reacheth even unto the neck, to sift the nations with the sieve of vanity . . . And the Lord shall cause his glorious voice to be heard, and shall shew the lighting down of his arm, with the indignation of his anger, and the flame of a devouring fire, with a blast, and tempest, and hailstones. For through the voice of the Lord shall the Assyrian be broken in pieces, etc.' (Is. xxx. 27–31). 'O God, thou hast cast us off, thou hast broken us down; thou hast been angry: . . . Thou hast made the land to tremble; thou hast rent it: . . . Thou hast shewed thy people hard things: thou hast made us to drink the wine of staggering' (Ps. lx. 1–3).

It is difficult to imagine how the prophets and psalmists could possibly have expressed more strongly the personal aspect of the wrath of God. While disaster is regarded as the inevitable result of man's sin, it is so in the view of the Old Testament, not by some inexorable law of an impersonal Nature, but because a holy God wills to pour out the vials of His wrath upon those who commit sin. Indeed, it is largely because wrath is so fully personal in the Old Testament that mercy becomes so fully personal; for mercy is the action of the same God who was angry, allowing His wrath to be turned away. It should be noted that many passages place the wrath and the mercy of God on the same plane as personal activities, as when we read: 'He retaineth not his anger for ever, because he delighteth in mercy' (Mi. vii. 18), or 'Thou hast forgiven the iniquity of thy people, thou hast covered all their sin. Thou hast taken away all thy wrath: thou hast turned thyself from the fierceness of thine anger' (Ps. lxxxv. 2f.).

It is true that there are some passages which speak of wrath in more or less impersonal terms, or which connect punishment directly with sin, but these will always be found to imply the continuing activity of Yahweh. For example Ps. xxxviii. 3 says: 'There is no soundness in my flesh because of thine indignation; neither is there any health in my bones because of my sin', words which might well be cited in support of the contention that wrath is impersonal retribution were it not that the two preceding verses strongly emphasize the personal divine activity. 'O Lord, rebuke me not in thy wrath: neither chasten me in thy hot displeasure. For thine arrows stick fast in me, and thy hand presseth me sore'. This will be found to be typical of the Old Testament position; God is personally active in deeds of wrath as in deeds of mercy.

Let us now notice some of the ways in which the wrath of God is said to be averted. One way is by purging out the sin, for example, by completely destroying an offending city (Dt. xiii. 15–17), slaying those who had sinned at Baal-peor (Nu. xxv. 4), releasing captives (2 Ch. xxviii. 11–13), putting away heathen wives (Ezr. x. 14). Sometimes the means is said to be a right inward state, as for example repentance (Jon. iii. 7, 10), or humbling oneself (2 Ch. xii. 7), while the passages referring to judgment (Je. xxi. 12) and circumcising the heart (Je. iv. 4) are not dissimilar. Both Moses and Jeremiah are said to have stood before God and turned away wrath from Israel, presumably by successful intercession (Ps. cvi. 23; Je. xviii. 20), while Job's prayer is similarly referred to (Jb. xlii. 7f.).

Underlying the fact that these and other things are said to turn away the divine wrath is the basic truth that God is by nature merciful rather than wrathful. Indeed wrath may be thought of as His 'strange work', as in Is. xxviii. 21: 'For the Lord shall rise up as in mount Perazim, he shall be wroth as in the valley of Gibeon; that he may do his work, his strange work, and bring to pass his act, his strange act'. While wrath is a dreadful reality, it must not be taken as the last word about God. This is not contradicted by the statement that 'God will not withdraw his anger' (Jb. ix. 13), for this means not that He is implacable, but only that He is not to be diverted from His purposes by puny man. It is a denial of the heathen idea of a gift being accepted to appease anger. But it does not follow that He habitually punishes men to the fullest extent, as we see from Jb. xxxv. 15, 'he hath not visited in his anger', or from the incredulous question of the psalmist, 'Hath God forgotten to be gracious? Hath he in anger shut up his tender mercies?' (Ps. lxxvii. 9). A beautiful statement of God's nature as merciful rather than wrathful comes from Mi. vii. 18f.: 'Who is a God like unto thee, that pardoneth iniquity, and passeth by the transgression of the remnant of his heritage? He retaineth not his anger for ever because he delighteth in mercy. He will turn again and have compassion upon us, he will tread our iniquities under foot: and thou wilt cast all their sins into the depths of the sea'.

Full of interest are ten passages in which God is said to be 'slow to anger' (Ex. xxxiv. 6; Nu. xiv. 18; Ne. ix. 17; Pss. lxxxvi. 15, ciii. 8, cxlv. 8; Je. xv. 15; Joel ii. 13; Jon. iv. 2; Na. i. 3). In reading such passages we are apt to fasten our attention on expressions like 'slow to anger and plenteous in mercy', but we should not overlook the fact that the writers could, in the immediate context, say such things as, the Lord 'will by no means clear the guilty' (Nu. xiv. 18), or 'turn ye unto me with all your heart, and with fasting, and with weeping, and with mourning' (Joel ii. 12). For those who wrote such words the idea that God is 'slow to anger' was not regarded as a truism, but as a surprising revelation, something to be received with awe and wonder.

This thinking reaches its climax in the passages where the removal of divine wrath is ascribed to God Himself. Thus Ps. lxxviii. 38 tells us that 'many a time turned he his anger away, and did not stir up all his wrath', and in Is. xlviii. 9 we read the words of the Lord, 'For my name's sake will I defer mine anger, and for my praise will I refrain for thee, that I cut thee not off.' Cf. Ps. lxxxv. 2f., where, incidentally, forgiveness and the turning away of wrath are nearly identical. Other passages could be quoted, but it seems hardly necessary, for the general picture which the Old Testament gives us of God is of One who is by nature merciful, and who cannot be swayed by man's puny efforts, so that forgiveness is always due in the last resort to God's being what He is, and not to anything that man may do. Because God is God, He must react in the strongest manner to man's sin, and thus we reach the concept of the divine wrath. But because God is God, wrath cannot be the last word. 'The Lord is good; his mercy endureth for ever' (Ps. c. 5).

IV. THE ἱλάσκομαι WORD GROUP IN THE SEPTUAGINT

a. The work of C. H. Dodd

Dodd's valuable treatment of the word group begins by showing that where the LXX does not use ἱλάσκομαι, etc., to translate *kipper*, it uses words with meanings like ' "to sanctify", "purify" persons or objects of ritual, or "to cancel", "purge away", "forgive" sins';

from which he concludes that 'We should therefore expect to find that they regard the ἱλάσκεσθαι class as conveying similar ideas'.[1] His next point is that, where ἱλάσκομαι, etc., are not the translation for *kipper* and its derivatives, 'they render words which fall into one or other of two classes: (i) with human subject, "to cleanse from sin or defilement", "to expiate"; (ii) with divine subject, "to be gracious", "to have mercy", "to forgive".'[2] His third main division is one in which he deals with those passages wherein ἱλάσκομαι, etc., render the *kipper* group, and here he concludes that 'the LXX translators did not regard *kipper* (when used as a religious term) as conveying the sense of propitiating the Deity, but the sense of performing an act whereby guilt or defilement is removed'.[3]

It might be urged in criticism of this method that it is capable of giving the meaning of the word group in question only in a very general way. Thus Dodd has to group together in his first main section words whose meaning differs as greatly as 'to sanctify' and 'to cancel'. When there is such a vast gulf between different members of the same group obviously we cannot expect to get a very precise meaning for the ἱλασκομαι group from them.

In the second place the method itself is open to dangers. To give an example, the A.V. of 1 Pet. iii. 3 renders κόσμος by 'adorning', whereas in most passages the meaning given is 'world'; yet we cannot argue from this that 'adorning' and 'world' are words of similar meaning. The fact is that κόσμος in Greek covers a range of meaning for which we have no exact English equivalent, so that we must make use of various words some of which differ considerably from one another in meaning. This commonplace of translation is relevant to our inquiry. It may be true to say *kipper* and ἐξιλάσκομαι mean very nearly the same thing; but that does not carry with it the corollary that other Hebrew words which ἐξιλάσκομαι renders are akin in meaning to *kipper*, or that other Greek words which translate *kipper* are necessarily of similar significance to ἐξιλάσκομαι. The very reason for the choice of the different word may be that the second context demands a word differing in meaning from that appropriate in the first passage.

---

[1] JTS, XXXII (July 1931), p. 353.
[2] Op. cit., p. 356.
[3] Op. cit., p. 359.

The way to clear up such points is to pay close attention to the context in order to see, not so much what word, but what idea ἱλάσκομαι, etc., translate. It may well be that, on occasion, the best word with which to render ἱλάσκομαι is 'forgive' or 'purge'; but if the particular forgiveness or purging of sin is one which involves, as a necessary feature, the putting away of the divine wrath, then it is idle to maintain that the word has been eviscerated of all idea of propitiation. Dodd totally ignores the fact that in many passages there is explicit mention of the putting away of God's anger, and accordingly his conclusions cannot be accepted without serious modification.

b. ἱλάσκομαι.

This verb occurs eleven times in all, always in the middle or passive, and always with the Lord as subject (sometimes in petition, 'Be thou, etc.').[1] The Hebrew verbs it translates convey thoughts like 'forgive', but we cannot glibly reason from this that therefore there is no thought of propitiation. For example, the word occurs in Ex. xxxii. 14 (translating *nḥm*) where RV reads: 'And the Lord repented of the evil which he said he would do unto his people.' But however we translate we must notice that, in the context, it refers to a removal of wrath, for earlier Moses has asked the Lord 'why doth thy wrath wax hot against thy people?' (verse 11), and has prayed, 'Turn from thy fierce wrath, and repent of this evil against thy people' (verse 12). The connection between wrath and the Lord's 'repenting' is plain. Similarly in La. iii. 42 ἱλάσκομαι translates *slḥ* and can be rendered 'forgive'. But the sort of forgiveness which is meant is one which includes a turning away of wrath, as we see as soon as we look at the expression in its context: 'We sinned, we behaved impiously and thou didst not forgive (or wast not propitiated). Thou didst visit in anger and pursue us'. So in Dn. ix. 19 (Th.) we read: 'O Lord, forgive', which is much the same as 'let thine anger and thy

---

[1] The verb is used absolutely four times, with dative of persons three times, with dative of sin three times, and with accusative of sin once. The underlying Hebrew is *slḥ* (six times), *kppr* (three times), *nḥm* (once), while there is no Hebrew corresponding to Est. xiii. 17.

wrath, I pray thee, be turned away from thy city Jerusalem'
(verse 16). In 2 Ki. xxiv. 3f. the explicit mention of the Lord's
anger, and the stress on the magnitude of Manasseh's sin, combine
to show that the verb carries the meaning 'propitiate',[1] while in
Ps. lxxvii (lxxviii). 38 the forgiveness idea conveyed by this verb
is practically identical with the averting of the divine wrath, 'But
he is compassionate and will forgive their sins, and he will not
destroy (them); and he will many times turn away his anger,
and will not kindle all his wrath'. We might make almost the
same remark about the occurrence of the verb in Ps. lxxviii
(lxxix). 9 (cf. verses 5ff.), and while wrath is not mentioned in
Ps. xxiv (xxv). 11 the psalmist's sin is said to be 'great', and he is
suffering what might well be understood as the wrath of God, for
he is desolate and afflicted, in trouble, distress, and travail, his
enemies are many (verses 16ff.).

Much is sometimes made of the fact that there is one passage
where sin is the object of the verb and it is urged that 'expiate'
rather than 'propitiate' must be the meaning (Ps. lxiv (lxv). 4).
But even if we dismiss the fact that some MSS read the dative
(Swete cites אֹ‎[c.a.], T) the context tells us that 'Words of law-
less men have overpowered us', and once more we see the kind
of thing which would naturally be associated with divine wrath.
So it is also with Est. xiii. 17 (Addition C verse 10), for here the
people are under sentence of death, while in the only remaining
passage, 2 Ki. v. 18 (where the verb occurs twice) Naaman asks
pardon for bowing down in the house of Rimmon, an action
prohibited in the Second Commandment on the grounds that
Yahweh is a 'jealous God'. Moreover Naaman has just come out
of heathendom, and might be expected to use the word in the
typically heathen fashion.

To sum up. Six times there is explicit mention of wrath
in the immediate context, once the people are under sentence
of death, twice the psalmist is greatly afflicted, and on the

---

[1] Some would take θυμός here to mean something like 'purpose' since
the Hebrew of the Massoretic text here is עַל־פִּי יהוה. But even if this be
accepted there is still the stress on the magnitude of the sin, and in any case that
Manasseh had aroused the anger of the Lord is clear from other passages such
as 2 Ki. xxiii. 26.

other occasion the action is that one above all others which the Old Testament regards as provoking God's wrath. We cannot say that the concept of the wrath of God is certainly absent from any of these passages, and in every one the rendering 'propitiate' is quite appropriate. In the face of all this it is manifestly impossible to maintain that the verb has been emptied of its force.[1]

c. ἱλασμός

This noun occurs ten times in a variety of contexts. Sometimes it is connected with kpr as in 'day of atonement', etc. (We will deal with the idea of atonement when we come to ἐξιλάσκομαι.)

The word is used of forgiveness in Dn. ix. 8 (Th.), 'To the Lord our God belong mercies and forgivenesses', and here again the whole situation involves the wrath of God, as we see from 'the curse has come upon us' (verse 11), He has brought 'great evils' upon His people (verse 12), and Daniel's prayer 'let thine anger and thy wrath, I pray thee, be turned away' (verse 16). The word occurs in Ps. cxxix (cxxx). 4, in a context of trouble: 'Out of the depths have I cried' (verse 1). Propitiation is clearly the meaning in 2 Macc. iii. 33, where it is applied to the sacrifice offered by Onias to deliver Heliodorus from further chastisement, and where the whole tenor of the passage leaves no doubt that averting of wrath is being signified.

Thus the propitiatory idea which we have seen to be involved in ἱλάσκομαι is to be discerned also in ἱλασμός. Wherever it means 'forgiveness', the circumstances indicate the turning away of the divine wrath.[2]

d. ἱλαστήριον

This word is used of the mercy seat over the ark of the covenant (twenty-two times) and of one of the ledges of Ezekiel's altar (five times). It means either 'place of atonement' (Manson) or

---

[1] The verb is also found in the Sixtine text of 2 Ch. vi. 30, but here again the context speaks of disasters which evidence the divine displeasure.

[2] ἱλασμός also occurs as the reading of A in Sir. xviii. 20, and of ℵ* in Sir. xxxii. 5, but in both places ἐξιλασμός is the better attested reading.

'means of atonement' (Büchsel, Deissmann, etc.), but in either case it is associated with the cultus, and we defer discussing the idea involved until we come to consider ἐξιλάσκομαι.

The term also occurs in 4 Macc. xvii. 22, though here it may be held to derive from the adjective rather than the substantive. The death of the seven brothers is spoken of: 'They having as it were become a ransom (ἀντίψυχον) for the nation's sin; and through the blood of these righteous men and their propitiatory death (or, the propitiation of their death) the divine providence delivered Israel'. Here the meaning 'propitiation' is plain, and this may be of significance for the interpretation of Rom. iii. 25.

e. ἵλεως

It hardly seems necessary to examine the thirty-five occurrences of this word in detail. In general we may say that the usage fits in with that of the other words of the word group, in that the term usually denotes the attitude of the Lord in turning His anger away from the people. The adjective occurs several times in the prayer of Solomon at the dedication of the Temple (see 1 Ki. viii; 2 Ch. vi), which prayer is of a cyclic character with the pattern 'When the people commit sin and thou afflict them in such and such a way, if they repent and confess, then hear thou and forgive'. All the afflictions are such as might be caused by the divine wrath (and in one place or another of the Old Testament each is expressly said to be the result of the anger of the Lord), and it would be going contrary to the whole tenor of Old Testament thought to regard the afflictions mentioned as other than the outworking of the divine wrath. In view of the setting, then, 'forgive' here seems to have the implication of the removal of wrath. So is it with Dt. xxi. 8 which deals with the finding of a murdered man and the slaying of a heifer by the elders of the nearest city. It is difficult to interpret this other than as a propitiatory rite, after which 'Be propitiated for thy people Israel' is quite in place. In other passages where the word is found we shall usually find that the wrath of God is mentioned or implied, and we may well feel that this word, like the others we have considered, has reference, in the last resort, to the removal of wrath.

f. ἐξιλάσκομαι

Although the verb ἐξιλάσκομαι does not occur in the New Testament, yet because of its close kinship in meaning with ἱλάσκομαι, and because of its importance in the Old Testament, it is well to consider its usage. It is found 105 times, the number being accounted for in large measure because it is the usual verb for rendering the recurring expression 'to make atonement' (Heb. *kipper*) in connection with the sacrificial system. The fact that ἐξιλάσκομαι renders *kipper* eighty-three times and other Hebrew roots a total of eleven times only, shows that the two words ἐξιλάσκομαι and *kipper* are nearly synonymous in meaning, or at least that the LXX translators thought so. Since this is the case it will repay us to make an examination of the meaning to be attached to this Hebrew word.

The usage of *kipper* divides naturally into two sections, according as atonement is thought of as coming by a cultic action or by non-cultic means, the former being by far the larger section. But for our present purpose the latter is the more important group, enabling us, as it does, to see what the verb means in itself quite apart from the conventional use of the cultus. For it seems probable that, in the case of *kipper* (as no doubt of other words also), a word well understood from its use in connection with ordinary affairs was adopted and adapted by exponents of the cultus because it so well expressed one of the aspects of the cultic approach to God. It is likely that, in the process, a conventional meaning will become attached to the word, and not at all improbable that the cultic use will differ somewhat from the secular use. That, however, will remain for examination, and does not affect our main contention that the non-cultic use is fundamental. This was noticed long ago by Dr. S. H. Langdon who said: 'Before examining the Hebrew cult term it will be much more logical to examine those passages in which the word is not employed in the rituals'.[1] But, unfortunately, he failed to notice more than a very few such passages. More recently Herrmann has also noticed the importance of the non-cultic passages.[2]

[1] ET, XXII, p. 323.

[2] TWNT, III, p. 302.

(i) *The non-cultic use of kipper.* The impressive thing about the passages in which *kipper* is used of atonement wrought without reference to the cultus, is the close kinship in meaning between it and the noun *kopher* which we have already had occasion to consider,[1] and which we saw almost without exception (perhaps without any exception) to denote payment for the redemption of forfeited life.

Especially important from our present point of view is Ex. xxx. 12–16 where *kipper* and *kopher* occur together, and their connection is clearly to be seen. The passage deals with the half shekel to be paid at the census as a *kopher* in order that there be no plague. The thought of payment for a man's life is clear, and the money in question is referred to both as *kopher naphsho* ('ransom for his soul', verse 12), and as *keseph hakippurim* ('atonement money', verse 16), while it is twice said 'to make atonement for your souls' (verses 15, 16). The verb *kipper* has here the sense of atonement, and of atonement by the payment of a sum of money as ransom. A similar meaning is to be found in passages like Nu. xxxi. 50 where the men of war offer a part of the spoil which they term 'the Lord's oblation', and which is 'to make atonement for our souls before the Lord'. Plainly here the verb *kipper* is in the nature of a denominative, meaning 'to offer a *kopher*'. This meaning is clear also in Gn. xxxii. 20, where Jacob thinks that his present to Esau will have the effect of 'ransoming' him from his brother's wrath,[2] and in Is. xlvii. 11, especially if the emendation of *shahrah* ('dawning thereof') to *shahadhah* ('to buy it off') be accepted, thus restoring an interesting parallelism. The thought of the verse would then run: 'Therefore shall evil come upon thee; and thou shalt not know how to buy it off (*shahadhah*): and mischief

---

[1] See above pp. 17ff.

[2] With this expression should be compared *hillah 'eth-pene-* which BDB explain as 'lit. *make the face of* any one *sweet* or *pleasant*', and thus 'mollify, appease, entreat the favour of'. The idea in *kipper* is similar, but carries with it the thought that the making of the face sweet is by specific means, namely, the offering of a gift. It is the turning away of anger by means of a *kopher*.

In passing we note that the suggestion often put forward that *'akhapperah phanayw* here means 'I will cover his face' will not fit the context, for Jacob goes on 'and afterward I will see his face'.

shall fall upon thee; and thou shalt not be able to ransom it away (*kapperah*)'[1]

In other instances the *kopher* is not money, but life. See Ex. xxxii. 30, where Moses says: 'Now I will go up unto the Lord; peradventure I shall make atonement for your sin'. But when he pleads with the Lord his method of 'making atonement' is by offering his own life for them as we see from verse 32. Here again *kipper* means 'to pay a *kopher*', but the *kopher* in question is a life. Most instructive for an understanding of *kipper* is 2 Sa. xxi. 1–14, where we read of a famine due to Saul's treatment of the Gibeonites. David called them and asked: 'What shall I do for you? and wherewith shall I make atonement ('*akhapper*), that ye may bless the inheritance of the Lord?' (verse 3). That the Gibeonites understood by '*akhapper* 'pay a *kopher*' is clear by their answer: 'It is no matter of silver or gold between us and Saul, or his house'; and their recognition of the life-for-life principle comes out in the second part of their answer: 'neither is it for us to put any man to death in Israel' (verse 4). Eventually seven descendants of Saul were delivered to the Gibeonites to be hanged and these formed the *kopher* demanded (though that term is not explicitly used). The whole passage is most instructive. Nu. xxxv. 33 falls to be considered here, for it is almost a statement of the very principle on which the Gibeonites acted. The two preceding verses have said that for murder no *kopher* may be paid, and the reasoning goes on: 'So ye shall not pollute the land wherein

---

[1] Cf. Herrmann: 'In Is. xlvii, 11 *kpr* means "pay *kopher*", "provide *kopher*"' "avert through *kopher*" in parallel to *shhd* ("provide *shohadh*", "avert through *shohadh*"), from which *kpr* appears to be a denominative from *kopher* just as *shhd* from *shohadh*; thereby it is a question of the averting of a destruction in death' (*Op. cit.*, p. 304).

BDB give *shahadhah* as the probable reading, citing in support a number of Hebraists. But it should be borne in mind that other scholars from the analogy of the Arabic read 'charm it away' with RV mg. (see authorities in BDB *sub shahadh* and *shahar* respectively). If this is accepted as the sense of the word there is again an interesting parallelism, and one in which the meaning of *kpr* remains as suggested above.

BDB bring out the connection of the verb with *kopher* in their section on *kipper* where the meaning of Is. xlvii. 11 is given as 'and disaster will fall upon thee, thou wilt not be able to propitiate it (by payment of a *kopher*, see Is. xliii. 3).' *shohadh* occurs in parallelism with *kopher* in Pr. vi. 35.

ye are: for blood, it polluteth the land: and no expiation can be made for the land for the blood that is shed therein, but by the blood of him that shed it'. In its context the last section of the verse must mean 'No *kopher* is acceptable for murder, other than the blood of the murderer', and once again we have strong evidence of the close connection between the two words. The Song of Moses (Dt. xxxii) gives us a further example of the same principle at work, when we read in verse 43 that Yahweh 'will make expiation (*wekhipper*) for his land, and for his people'; for in verses 41, 42 we have the blood of the enemy specifically indicated, and that it is a life-for-life transaction the expression 'For he will avenge the blood of his servants' (verse 43) clearly indicates.

It is this necessity for paying for blood with blood that is behind Dt. xxi. 1-9, where we get the further idea of propitiating the divine wrath by means of a *kopher*. A murder has been committed, the body being left lying in a field, and the perpetrator of the crime is unknown. Since no *kopher* has been paid by 'the blood of him that shed' blood (Nu. xxxv. 33), the wrath of God must be assumed to rest on the community, and in order to remove it the elders of the nearest city are to take a heifer to a prescribed place and there to break its neck. It is difficult to see in this anything other than an offering of a propitiatory character,[1] wherein the blood of the beast is the *kopher* for the blood of the man. On the ground of this Yahweh is prayed to grant His people atonement, and the passage assures them that the blood will thus be atoned (verse 8).

There are other occurrences of *kipper* where the cultus is not in question, most of which are readily understood in the way we have outlined above. Thus, when we read in Pr. xvi. 6, 'By mercy

---

[1] Driver goes rather further than I would think justified when he says, 'the heifer in this rite is manifestly designed as a substitute for the unknown murderer, and bears the penalty which ought properly to be his' (*Deuteronomy*, I.C.C., *in loc.*). We see the force of this rite if we imagine that after it has been performed the murderer is discovered. Presumably in this case he would not be allowed to go scot free, which ought to be the case if the penalty has been borne. The real significance of the rite is that it averts the divine wrath from the community; it is the *kopher* whereby immunity from punishment for the crime is purchased.

The Mishna says that if the slayer were found after the killing of the heifer, he was to be put to death (Sot. ix. 7).

and truth iniquity is purged', the meaning would seem to be that these qualities are a sort of price paid—the language is figurative— whereby the wrath attendant on iniquity is bought off. A few verses later we have the verb again in the statement that 'The wrath of a king is as messengers of death: but a wise man will atone it',[1] i.e. will provide a *kopher* for it.

The idea that is to be discerned in the last mentioned passage of a gift turning away wrath probably underlies other passages wherein the thought is of forgiveness, so that the forgiveness that is thought of when *kipper* is used is one which involves the turning away of wrath, and the imagery of the word implies that it is by the offering of a *kopher*. Thus in Is. xxvii. 9 we have the thought of forgiveness, but it is a forgiveness that is brought about when Jacob 'maketh all the stones of the altar as chalkstones that are beaten in sunder, so that the Asherim and the sun-images shall rise no more'. The nation is being castigated for idolatry, which is probably the sin above all others that is said in the Old Testament to arouse the wrath of God, and the path of expiation is the beating small of the idolatrous altars and the abolition of the worship served by them. This is regarded as the *kopher* by which forgiveness is obtained.

The particular *kopher* which is to be offered is not mentioned in some other places such as Ezk. xvi. 63, but the explicit mention of the wrath of God (verses 38, 42) makes it clear that we are still moving in the same circle of ideas. So is it with Ps. lxxviii. 38 where the parallelism makes 'forgive (atoned) their iniquity' almost equivalent to 'turned he his anger away', and similarly in Ps. lxxix. 9, the removal of wrath as the way of purging sins is clear from the references to the divine anger in the situation (verses 5, 6, 8). In Ps. lxv. 3, 'As for our transgressions, thou shalt purge them away', there is by no means as clear a reference either to a *kopher* or to divine anger, though the magnitude of the sin is stressed in the preceding 'Iniquities prevail against me', which perhaps points to the arousing of such an anger. The precise meaning of Dn. ix. 24 is not easy to determine, but the expression 'Seventy weeks are decreed upon thy people and upon thy holy

---

[1] Pr. xvi. 14. BDB under *kipper* comment 'pacify the wrath of a king, Pr. xvi. 14 (e.g. by a gift)'.

city, to finish transgression, and to make an end of sins, and to make reconciliation for iniquity' seems to indicate, at any rate, that the 'troublous times' of the period mentioned are in the nature of a *kopher* playing its part in making the reconciliation.

There is a similar idea behind Jeremiah's prayer against his enemies: 'Forgive not their iniquity . . . deal thou with them in the time of thine anger' (Je. xviii. 23). The anger of the Lord and the refusal to accept a *kopher* are here in close connection.

The thought of propitiation is very clear in the incident related in Nu. xxv wherein Phinehas slew Zimri and Cozbi at the time of the sin of Baal-Peor to stay the plague which followed the kindling of the Lord's anger (verses 3, 9). Of this action we read: 'Phinehas, the son of Eleazar, the son of Aaron the priest, hath turned my wrath away from the children of Israel, in that he was jealous with my jealousy among them, so that I consumed not the children of Israel in my jealousy . . . he was jealous for his God, and made atonement for the children of Israel' (Nu. xxv. 11–13). Here the zealous priest by offering up the lives of the evil-doers is thought of as rendering the *kopher* which averts the divine wrath. There can hardly be serious doubt that here we have propitiation in the fullest sense,[1] or that this propitiation is the turning away of wrath by the offering of a *kopher*.

There remain two passages, 2 Ch. xxx. 18 and Is. vi. 7, in both of which the reference is to the purging away of uncleanness. In neither case can it be said that the payment of a *kopher* seems indicated, though neither is inconsistent with a propitiation of the divine wrath, for ritual defilement is thought to provoke the anger of the deity in many religions. But it should be noticed that these passages are both later than 1 Sa. iii. 14 where *kipper* has begun to have a cultic application. It is accordingly not impossible that cultic ideas are behind the use of the word in these passages. If this is so, the general argument from the secular use of the word would, of course, remain unaffected.

From the foregoing examination of the evidence it would appear that, when *kipper* is used in the Old Testament to denote the making of an atonement by means other than the use of the cultus, it usually bears the meaning 'to avert punishment, especially

---

[1] Cf. Dodd in JTS, xxxII (July 1931), p. 355.

the divine anger, by the payment of a *kopher*, a ransom', which may be of money or which may be of life. Thus extra-cultic *kipper* denotes a substitutionary process. This is so plain as to need no comment in the cases where life is substituted for life, and the principle is really the same when the sentence is commuted for a money payment. In each case the essence of the transaction is the provision of an acceptable substitute.

The fact that, in practically all of the passages we have examined, *kipper* and *kopher* are seen to be closely connected seems very significant, for when we are seeking to establish the meaning of a word it is the *usage* in Hebrew that is decisive.[1] In examining the meaning of *kipper* scholars often adduce words from other Semitic languages; but while due allowance must be made for the importance of such evidence, in the last resort it is the way the Hebrews actually used the word which really counts. The importance of this is that the usage of the two words *kipper* and *kopher* indicates, as we have seen, that *kopher* is probably the more original, and that *kipper* may well be regarded as a denominative from *kopher*. The seven places where atonement is made through offering a *kopher* of life, and the nine where the *kopher* is money or goods or a metaphorical price, seem to be conclusive, embracing as they do the majority of the non-cultic occurrences of the term.

(ii) *The cultic use of kipper.* When we turn our attention to the use of *kipper* with respect to the sacrifices it is not easy to find out exactly how atonement was thought to be made, as the verb acquired a technical meaning which completely overshadowed any other, so that in most places it means 'to accomplish reconciliation between God and man' without anything to indicate how that reconciliation is held to be obtained. The word has taken on a conventional meaning. However, indications are not lacking that the above-mentioned relationship between *kopher* and *kipper* gives us the key to the understanding of the cultic references.

---

[1] Cf. G. F. Moore: 'by a fault of method which has been fruitful of error in the study of the OT, the investigation has frequently set out from etymological assumptions instead of from the plain facts of usage' (*Enc. Bib.*, IV, col. 4220). So also König: 'the Heb. usage of the word *kipper* is the *only* starting-point from which to determine the original significance of the word' (ET, XXII, 380).

Thus if we take the incident narrated in Nu. xvi. 41–50 we have a making of atonement which may be held to be a link between the cultic and the non-cultic usages. Here the congregation has murmured against Moses and Aaron and a plague has broken out as a consequence of the Lord's anger against the people (verse 46). The means of averting the wrath is by Aaron's making an offering of incense (verses 46f.), and such an action by a duly consecrated priest must surely be regarded as within the scope of the cultus. But it was not one of the prescribed offerings, being purely an oblation made in time of grave emergency for the specific purpose of turning away the anger of the Lord, and the affinities of this with a *kopher*-payment are obvious. If it be objected that there was no great money value in the offering of a small quantity of incense, so that the atonement obtained is out of all proportion to the price paid, the answer must be that the atonement obtained is always out of all proportion to the price paid,[1] even in the case of the non-cultic atonements, as for example the half-shekel, or the payment to secure immunity when one's ox has gored a man. There is always an element of grace in atonement. But just as, notwithstanding this, we can appreciate the place of the *kopher*-payment in non-cultic practice, so in the processes of the cultus we may recognize both the element of grace and the necessity for the worshipper to make his offering if he would be forgiven his sin.

We have already noted the incident in Nu. xxxi wherein the men of war offered part of the spoil which they called 'the Lord's oblation' and which was 'to make atonement for their souls before the Lord'. There seems no reason to regard this as other than a non-cultic process, for there is no hint of sacrifice being offered, but there is not a great deal of difference between this and the offering of the princes in Nu. vii, for included in their oblation (*qorban*) were 'one silver charger, the weight thereof was an hundred and thirty shekels, one silver bowl of seventy shekels, after the shekel of the sanctuary . . . one golden spoon of ten

---

[1] Cf. the Midrash on Numbers: 'Moses pondered: Who is in a position to give ransom for his soul? . . . The Holy One, blessed be He, told him: I do not ask for ransom in accordance with My means, but in accordance with theirs' Nu. R. xii. 3 (Soncino trans. pp. 451f.).

shekels', which objects of precious metal seem similar to the offering of the men of war. But we cannot separate the gift of the princes from the cultus, because under the comprehensive term *qorban* are included not only the precious metal, but also burnt, sin and peace offerings.

The affinity of the cultus with *kopher* seems clear also in Nu. xv. 25 where we read, 'And the priest shall make atonement (*wek-hipper*) for all the congregation of the children of Israel, and they shall be forgiven; for it was an error, and they have brought their oblation ('*eth-qorbanam*), an offering made by fire unto the Lord, etc.' Here the sacrifice that makes atonement is expressly said to be *qorban*, a word which, as G. Buchanan Gray puts it, 'vividly expressed the sense of gift'.[1] It seems impossible to escape the conclusion that in this passage *kipper* stands for a process of making atonement by the offering of a suitable gift. For other passages with the idea of the gift element in sacrifice see Dt. xvi. 16; Jdg. vi. 18–19; Is. xviii. 7; Zp. iii. 10, etc.[2]

It would seem that it is in this circle of ideas that we are to understand the statement in 1 Sa. iii. 14 that 'the iniquity of Eli's house shall not be atoned with sacrifice nor offering for ever'. The house in question had been guilty of sin against the Lord which aroused His wrath against them. Perhaps this wrath could be turned away (according to the thought of the day) by payment of a *kopher* and the lives now forfeit be in this manner redeemed? The words of verse 14 emphatically repudiate this idea. No sacrifice or offering will form a *kopher* under these circumstances. It is very interesting that in this undeniably early passage the cultus is regarded as a means of offering a *kopher*, and this is probably significant for an understanding of the cultus.

It may not be inappropriate to remark here that this was apparently the way the cultus was regarded by the Jews at Yeb, in Egypt; for when the priests wrote to Bigvai, the governor of

---

[1] *Sacrifice in the Old Testament*, Oxford, 1925, p. 51.

[2] Davidson says: 'whatever older or more primary ideas of sacrifice may have been, in the Old Testament at least sacrifice is of the nature of a gift to God' (*The Theology of the Old Testament*, Edinburgh, 1904, p. 353). He also says: 'The traditional explanation has been that the death of the victim was a *poena vicaria* for the sin of the offerer. And it is probable that this idea did become attached to sacrifice' (*Ibid.*), though he questions whether this thought is to be found in the law.

Judea, urging him to give command concerning the rebuilding of their temple, they said that, if he acceded to their request, they would offer sacrifices on his behalf and pray for him, 'and it shall be a merit to you before Ya'u the God of Heaven more than a man who offers to him sacrifice and burnt-offerings worth as much as the sum of a thousand talents'.[1] The mention of the money equivalent indicates clearly that the thought of a gift availing before God is for the writers the rationale of sacrifice.

Possibly the provision in the case of the guilt offering for an extra one fifth to be added to full restitution in certain cases points in the same general direction. Thus, in the matter of an unwitting trespass 'in the holy things of the Lord', it is provided that 'he shall make restitution for that which he hath done amiss in the holy thing, and shall add the fifth part thereto, and give it unto the priest: and the priest shall make atonement for him with the ram of the guilt offering, and he shall be forgiven' (Lv. v. 16). Here the extra fifth looks uncommonly like a sort of *kopher*, and the same may be said for other examples of the guilt offering.

It is especially interesting to note that when restitution was owed to a man, but could not be paid because the man was dead, and there was no kinsman, it was still necessary for the restitution (the full amount owed plus one fifth) to be paid, but to the Lord (Nu. v. 8). It would seem that there was a principle involved, namely that a *kopher* must be paid if atonement was to be effected.

To adduce further examples would entail a long discussion such as would be out of place here. If there is anything in the thesis which is being maintained then the use outside the cultus coupled with these few examples of the continuity of the cultic with the non-cultic use should suffice to demonstrate the point. The general impression produced by the sacrificial system, that an offering of a propitiatory character is being made, is perhaps worthy of notice also. It is not so much from consideration of details as from the general sweep of the whole that conviction is obtained.[2]

It is also worth noticing that the prophets witness to a belief in sacrifice as the offering of such a gift to Yahweh as would incline

---

[1] Cowley, *Aramaic Papyri of the Fifth Century B.C.*, Oxford, 1923, No. 30, lines 27f.

[2] Cf. the statement quoted from the Jewish Encyclopedia on p. 156 below.

Him to be favourable. Passages like Is. i. 11ff.; Mi. vi. 6ff., show clearly that such a theory of sacrifice was present to the minds of the worshippers. The prophets denounce much in the attitude of the people, in particular pointing out the prime importance of ethical considerations; but it may be significant that they nowhere suggest a different theory of sacrifice. It seems reasonable to expect that had they held this theory to be wrong they would have both said so, and also have indicated the better theory.

Thus it would seem that the verb *kipper* carries with it the implication of a turning away of the divine wrath by an appropriate offering, a meaning which accords well with the general usage of ἐξιλάσκομαι and which we may take as indicated also in the LXX by virtue of the ideas contained in the verb it is used to translate.

It remains to be considered whether the conclusions we have reached regarding the ἐξιλάσκομαι=*kipper* equation are affected by the evidence afforded by those passages where ἐξιλάσκομαι in the LXX renders Hebrew words other than *kipper*. We have already noted that this Greek verb is the translation of *kipper* eighty-three times; for the rest it translates *ḥṭṭ'* five times, *ḥllh* three times, *plll* and *'shm* once each (also *yd'* once, but this seems to rest on a misunderstanding of the Hebrew[1]), and eleven times there is no Hebrew equivalent.

So far as *ḥṭṭ'* 'to un-sin, to make a sin offering', is concerned, very little needs be said. Its use is practically indistinguishable from that of *kipper* in the places where ἐξιλάσκομαι translates it. Thus in 2 Ch. xxix. 24 the verb signifies 'they made their blood a sin offering', which is close to the usage we have already noted, especially to that non-cultic use of *kipper* wherein there is a life-for-life conception. In Ezekiel, where all the remaining examples are found, it is very difficult to find any difference between this use of ἐξιλάσκομαι and that where *kipper* is the underlying Hebrew, this being especially plain in Ezk. xliii. 20 where it is impossible to say which of the two Hebrew verbs the Greek word translates.

ḥillah is a verb meaning 'to appease, mollify', and three times it occurs as the ground word for which ἐξιλάσκομαι is the transla-

---

[1] Or perhaps a different (and now lost) reading. Either way it sheds no light on our problem.

tion, namely in Zc. vii. 2, viii. 22; Mal. i. 9. Each time the thought of propitiation is quite clear, as Dodd notes when he calls these three occurrences 'unmistakable examples of the ordinary classical and Hellenistic sense of ἐξιλάσκεσθαι "to propitiate".'[1]

The use of ἐξιλάσκομαι to translate *plll* ('to interpose', hence 'to do judgment', or by another line of development, 'to pray') in Ps. cv (cvi). 30 is very unusual, and despite Dodd's objection is probably to be understood in the light of the story in Numbers. The psalmist is recalling the atonement wrought by Phinehas at the time of the sin of Baal-Peor and the LXX translator substitutes 'and he made propitiation' for 'and he interposed', or 'wrought judgment'.

The one occurrence of ἐξιλάσκομαι as the translation of *'shm* presents us with a difficulty, as the Hebrew verb means 'to be guilty' and it is hard to fit ἐξιλάσκομαι into this circle of ideas. Probably, as Dodd suggests, the translators of the LXX were influenced by the close kinship between *'shm* and *ḥṭ'* in which case we must think of the passage for our present purpose as coming close to the group already considered.

Thus there is nothing in the use of ἐξιλάσκομαι to translate other Hebrew roots which conflicts with what we have already seen may be deduced from its connection with *kipper*. The thought of the offering of a ransom which turns away the divine wrath from the sinner still seems to be the basic meaning of the verb.

We conclude this section by noticing the constructions used with ἐξιλάσκομαι. Since it is sometimes said that the verb is often used in the sense 'to expiate' it is worth noting that it is never followed by an accusative of sin in the canonical Scriptures of the Old Testament.[2] There are seven occurrences of this construction, one being in Theodotion's Daniel, namely ix. 24, where the 'seventy weeks' decreed upon the people look like a manifestation of divine wrath; the remaining six are in Sirach, three of them certainly referring to removal of wrath (Sir. iii. 30, v. 6, xxviii. 5), and probably two more also (Sir. xx. 28, xxxi. 33). This evidence cannot be said to be very strong, and it can be supported by only

---

[1] JTS, XXXII, 355.

[2] Here and elsewhere I use this term to denote the Greek translation of the Scriptures of the Hebrew canon. I exclude the Apocrypha and the Theodotianic version of Daniel.

two passives with sin as subject (Dt. xxi. 8; 1 Sa. iii. 14), in both of which it is possible to think of propitiation. The grouping of the nine accusatives of a cultic object (altar, sanctuary, etc.) with this class is not warranted, for the meaning is not the same (Lv. xvi. 16, 20, 33 (twice); Ezk. xliii. 20, 22, 26, xlv. 18, 20; cf. also the curious accusative of 'blood' in 2 Ch. xxix. 24). If one expiates a sin it is clean gone, but if one cleanses an altar it is still there. It seems best to recognize that the verb had a complex meaning, but to see the removal of wrath as the basic idea. Wrath could be removed with reference to a sin, or with reference to an (unclean) altar, etc.

Again, God is the subject of the verb three times, followed by dative of person (Ezk. xvi. 63), by περί (Sir. xvi. 7), and by ὑπέρ (2 Ch. xxx. 18); but not much can be made of this because in the first and last of these the verb is in the passive. With these two passives which have God as the subject should be classed three passages with God as the object and where the meaning clearly is 'propitiate', namely Zc. vii. 2, viii. 22; Mal. i. 9. The idea of propitiation is also found with a human object in Gn. xxxii. 20, while the one accusative of 'wrath' (Pr. xvi. 14) has much the same meaning. This brings us to the thought that the verb is most often used in a personal sense, the most common construction being περί with genitive of person, 'to make propitiation concerning a person', this construction being found fifty-eight times (e.g. Ex. xxx. 15, 16; Lv. i. 4. Sometimes περί of sin is added, as in Lv. iv. 35, or ἀπό of sin, as in Lv. iv. 26, or of uncleanness, as in Lv. xv. 15, 30. Once, Ezk. xlv. 17, we find ὑπέρ of person, and once, Lv. xvi. 10, ἐπί with animal).

For the rest the verb is used absolutely ten times (as Lv. vi. 30), with περί of sin twice (Ex. xxxii. 30; Lv. v. 10), with περί or ἐπί of things four times (Ex. xxx. 10; Lv. viii. 15, xiv. 53, xvi. 18), and there are two passives, one with the land as subject, while the verb is impersonal with dative of person in the last case (Nu. xxxv. 33; 1 Sa. vi. 3).

These constructions reveal that the word is used in a variety of ways, but there is no preponderance of expressions which could be construed of expiation of sin. Rather the emphasis seems to be on the relation between persons, a fact which accords better with a meaning like 'propitiate' than 'expiate'. It is clear that ἐξιλάσκομαι in the LXX is a complex word, but the averting of anger seems to represent a stubborn substratum of meaning from which all the usages can be naturally explained, even those with God as subject, for while the Old Testament is emphatic about the reality and seriousness of the wrath of God, the removal of that wrath is due in the last resort to God Himself, for as the LXX of Ps. lxxvii (lxxviii). 38 says 'He will many times turn away His anger'.

Pausing now to summarize the results of our investigation of the use of this word group in the Septuagint, we accept the verdict of such scholars as Westcott and Dodd in their demonstration that in the Old Testament there is not the usual pagan sense of a crude propitiation of an angry deity, and that this is shown in the LXX use of ἰλάσκομαι, etc. The usage with God as the subject of the verb, the paucity of examples of its use with Him as the object, the study of the Hebrew words translated by ἰλάσκομαι and its cognates all alike draw us to this conclusion, and though in the foregoing treatment we have not been greatly concerned to defend this point of view, that should not be understood as minimizing its importance. It is of the utmost importance that we should understand that propitiation in the crude sense is not possible with the God of Israel, and that the Greek words used reflect this view of the deity. We cannot be too grateful to Dodd and others for their convincing demonstration of this truth.

However, it is the present writer's conviction that, in stating this great truth, most who have treated it have tended to go too far. When we reach the stage where we must say 'When the LXX translators used "propitiation" they did not mean "propitiation"', it is surely time to call a halt. No sensible man uses one word when he means another, and in view of the otherwise invariable Greek use it would seem impossible for anyone in the first century to have used one of the ἰλάσκομαι group without conveying to his readers some idea of propitiation.

It is contended that while care is taken to avoid the crude use natural to pagans, yet the words of the ἰλάσκομαι group as used in the LXX were not eviscerated of their meaning, nor were they given an entirely new meaning. Rather there is a definite continuity, and in particular the removal of wrath seems to be definitely in view when this word group is used. We have noticed that in many passages where one or other of these words is used there is a plain statement that Yahweh is angry, and in others there is a clear implication that this is so, and these passages (taken in conjunction with the essential meaning of ἱλάσκομαι, etc.) must be held to set the tone for the rest.

Examination of this word group brought us inevitably into the circle of ideas associated with *kipper*, where we have seen reason for postulating a close connection between *kipper* and *kopher*, which further strengthens the conclusion that ἱλάσκομαι, etc., retain the idea of putting away the divine anger, since we see that in the cultus itself there is the thought of a ransom being paid, a ransom which we may not unjustly regard as a propitiation. As the Jewish Encyclopedia puts it: 'Every sacrifice may be considered thus as a kofer, in the original sense a propitiatory gift'.[1]

Thus we conclude that the sense of propitiation seems to be established from the passages in which ἱλάσκομαι and its cognates occur.

V. CONCLUSION

The preceding sections have shown that the wrath of God is a conception which cannot be eradicated from the Old Testament without irreparable loss. It is not the monopoly of one or two writers, but pervades the entire corpus so that there is no important section of which it can be said 'Here the wrath of God is unknown!' The ubiquity of the concept must be stressed, because of the tendency in some circles today to overlook it or to explain it away. The concept may need to be understood carefully, but it is so much part and parcel of the Old Testament that, if we ignore it, we cannot possibly enter into a proper appreciation of the Hebrew view of God or of man.

Above everything else, the concept of the wrath of God stresses the seriousness of sin. On the Old Testament view sin is not just a mere peccadillo which a kindly, benevolent God will regard as of no great consequence. On the contrary, the God of the Old

[1] Vol. II, p. 247. Driver makes a thorough examination of *kipper* in his article on 'Propitiation' in HDB and concludes that, when the verb is used in a ritual sense, it means 'to make propitiation', and in other places it signifies 'deal propitiously with', or 'be propitious to'. See also his commentary on Deuteronomy (I.C.C.) pp. 425f.

Testament is One who loves righteousness (Pss. xxxiii. 5, xlviii.
10, etc.), and whose attitude to unrighteousness can be described
as hatred. 'These are the things that ye shall do; Speak ye every
man the truth with his neighbour; execute the judgment of truth
and peace in your gates: and let none of you imagine evil in your
hearts against his neighbour; and love no false oath; for all these
are things that I hate, saith the Lord' (Zc. viii. 16f.) is a typical
statement. Also Scripture not only speaks of the Lord hating sin,
but of those who commit sin as well, for as the psalmist puts it:
'The Lord trieth the righteous; but the wicked and him that loveth
violence his soul hateth. Upon the wicked he shall rain snares; fire
and brimstone and burning wind shall be the portion of their cup.
For the Lord is righteous; he loveth righteousness, etc.' (Ps. xi.
5–7). Such passages reveal the strongest possible repulsion in the
face of everything that is evil; and it is from the very heart of a
God who loves His people and hates evil that there proceeds such
pleading as 'I sent unto you all my servants the prophets, rising up
early and sending them, saying, Oh do not this abominable thing
that I hate' (Je. xliv. 4). So, too, we find passages in which those
who love God are called upon to exercise the same attitude to
evil, 'O ye that love the Lord, hate evil' (Ps. xcvii. 10).

Modern men find a difficulty with this aspect of the Old
Testament teaching, in part at least because they have so well
learned that God is love. But it is important to notice that this was
a truth known and valued by men of Old Testament times, and
they apparently did not find it insuperably difficult to combine
the ideas that God loved them and that He hated all that is evil
and would punish it severely. For example we find both thoughts
emphasized in Hosea's prophecy. On the one hand we have the
beautiful picture of Yahweh wooing the nation in ii. 14f., expressed in statements such as 'I drew them with cords of a man,
with bands of love' (Ho. xi. 4), or 'How shall I give thee up,
Ephraim? how shall I deliver thee, Israel? how shall I make thee as
Admah? how shall I set thee as Zeboim? mine heart is turned
within me, my compassions are kindled together. I will not
execute the fierceness of mine anger, I will not return to destroy
Ephraim' (Ho. xi. 8f.), and the unforgettable picture of a father
teaching a baby son to walk in xi. 1–3. On the other hand we have
the most categorical statements of God's loathing of the evil that

was in the nation and the certainty of divine visitation and punishment in consequence. 'All their wickedness is in Gilgal; for there I hated them: because of the wickedness of their doings I will drive them out of mine house: I will love them no more; all their princes are revolters. Ephraim is smitten, their root is dried up, they shall bear no fruit: yea, though they bring forth, yet will I slay the beloved fruit of their womb. My God will cast them away, because they did not hearken unto him: and they shall be wanderers among the nations' (Ho. ix. 15–17). 'He hath cast off thy calf, O Samaria; mine anger is kindled against them' (Ho. viii. 5). 'For Israel hath forgotten his Maker, and builded palaces; and Judah hath multiplied fenced cities: but I will send a fire upon his cities, and it shall devour the castles thereof' (Ho. viii. 14).

Such examples could be multiplied from many parts of the Old Testament, and they demand some explanation. It is open to us to say that there are divergent ideas which have not been harmonized; but if we are to be true to the records we cannot simply say that half the evidence does not exist. But in view of the fact that we have both truths expressed, and expressed very strongly, by one man as we have just seen (and what is true of Hosea is also true of other Old Testament figures) it seems better to say that divine love and the divine wrath are compatible aspects of the divine nature. There is a divine wrath, but if we may put it this way, it is always exercised with a certain tenderness, for even when He is angry with man's sin God loves man and is concerned for his well-being in the fullest sense. There is a divine love, but it is not a careless sentimentality indifferent to the moral integrity of the loved ones. Rather it is a love which is a purifying fire, blazing against everything that hinders the loved ones from being the very best that they can be.

Indeed wrath may be thought of as especially wrath against the loved ones for, as Fichtner points out,[1] wrath is connected much more often with the covenant name 'Jehovah' than with any other of the divine names. There are times when the wrath of God is spoken of as directed against the heathen, and the importance of these passages should not be minimized (wrath is directed

[1] TWNT, v, p. 396.

against *all* evil); but in one aspect it is God's reaction against sin in His chosen people, in those whom He loves.

Much, it would seem, depends on what we understand by wrath. If we think of an uncontrollable outburst of passion, then we have a pagan conception, completely inapplicable to the God of the Old Testament.[1] But if we think rather of a wrath which is the reverse side of a holy love, a flame which sears but purifies, then we have a conception which is valuable not only for an understanding of the ancient Scriptures, but also for any right conception of the nature of God. 'Neither doth he abhor anything that is evil' (Ps. xxxvi. 4 Prayer Book version) is a terrible condemnation of a man's character. The Hebrews did not ascribe such moral flabbiness to the God they worshipped.

It is against such a background that the Old Testament idea of propitiation is to be studied. Where there is sin, the Old Testament teaches, there is wrath; but this does not mean that all men are to be consumed, for that wrath is the wrath of a loving father who yearns for His children to come to Him.[2] There is forgiveness with God, and this forgiveness necessarily involves the laying aside of wrath.[3] But it is important to note that the removal of this wrath is not due to man's securing such an offering that God is impressed and relents. It is due to God Himself, and this alone is sufficient to show that we are not dealing with the pagan idea when we speak of propitiation. Such a passage as Lv. xvii. 11, 'For the life of the flesh is in the blood: and *I have given it to you upon the altar to make atonement* for your souls', clearly indicates the position.[4] The cultus

[1] Cf. G. O. Griffith: 'We picture "wrath" as we might think of the fury of a storm. The Hebrew Prophets, when they spoke of "the wrath of God", ethicized the idea of anger so that it meant the absolute implacable hostility of the Divine Holiness to every form of moral evil' (*St. Paul's Gospel to the Romans*, Oxford, 1949, p. 20), or again: 'The wrath is no fitful outburst of personal anger, but the implacable antagonism of holiness for evil, an antagonism that burns eternally' (*Op. cit.*, pp. 85f.).

[2] Cf., for example, Ho. xi. 1–4 with Ho. xi. 5f.

[3] G. Buchanan Gray says: 'The ideas of expiation of sin and propitiation of God are in Hebrew thought closely related' (*Op. cit.*, p. 74).

[4] Cf. P. T. Forsyth: 'Given! Did you ever see the force of it? "I have given you the blood to make atonement. This is an institution which I set up for you to comply with, set it up for purposes of My own, on principles of My own,

[*continued on p. 160*]

may well be regarded as a means of turning away the wrath of God from the sinner by the offering of a *kopher*; but it is so, not because the God of Israel can be bought, but because He has *given* to the people this means of averting wrath. That it is not an unconditional means many passages in the prophets and elsewhere plainly show. The cultus does not work like a bribe, but it is the divinely appointed way of removing wrath, of propitiation. As P. T. Forsyth puts it: 'Atonement in the Old Testament was not the placating of God's anger, but the sacrament of God's grace. It was the expression of God's anger on the one hand and the expression and putting in action of God's grace on the other hand. . . . The sacrifices were in themselves prime acts of obedience to God's means of grace and His expressed will.'[1]

Thus, our conviction that ἱλάσκομαι and its cognates include as an integral part of their meaning the turning away of wrath rests partly on the examination of the occurrences of these words in the Septuagint, and partly on the fact that, quite apart from the words themselves, there is a formidable body of evidence that the wrath of God was a conception to be reckoned with on the Old Testament view. These two lines of thought reinforce one another and lead us to the conclusion that, on the biblical view, an element of wrath inheres in the divine nature, but that, by God's own appointment, this wrath may be averted. This averting we may properly term 'propitiation', if that word is understood as excluding the pagan idea of a process of celestial bribery. It may have to be used with care, but there is no reason for jettisoning it altogether.

---

[1] *Ibid.*, p. 90. It is of interest in connection with the foregoing that H. Wheeler Robinson regards 'propitiatory' as one of the four chief ways of regarding the sacrifices (*Redemption and Revelation*, London, 1942, pp. 249f.).

---

but it is My gift". The Lord Himself provided the lamb for the burnt offering' (*The Work of Christ*, London, 1948, p. 90).

PROPITIATION (2)

IN THE preceding chapter we noted that there are four passages in the New Testament which are specially important for an understanding of propitiation, but that is not to say that we have exhausted the concept of propitiation when we have examined them. In the New Testament, as in the Old, a good deal depends upon our conception of the place and nature of the wrath of God. If this wrath is regarded as a very real factor so that the sinner is exposed to its severity, then the removal of the wrath will be an important part of our understanding of salvation; whereas if we diminish the part played by the divine wrath we shall not find it necessary to think seriously of propitiation. Accordingly we begin our discussion of the New Testament teaching on this subject by examining those passages where the wrath of God is mentioned.

I. THE WRATH OF GOD IN THE NEW TESTAMENT

There is neither the same richness of vocabulary nor the same frequency of mention in the New Testament treatment of the wrath of God as in the Old, but, nevertheless, an examination of the relevant passages seems to show that for the early Christians the divine wrath was just as real as it was for the men of the old covenant. In our section on wrath in the Old Testament we noted the view held by some that wrath for the prophets signifies nothing more than an impersonal process of retribution. Such views are held, too, with regard to the New Testament. For example, C. H. Dodd says that, in the teaching of Jesus, 'anger as an attitude of God to men disappears, and His love and mercy become all embracing'.[1] St. Paul, he thinks, agrees with this in substance and retains the concept of the wrath of God 'not to describe the attitude of God to man, but to describe an inevitable process of cause and effect in a moral universe'.[2] In support he appeals to

[1] *Romans* (MNTC), p. 23.　　　　[2] *Ibid.*

Rom. i. 18f. We do not think that such views can be substantiated. Let us examine, therefore, the witness of the New Testament.

There are two Greek words particularly used to denote the divine anger, namely θυμός and ὀργή. The two seem at times to be used synonymously; Büchsel, indeed, denies that we can distinguish between them. Etymologically there is a distinction, for θυμός derives from θύω which means to rush on or along, and, as Grimm-Thayer put it: 'be in a heat, breathe violently; hence Plato correctly says, Cratyl. p. 419e θυμὸς ἀπὸ τῆς θύσεως κ. ζέσεως τῆς ψυχῆς; accordingly it signifies both *the spirit* panting as it were in the body, and the *rage* with which the man pants and swells'.[1] ὀργή on the other hand is from ὀργάω which signifies 'to be getting ready to bear, growing ripe for something',[2] and comes to mean the natural disposition or character, any movement of soul, especially strong emotion, and so anger. This leads to a distinction between the two words such that θυμός more readily denotes passionate anger, arising and subsiding quickly, whereas ὀργή is adapted to a more settled emotion,[3] and Grimm-Thayer cites Plato and Gregory Nazianzum to show this.

This original distinction is not always observed, but from it we can see that ὀργή is a more suitable term for the divine wrath than θυμός, and, in point of fact, the latter term is used only once of God's anger outside the Apocalypse in which book the thought of a passionate wrath is in keeping with the vivid imagery used throughout.[4] The point of all this is that the biblical writers habitually use for the divine wrath a word which denotes not so much a sudden flaring up of passion which is soon over, as a

---

[1] Lexicon *sub* θυμός.

[2] Liddell and Scott (new edn.). The Eighth edn. says the word means 'prop. to swell and teem with moisture'.

[3] Thus Stählin says of ὀργή: 'Nevertheless this word includes an element of consciousness, even of deliberation, which is absent from θυμός; in Jas. i. 19 (βραδὺς εἰς ὀργήν) for example ὀργή could hardly be replaced by θυμός' (TWNT, v, p. 419).

[4] To cite Stählin again: 'But one could well say that θυμός, to which there cleaves the idea of outbursting passion, is well suited for the representation of the vision of the seer, but not as a designation for the Pauline conception of the wrath of God' (*Op. cit.*, p. 423).

strong and settled opposition to all that is evil arising out of God's very nature.

Beginning our examination of the evidence with the Gospels we find that, though the actual term 'wrath' is not of frequent occurrence,[1] Jesus Himself is once said to have been angry (Mk. iii. 5), and He spoke of the siege of Jerusalem as 'wrath unto this people' (Lk. xxi. 23), while His forerunner warned men of 'wrath to come' (Mt. iii. 7; Lk. iii. 7). We also read of the disobedient (or unbeliever; ὁ ἀπειθῶν τῷ υἱῷ) that 'the wrath of God abideth on him' (Jn. iii. 36), where wrath is the portion of the sinner, corresponding to the believer's reception of eternal life.

But in other places where the term 'wrath' does not occur we find strong expressions for the divine hostility to all that is evil. Thus Jesus taught explicitly that men stand in danger of a hell which may be described as a 'hell of fire' (Mt. v. 22, etc.), or as 'the eternal fire' (Mt. xviii. 8), a place where 'their worm dieth not, and the fire is not quenched' (Mk. ix. 48). God is to be feared, for He, 'after he hath killed hath power to cast into hell' (Lk. xii. 5). Jesus' severe strictures on Capernaum and other cities (Mt. xi. 20, 24), and on the Pharisees (Mt. xxiii), show an intolerance of evil, which we see again in the 'except ye repent, ye shall all in like manner perish' of Lk. xiii. 3, 5, and the saying that 'whosoever shall blaspheme against the Holy Spirit hath never forgiveness, but is guilty of an eternal sin' (Mk. iii. 29). It is in keeping with this general attitude that we read of Judas, 'good were it for that man if he had not been born' (Mk. xiv. 21), and that, on the day of judgment, the verdict on some will be, 'Depart from me, ye cursed, into the eternal fire' (Mt. xxv. 41 and cf. verse 46). In the parables judgment is a persistent theme as we see for example from Mt. xiii. 42, 50, xviii. 34, xxi. 44, xxii. 7, 33. So, too, is the idea of the 'outer darkness' where there will be 'weeping and gnashing of teeth' (Mt. viii. 12, xiii. 42, 50, xxii. 13, xxiv. 51, xxv. 30; Lk. xiii. 28). In the face of all this it is difficult to maintain that Jesus had discarded the conception of the wrath

[1] Stählin introduces his section on 'The Revelation of the Divine Wrath' by saying: 'Wrath is an integral trait in the evangelists' portrait of Jesus. To be sure, the subject is mentioned only seldom in express words . . . but the fact is clearly more often there' (*Op. cit.*, p. 428).

of God. For Him the divine reaction in the face of evil was a solemn and terrible reality.

Nor is the case different when we turn to the rest of the New Testament. It is sometimes said that there is significance in the fact that 'the wrath' occurs often without being definitely associated with God, and that this points to a semi-personalization, wrath being conceived of as something different from, and almost independent of, God.[1] To this there are two answers. The first is that more than one conclusion can be drawn from the occurrence of 'the wrath'. It is quite legitimate for us to hold that the prophets who spoke of the coming day of wrath when God would punish sin had done their work so well that the fact that the wrath that was to be revealed was God's wrath did not require emphasis. The second is that the association of 'the wrath' with God is not so tenuous as some would have us believe. 'The wrath' (ἡ ὀργή) is specifically said to be of God in Jn. iii. 36; Rom. i. 18; Eph. v. 6; Col. iii. 6; Rev. xix. 15. In addition ἡ ὀργή σου of Rev. xi. 18 and τῆς ὀργῆς αὐτοῦ of Rev. xiv. 10, xvi. 19 obviously refer the wrath to God, while most people would agree that Rom. ix. 22 is correctly translated by 'What if God, willing to shew his wrath' (with EV). Again 'the wrath of the lamb' (Rev. vi. 16) associates wrath personally with a divine Being. θυμός is used to convey the idea of an anger specifically linked with God in Rev. xiv. 10, 19, xv. 1, 7, xvi. 1, xix. 15, while in Rev. xvi. 19 the anger is clearly that of God. Nor have we told the whole story when we have listed the passages where there is an explicit connection of 'wrath' with God, for there are some passages without this where it is quite plain that such a link must be postulated. Thus C. Anderson Scott includes in a list of passages where 'Directly or indirectly St. Paul connects God with the idea of anger or wrath'

---

[1] So Sydney Cave (to whose writings the present writer owes a debt he can never repay): 'they (i.e. Law and Wrath) are almost personified powers, which, owing to God their origin, act on in partial independence of God, and are hostile to men as He is not' (*The Doctrine of the Work of Christ*, London, 1937, p. 43). The idea is categorically rejected by F. V. Filson: 'It is unwarranted to separate wrath from God, personalize it, and so make it a personal power independent of God . . . Paul was not thinking of a separate being called Wrath' (*St. Paul's Conception of Recompense*, Leipzig, 1931, p. 40, n. 2). Similarly Stählin (*Op. cit.*, p. 425).

Rom. ii. 5, iii. 5, v. 9; 1 Thes. i. 10, ii. 16, while he thinks 'the same reference is less clearly expressed' in Rom. iv. 15; Eph. ii. 3; 1 Thes. v. 9.[1]

Nor have we yet finished. What are we to make of such a passage as 2 Thes. i. 7–9 where we read of 'the revelation of the Lord Jesus from heaven with the angels of his power in flaming fire, rendering vengeance to them that know not God, and to them that obey not the gospel of our Lord Jesus: who shall suffer punishment, even eternal destruction from the face of the Lord and from the glory of his might'? Surely it is clear from this that the apostle expected a day to come when that which he elsewhere designates as 'the wrath of God' will have full operation. As we read these words we cannot think that he is referring to an impersonal retribution, for he speaks of the revelation of a person. Similarly, when we read Rom. ii. 5–9, although we do not encounter the phrase 'the wrath of God', we cannot feel that the apostle is thinking of an impersonal retribution which operates while God remains apart, little more than a spectator. Paul's vigorous language gives us rather a picture of a God who is personally active in dealing with sinners. As Heb. xii. 29 puts it 'our God is a consuming fire.'[2]

P. T. Forsyth has a valuable Addendum to his *The Work of Christ* in which this question is discussed with great force. He asks: 'When a man piles up his sin and rejoices in iniquity, is God simply a bystander and spectator of the process? Does not God's pressure on the man blind him, urge him, stiffen him, shut him up into sin, if only that he might be shut up to mercy alone? Is it enough to say that this is but the action of a process which God simply watches in a permissive way? Is He but passive and not positive to the situation? Can the Absolute be passive to anything?

---

[1] *Christianity According to St. Paul*, Cambridge, 1927, p. 78.

[2] R. V. G. Tasker speaks of some severe sayings of Jesus and comments: 'These are sayings of terrible severity, but they are just as much part of the revelation of God made known in Christ Jesus as those sayings and deeds of the Master which so conspicuously display the divine love and mercy. To thrust these severe sayings on one side and to concentrate attention solely upon passages of the Gospels where the divine Fatherhood is proclaimed is to preach a debilitated Christianity, which does not and cannot do what Christ came into the world to do, viz. save men from the wrath to come' (*The Biblical Doctrine of the Wrath of God*, London, 1951, p. 36).

If so, where is the inner action of the personal God whose immanence in things is one of His great modern revelations?'[1]

We saw earlier that Dodd sees in Rom. i. 18f. the concept of 'the wrath of God' used 'to describe an inevitable process of cause and effect in a moral universe'. But in these very verses we find the personal activity of God brought out, for when St. Paul might well say that the sins of the heathen produced inevitable results, or might make use of some similar expression, he seems to go out of his way to lay stress upon the divine activity. 'God gave them up . . . unto uncleanness' (verse 24); 'God gave them up unto vile passions' (verse 26); 'God gave them up unto a reprobate mind' (verse 28). It is true that sin has its consequences; but for St. Paul this does not take place apart from God, for His activity is to be discerned in those consequences. Indeed the whole of this section might be regarded as an expansion of the opening words, 'For wrath of God is being continually revealed from heaven upon all impiety and unrighteousness of men'. And, as H. Wheeler Robinson says: 'This wrath of God is not the blind and automatic working of abstract law—always a fiction, since "law" is a conception, not an entity, till it finds expression through its instruments. The wrath of God is the wrath of divine Personality'.[2]

II. THE ἱλάσκομαι WORD GROUP IN THE NEW TESTAMENT

We turn now to the actual terminology of the word group which has generally been understood to convey the thought of propitiation. There are four passages to be discussed, the remainder being

[1] Op. cit., p. 242. He also says: 'The love of God is not more real than the wrath of God' (Ibid). Cf. Emil Brunner: 'His Holy Will is unconditionally active: if it is not effective for blessing or salvation, then, in consequence of the human break in the divine order, it works in the opposite direction, and produces disaster. But this will is personal. God is present in this anger, it is actually His anger' (The Mediator, London, 1942, p. 518). So Althaus: 'So long as God is God He cannot deny in Himself His holiness and His wrath' (Mysterium Christi, London, 1930, p. 198); or again: 'Sin has not only determined the attitude of men but also the relation between God and men. Man's attitude is only a part of the relationship; the whole relationship is determined by the wrath of God' (Op. cit., p. 200).

[2] Redemption and Revelation, London, 1942, p. 269.

concerned with matters other than the interpretation of the work of Christ. Logically, perhaps, we should first examine the occurrence of the verb ἱλάσκομαι; but in view of the importance and difficulty of the passage in which ἱλαστήριον occurs we shall begin with this word.

a. ἱλαστήριον[1]

This word occurs only in Rom. iii. 25 in what is perhaps the most critical section in the most important of the Epistles, so that its context may fairly demand for it the most careful and critical examination, and there have not been wanting a host of commentators to explain it. However, there cannot be said to be any considerable measure of agreement, although many commentators support one or other of two opinions, the first which sees in ἱλαστήριον essentially a word with propitiatory significance, and the second which regards the term as conveying only the thought of expiation. The situation is made difficult in that there is nothing in the verse in which the term occurs to make it clear which meaning is to be preferred, the qualifying 'through faith' and 'in His blood' being capable of application to either interpretation.

But we may find help if we look to the wider context. We have already noted that Rom. iii. 25 is in a passage of critical importance, and that means that a survey of the argument should help us to see what sense is required. The first three chapters of Romans (after the opening remarks) form a closely-knit piece of reasoning in which the apostle unfolds his conception of the way in which a man comes to be accepted with God. In i. 15 he mentions preaching the gospel, and this leads him to consider the essential constitution of the gospel, which he sees in the thought of 'a righteousness of God' being at work, and of the just living by faith (Rom. i. 16, 17).

It is not always realized that this first mention of justification by faith leads on immediately in logical sequence to the thought of God's wrath. 'For (γάρ) wrath of God is being continually revealed from heaven upon all impiety and unrighteousness of men, etc.' (Rom. i. 18). Agar Beet is not overemphasizing the importance of this point when he says: 'The entire weight of

[1] Since the first edition of this work I have examined this term more fully in *New Testament Studies*, II, pp. 33–43.

verses 16, 17, which contain a summary of the Epistle, rests upon
the assumption that all men are, apart from the Gospel, under the
anger of God.'[1] Salvation for Paul is essentially a salvation *from*
as well as a salvation unto.

Having introduced the thought of the divine wrath, the apostle
proceeds to enlarge upon the theme by showing more fully that
this wrath is to be discerned in its outworkings consequent upon
man's sin. The thought of God's wrath is never out of sight
throughout the remainder of this section of the Epistle as Paul
builds up his case that Gentiles and Jews are alike sinners and
alike come under the wrath and judgment of God, which in this
situation he regards as being much the same thing, as we see from
ii. 5 and iii. 5, 6, where judgment and wrath are inseparable.

In the remainder of chapter i Paul shows how the wrath of God
rests upon the pagan world. And just as the present aspect of this
wrath comes out in this chapter, so the future aspect[2] of wrath is
developed in chapter ii with its 'thou condemnest thyself' (verse 1);
'We know that the judgment of God is in accordance with truth
upon them that practise such things' (verse 2); 'And dost thou
reckon . . . that thou wilt flee away from the judgment of God?'
(verse 3); 'Thou storest up for thyself wrath in a day of wrath and
revelation of God's righteous judgment' (verse 5); 'To them that
are factious . . . wrath and anger, affliction and anguish' (verses
8f.); 'For them that without law have sinned, without law also
shall perish: and them that in law have sinned, through law shall
be judged' (verse 12); 'God will judge the secrets of men' (verse
16). Such words as these leave no doubt as to the apostle's burning
conviction that the wrath of God is a terrible reality, and that the
evil-doer has a frightful prospect before him. The remainder of
the chapter shows the Jew to be guilty before God, just as the

---

[1] *Romans*, pp. 50f. Cf. Godet: 'The transition from verse 17 to verse 18,
indicated by *for*, can only be this: There is a *revelation of righteousness* by the
gospel because there is a revelation of *wrath* on the whole world' (*Romans*, I, p.
164).

[2] 'But the future wrath is certain. A religious man like Paul never doubts
this. On the contrary, he is convinced that this delay is a storing up of wrath
for the great last day of wrath, and those who do not receive punishment for sin
now will certainly receive it in full measure then. The contentious, disobedient
and unrighteous will receive full retribution from the wrath and anger of God'
(F. V. Filson, *op. cit.*, p. 48).

Gentile is, and chapter iii carries on to show that this does not conflict with the fact that the Jews are the chosen people. Then he is able to sum up his argument so far in the words 'we have already accused both Jews and Greeks of being all under sin' (iii. 9). He emphasizes this with a catena of quotations from the Old Testament, and reinforces it with a statement that the purpose of the law was 'that every mouth might be sealed, and all the world be brought to trial before God' (iii. 19).

It is in this context that the critical passage iii. 21-26 must be studied. The whole force of the preceding portion of the Epistle has been to demonstrate that all men, Jews and Gentiles alike, lie under the condemnation and the wrath of God. The two conceptions we have seen to be intertwined, and neither can be separated out from the argument. But now, Paul says, a new factor enters the situation. The whole effect of the law had been to show that men are blameworthy before God, that they are sinners (Rom. iii. 20). But now, quite apart from the law, there is a righteousness of God revealed, a righteousness leading to the sinner's justification through the work of Christ 'whom God set forth ἱλαστήριον'. There has been, and still is, vigorous debate as to just exactly what we should understand by this Greek term; but if we begin with the context, we can say that a meaning including an element of propitiation would be natural. Indeed it is demanded, for Paul has brought heavy artillery to bear in demonstrating that God's wrath and judgment are against the sinner.[1] And while other expressions in verses 21-26 may be held to deal with the judgment aspect, there is nothing other than this word to express the turning away of the wrath. Wrath has occupied such an important place in the argument leading up to this section that we are justified in looking for some expression indicative of its cancellation in the process which brings about salvation. More than expiation is required, for to speak of expiation is to deal in sub-personal categories, as Horace Bushnell long ago pointed

[1] Cf. R. W. Dale: 'St. Paul's intention was to demonstrate that the whole world was exposed to the Divine wrath, and that if men are to be saved, that wrath must be somehow averted. That this was his intention, becomes clearer the more rigorous the examination to which the whole argument is subjected' (The Atonement, London, 1902, p. 232).

out,[1] whereas the relationship between God and man must be thought of as personal in the fullest sense.

We pass now from considerations of context, to examine the only occurrence of the word in the LXX in a passage not denoting a cultic object. This is 4 Maccabees xvii. 22 where the death of the seven brothers is referred to thus: '. . . they having as it were become a ransom (ἀντίψυχον) for the nation's sin; and through the blood of these righteous men and their propitiatory death (or the propitiation of their death) the divine Providence delivered Israel that before was evil entreated.' Whether we regard the word ἱλαστήριον as a noun or an adjective, in either case the thought of the passage demands that it be given a propitiatory meaning. The wrath of God rested upon the people (elsewhere this is explicitly stated with regard to this very incident; see 2 Macc. vii. 32–38), and the death of the brothers is viewed as a propitiatory offering which would avail to turn away this wrath. The undoubtedly propitiatory significance of the word in 4 Maccabbees strongly supports a similar significance in Rom. iii. 25, especially as in both cases it is conjoined with an expression referring to the blood shed in a vicarious death.[2]

So much seems clear. What is not so clear is whether we should understand ἱλαστήριον in Rom. iii. 25 as a noun or an adjective, and if a noun whether we should take it as signifying 'propitiation' or 'the mercy-seat', a strong argument in favour of this latter interpretation being that the LXX uses the word in this sense. The article meant is the gold slab or plate with the cherubim at either end which was set on top of the ark of the covenant in the holy of

---

[1] '. . . we propitiate only a person, and expiate only a fact, or act, or thing' (*Forgiveness and Law*, London, 1874. p. 83).

[2] Cf. Büchsel: 'In 4 Macc. xvii also it is God who provides the means of atonement and thus saves; only through substitutionary suffering, through personal self-offering is the community atoned' (TWNT, III, p. 323). He draws attention also to i. 11, vi. 28f., and he renders the important part of the latter: 'Make my blood a means of atonement for them and take my soul substitutionarily for their souls' (*Ibid.*, n. 23).

4 Maccabees is generally regarded as more Greek than Hebrew in its outlook, but its community of thought in respect of this incident with the earlier books of Maccabees makes the expression cited important. Rashdall regards it as 'highly probable' that this passage was the source of St. Paul's 'thought and expression' (*The Idea of Atonement in Christian Theology*, London, 1925, p. 132).

holies. It was regarded as in especial measure the place of God's presence, and on the day of atonement it was the place where the blood was sprinkled. The appeal to the use of the LXX is a strong one. It has been reinforced by an examination of the use of ἱλαστήριον made by Dr. T. W. Manson, in which he finds the word used often of places, and concludes that the most probable meaning of the word in Rom. iii. 25 is 'the place where God shows mercy to men.'[1] Another who accepts the idea of place is Karl Barth, who seems, moreover, to accept the idea of propitiation and not to reduce the thought to one of expiation, for he says: '. . . it is pre-eminently, however, the place where, on the great day of atonement, the people were reconciled to God by the sprinkling of blood . . . By the express counsel of God, Jesus has been appointed from eternity as the place of propitiation above which God dwells and from which He speaks.'[2] This is an attractive interpretation and one to which the mind returns, although it should be noted that there are some objections.

Thus it has been urged that it is harsh to make Christ at one time priest, victim and place of sprinkling, even though it is noted that there is warrant for regarding Him as priest and victim. Again the Christian place of sprinkling seems rather to be the cross than the Christ. Some find force in the fact that the sprinkling was done in the tabernacle in a place hidden from the people's gaze whereas in Rom. iii. 25 the verb προτίθημι is used. Against this, however, it may be argued, in the first place, that there could well be a contrast intended between the secret sprinkling under the old covenant, and the public setting forth of Christ under the new, and in the second, that it is not absolutely certain that the verb does connote a public setting forth. In the only two other places where it occurs in the New Testament, namely Rom. i. 13 and Eph. i. 9, it certainly means 'to set before the mind, to purpose', and this may well be the sense in the passage under discussion.

A more cogent objection is that the Epistle to the Romans

---

[1] JTS, XLVI, p. 4.

[2] *Romans*, p. 105. A little later he says: 'The propitiation occurs at the place of propitiation—only by blood, whereby we are solemnly reminded that God gives life only through death' (*Ibid.*).

does not move in the sphere of Levitical symbolism, and that, accordingly, it is unlikely that a reference should be suddenly introduced to a single article of the tabernacle furnishings without a word of explanation.[1] Moreover, to the present writer at least, it seems that the context requires rather a general reference to propitiation than an allusion to a specific cultic place or object.

Deissmann has written about this subject in more than one place, and in *Enc. Bib.* he retracts from the position he took up in *Biblestudien*, and, according to Manson,[2] he maintains the same position in ZNW as in *Enc. Bib.* In the latter article he shows that ἱλαστήριον is used to denote a great variety of objects including votive offerings to heathen deities, the golden plate above the ark, the ledge of the altar, the place of the altar, the altar itself, Noah's ark, a monastery and a church. This is a wide range of usage, and Deissmann concludes from it that '(α) ἱλαστήριον, wherever it occurs, always and invariably means "that which propitiates", "the means of propitiation", "the propitiating thing". (β) Any object whatever, as long as a propitiatory significance is attached to it, can be designated as a ἱλαστήριον'.[3] It is difficult to see how this conclusion can be resisted. Manson does so at the expense of passing over the references to the votive offerings which Deissmann says 'are most frequently of all so designated', and this does not seem warranted.

In view of the wide range of the usage, and the absence of any factor in the context of Rom. iii. 25 which indicates a specific limiting of the term, it seems best to understand it as signifying 'means of propitiation', the means being indicated by the following 'in his blood'.[4]

---

[1] Cf. Deissmann: 'The out-of-the-way passages referring to the ἱλαστήριον may very well have remained unknown even to a Christian who was conversant with the LXX: how many Bible readers of today, nay, how many theologians of today—who, at least, should be Bible readers—if their readings have been unforced . . . are acquainted with the *kapporeth*?' (*Bible Studies*, Edinburgh, 1901, p. 132).

[2] *Op. cit.*, p. 1.

[3] *Enc. Bib.*, col. 3033.

[4] J. Scott Lidgett says: 'Whether the word be translated by "a propitiatory sacrifice", or "a means of propitiation", its general significance, taken by itself,

[continued on p. 173]

It remains to be noticed that there is a substitutionary thought in the passage. We have already drawn attention to the similarity between this passage and 4 Macc. xvii. 22, and in this latter passage the offering is definitely said to be ἀντίψυχον, a term which cannot be emptied of the thought of substitution. This does not prove that substitution is involved in the passage in Romans, but it does show that substitution represents a natural way of understanding that passage.

Substitution, too, is implied in the context. As we have seen, our verse comes as the climax of an argument in which Paul had developed the thesis that all men are under the wrath of God with all that that means, but that now a new way appears. By the blood of Christ a propitiation is effected so that those who are of faith no longer need fear the wrath. Thus we see that, whereas originally sinners were liable to suffer from the outpouring of the wrath of God, Christ has suffered instead of them, and now they may go free. But to say this is to say substitution.

This does not conflict with the fact that a main thought of this passage is of the righteousness of God being revealed in the means whereby men are justified. It is true that there is a certain stress on this revelation (cf. verses 21, 25, 26); but mere revelation as such has no power to free men from sin. What has the power to do this is the particular action which is revealed, a propitiatory action whereby the wrath of God is averted and men are brought into a new relationship with God, and this action is essentially

---

seems clear. It is that by which those who are out of favour may be restored to favour . . . in consequence of the changed condition of mind it brings about, not in those who present it, but in him to whom it is presented' (*The Spiritual Principle of the Atonement*, London, 1898, pp. 50f.); he says, also, that in Rom. iii. 25, 'The word propitiation is used, and with its essential meaning unaltered' (p. 53). He is careful, of course, to show that it does not contain unworthy ideas. Platt says: 'Its interpretation as "a propitiatory offering"—a means of rendering God consistently favourable towards sinful men and the means of reconciliation between God and man—is the most natural, and is indeed the only meaning suitable to the context of Rom. iii; other Pauline passages harmonize with it better than with any other meaning' (HDAC, II, p. 283). Similarly Deissmann: 'The crucified Christ is the votive-gift of the Divine love for the salvation of men' (*Op. cit.*, p. 133), and Vincent Taylor also refers to 'the votive-gift of Christ, in virtue of which He is the "means of atonement"' (ET, L, p. 300).

substitutionary. As Büchsel puts it: 'But revelation and substitution form here no contradiction, but the revelation among men only takes place when simultaneously a substitution for men finds place . . . a revelation without substitution would not surpass the law in legal efficacy, and thus would not bring men effectual ἀπολύτρωσις.'[1] Or again, he says in a note that that which is only a declaration 'would bring no more than a condemnation of sin, not an overcoming of sin, which comes about through this that He who reveals God, dying for the sinner, stands in his place'.[2]

b. ἱλάσκομαι

Since the verb is used but twice in the whole New Testament, and one of these occurrences, Lk. xviii. 13, does not refer to the work of Christ for men, this section requires only an examination of Heb. ii. 17 where the true humanity of Christ is said to be necessary so that He might become a merciful and faithful high priest in the things of God εἰς τὸ ἱλάσκεσθαι τὰς ἁμαρτίας τοῦ λαοῦ. This verse presents us with some difficulties and we will examine them in order.

First of all we notice that, whereas we have seen in many of the Old Testament passages in which this and cognate words are used a reference implicit or explicit to the wrath of God, there does not seem to be such a reference here. This, however, is not conclusive, if only for the reason that there is nothing in the context to compel us to give up the idea of wrath. Accordingly, in the last resort, we must be guided by the plain meaning of the term in contexts where the wrath is unmistakable. But there are some indications that wrath may be in mind here. One of them is the fact that Christ is said to be a 'merciful' high priest in His atoning action. This word indicates that sinners were in no good case, and that they could look only for a severe punishment as a recompense for their evil deeds, a thought which reminds us of what is called 'the wrath of God' in other passages. Another is that Christ is said to be a high priest 'in things pertaining to God', thus directing our minds to the Godward rather than the manward

---

[1] TWNT, III, p. 323.

[2] *Op. cit.*, p. 323, n. 24.

aspect of atonement.[1] A Godward aspect expressed by ἱλάσκομαι is likely to include propitiation, to put it mildly.

Then the accusative after the verb attracts our attention, for despite much that is written these days it is a very unusual construction. We have already examined the one example in profane Greek[2] and have seen that it may well be held to involve the idea of propitiation. Much is made by some scholars of the fact that it is to be found in the Greek Old Testament, but here again there is only one accusative of sin after ἱλάσκομαι, while after ἐξιλάσκομαι there are no accusatives of sin in the canonical Scriptures, though one occurs in the Theodotianic text of Dn. ix. 24 and there are six examples in Sirach. In one or possibly two places the verb is in the passive with sin as its subject. This cannot be said to be a very impressive list when we remember that the two verbs occur 116 times between them, and that there are four or five places where the construction is accusative of person with the plain meaning 'appease, propitiate'.

The six examples of the accusative of sin in Sirach are of interest, more especially in view of the fact that it is sometimes said that with this construction these verbs have the meaning 'expiate'. But when we examine these passages we find statements like: 'And say not, His compassion is great; he will be pacified for the multitude of my sins: for mercy and wrath are with him, and his indignation will rest upon sinners' (Sir. v. 6), wherein the meaning obviously is that the man who complacently trusts that God's mercy will be his salvation will find that God's wrath is extended towards him. Even though there is an accusative of sin the context shows that the verb includes an element of propitiation, and it is the belief of the present writer that the same is true in probably five out of the six examples.[3] Since it is at least arguable that the examples in Ps. lxiv (lxv). 4 and Dn. ix. 24 (Th.) are also best understood if the thought of propitiation is

---

[1] Cf. Milligan: 'It was in the performance of that which was necessary towards God, and not in priestly privileges towards man, that the essence of Christ's Priesthood lay' (*The Theology of the Epistle to the Hebrews*, p. 103, n. 3).

[2] See p. 128.

[3] Cf. also Sir. xvi. 11 where the comment of Delitzsch seems to give the sense 'The atonement, ἐξιλασμός, is the removal of the ὀργή' (*Hebrews*, II, p. 456).

included, it would seem that there is not much ground for thinking that this construction does away with the thought of averting
wrath. Rather the contrary would seem to be true, that the
accusative of sin after ἱλάσκομαι or ἐξιλάσκομαι, in the few places
where it occurs, seems generally to imply the thought of
propitiation.

It should further be borne in mind that in the New Testament
period the accusative often replaces a prepositional construction
with little if any change of meaning. Thus ἀπορέω 'to be per-
plexed' is followed by περί in Lk. xxiv. 4 and Jn. xiii. 22; but in
Acts xxv. 20 we have the accusative, although the meaning
appears to be much the same. Similarly εὐδοκέω is usually
followed by ἐν as in Mt. iii. 17; 1 Cor. x. 5, etc., but the direct
object is found in Mt. xii. 18.[1] Compare also πενθέω ἐπί (Rev.
xviii. 11), accusative (2 Cor. xii. 21); κλαίω ἐπί (Lk. xix. 41,
xxiii. 28), accusative (Mt. ii. 18); θαυμάζω ἐπί (Lk. ii. 33), or
περί (Lk. ii. 18), accusative (Lk. vii. 9, xxiv. 12); ὑπομιμνήσκω
περί (2 Pet. i. 12), accusative (Jn. xiv. 26); διαμαρτύρομαι ἐνώπιον
(2 Tim. iv. 1), accusative (2 Tim. iv. 1).[2] The point of such
examples as these is not that they form exact parallels to
ἱλάσκομαι, for this might well be disputed at least in some of the
cases, but that they demonstrate that among the New Testament
writers there was great freedom in the use of constructions, and
that in particular the accusative was often used in places where we
would hardly have anticipated it, and where satisfactory prepositional constructions were available and in use. Under these
circumstances it does not seem wise to lay great stress upon the
occurrence of the accusative in Heb. ii. 17. In the case of none of
the verbs above can it be said that its meaning has been seriously
modified by using the accusative instead of the prepositional
construction, and accordingly it may fairly be asked, Why should
we believe that it is otherwise with ἱλάσκομαι?

Thus it seems best to take the accusative in Heb. ii. 17 as an
accusative of general respect and to understand the meaning of the
expression as 'to make propitiation with regard to the sins of the

---

[1] The accusative is read by ℵ* ,B, 115, 244, 892, etc., though εἰς ὅν is also
found.

[2] Cf. Blass-Debrunner, *Grammatik*, Göttingen, 1931, pp. 89f.

people'. This seems a better course than ignoring the usual meaning of the verb and making it signify here nothing more than 'expiate'. To take this line is to give the verb its sense from its object, a procedure to which John Owen raised his objection long ago.[1] Though I would not be prepared to endorse every detail of his treatment of this passage, his observation on the verb under discussion is surely valid: 'in the use of this word, then, there is always understood—(1st) An *offence*, crime, guilt, or debt, to be taken away; (2dly.) A *person offended*, to be pacified, atoned, reconciled; (3dly.) A *person offending*, to be pardoned, accepted; (4thly.) A *sacrifice* or other means of making the atonement. Sometimes one is expressed, sometimes another, but the use of the word hath respect unto them all.' It is a valuable point that the verb often implies more than is explicitly expressed.

A further point is that there are some manuscripts which read ταῖς ἁμαρτίαις instead of τὰς ἁμαρτίας in this verse; Moffatt cites 'A 5. 33. 623. 913, Athan. Chrys. Bentley, etc.' This is a surprisingly impressive list, although we need not take the reading very seriously if we are endeavouring to arrive at the true text. There seems no doubt that some scribe or scribes altered the accusative to the dative, a case which occurs much more often in this connection. But the fact that this variant has arisen shows that the accusative was felt to be a difficult construction after ἱλάσκομαι. This seems to indicate that the alleged meaning of 'expiate' was not one which was accepted in the circles in which this variant arose.

Thus there seems to be no really good reason for denying to ἱλάσκομαι in this verse its usual significance. The objections usually alleged are seen on examination to be of little weight, whereas there are not wanting some indications that the word is used in its normal sense. As we saw in our section on the Old Testament usage, the normal use of the verb with regard to the sacrifices is one which includes an element of propitiation, and this element seems clearly to be implied in this verse also in the priestly activity of Christ.

c. ἱλασμός

This word occurs twice, both times in the First Epistle of St. John,

---

[1] *An Exposition of the Epistle to the Hebrews*, III, pp. 474ff.

and on both occasions it occurs in an expression referring to Christ as 'the propitiation for our sins'. The first passage assures us that 'if any man sin, we have an Advocate with the Father, Jesus Christ the righteous: and he is the propitiation for our sins' (1 Jn. ii. 2), while the second is concerned with the love of God, 'Herein is love, not that we loved God, but that he loved us, and sent his Son to be the propitiation for our sins' (1 Jn. iv. 10). Here again objections have been raised to the traditional rendering, as by Dodd who says: 'The common rendering "propitiation" is illegitimate here as elsewhere'.[1]

The reasons alleged are those we have already noticed, namely that ἱλάσκομαι, etc., are thought to have evolved in the LXX a meaning strange to non-biblical Greek, and no new consideration is brought forward in connection with the Johannine passages. Indeed it is noticeable that there is a certain caution in Dodd's approach for he says: 'Here we have less confidence in appealing to LXX usage than in the case of Paul and Hebrews, for the Johannine Epistles are probably less influenced by the LXX than any other New Testament writings'.[2] However, he notes that hatta'th is variously rendered ἱλασμός and τὸ περὶ ἁμαρτίας and he thinks that 'the Johannine expression looks like a combination of these alternative translations'.[3] On these grounds he groups the Johannine usage with those previously considered and thinks the term means simply a cancelling of guilt and purification of the sinner. But Dodd has shown only that the Johannine passages link up with the LXX, and if our conclusion that in the LXX this word group conveys the thought of propitiation is sound, then a similar meaning will be required here.

In support of this there are one or two considerations which may be noted. The first of these is the context; and in connection with the first of these sayings even Dodd can say, '. . . in the immediate context it might seem possible that the sense of "propitiation" is in place'.[4] The point is that Christ is said to be 'an Advocate with the Father', and if we sinners need an advocate

---

[1] *The Bible and the Greeks*, London, 1935, p. 95.
[2] *Op. cit.*, p. 94.
[3] *Op. cit.*, p. 95.
[4] *The Johannine Epistles* (MNTC), p. 26.

with God, then obviously we are in no good case, our misdeeds prevail against us, we are about to feel the hostility of God to all that is sinful. Under these circumstances we may well speak of Christ turning away the wrath of God, and thus ἱλασμός is a natural word in the context.

Another feature of the passage is that, in addition to the word of the ἱλάσκομαι group, we have a reference to Christ as 'the righteous', and a few verses earlier there is a mention of His blood (1 Jn. i. 7). In these things we may discern a striking coincidence with Rom. iii. 25, where the propitiation occurs in a passage which several times refers to God's righteousness, and which says the propitiation is in Christ's blood. As our examination of the Romans passage demonstrated, as we believe, that the thought of propitiation is to be discerned there, the coincidences of language suggest that this idea is to be found also in 1 John.

Concerning the use of the term in 1 Jn. iv. 10 we would simply observe that, if ἱλασμός be given its usual meaning, we have here one of those resounding paradoxes which mean so much for the understanding of the Christian view of sacrifice, for then we would have the thought that it is to God Himself that we owe the removal of God's wrath (cf. Col. i. 21f. for a similar statement with regard to the removal of enmity), whereas, if the more colourless meaning 'expiation' is understood, the verse is much less striking.

A further point is that the nature of the allusion is such as to stress the fact that Christ is the offering which turns away the wrath, rather than to draw attention to any activity in thus averting the wrath. This is well put by Westcott when he says: 'Christ is said to be the "propitiation" and not simply the "propitiator" (as He is called the "Saviour" iv. 14), in order to emphasize the thought that He is Himself the propitiatory offering as well as the priest (cf. Rom. iii. 25). A propitiator might make use of means of propitiation, outside himself. But Christ is our propitiation'.[1]

In all this there is nothing to make us alter our previous conclusions with regard to the meaning of this word group. There is

[1] *The Epistles of St. John*, p. 44.

no crude process of celestial bribery thought of, but in speaking of our acceptance with God a word is chosen which reminds us of the very real wrath of God[1] manifested against all unrighteousness, a wrath which we need no longer fear, for Christ is 'the propitiation for our sins'.

A not unimportant consideration is that the ἱλάσκομαι words were not understood by the early Christians as signifying expiation. Both 1 Clement and Hermas, for example, use the verb ἐξιλάσκομαι with the accusative of the Deity in the sense 'propitiate',[2] so that if the LXX translators and the New Testament writers evolved a new sense for the word group it perished with them. But in view of the universal usage among pagan writers, early and late, in Philo and Josephus, in such Christian writers as those mentioned, it is much better to understand the New Testament writers in the normal fashion as referring to propitiation and not expiation.

III. CONCLUSION

What are we to say of all this? Some theologians unhesitatingly reject the whole idea of the wrath of God and of propitiation as being unworthy of the Christian view of God. Thus Berdyaev can say: 'The wrath of God described in the Bible is only an exoteric expression of the Divine Countenance as it appeared to the Hebrew mind'. Or again: 'Anger in every shape and form is foreign to God, Whose mercy is infinite'.[3] Such citations could be multiplied almost indefinitely, for there are many modern writers to whom the concept of the wrath of God is anathema.

One must have a certain sympathy with such positions, for nothing can be more certain than that the Christian view of God is that He is love, and nothing can be held for one moment which interferes with the clear perception of this basic truth. Without it Christianity becomes meaningless. Nevertheless the fact must be

---

[1] Cf. Brunner: 'This revelation of the divine mystery of love in the midst of the reality of wrath is the "propitiation" (ἱλασμός)' (*The Mediator*, London, 1944, p. 520).

[2] 1 Cl. vii. 7, Herm. v. 1, 2, 1. The passages are quoted in TWNT, III, p. 315, n. 67.

[3] *Freedom and the Spirit*, London, 1944, p. 92.

faced that the Bible in both Old and New Testaments speaks often
of God's wrath.

Perhaps the difficulty arises because we are making a false
antithesis between the divine wrath and the divine love. We are
handicapped by the fact that we must necessarily use terms
properly applicable to human affairs, and for us it is very difficult
to be simultaneously wrathful and loving. But, upon analysis,
this seems to be largely because our anger is such a selfish passion,
usually involving a large element of irrationality together with a
lack of self-control. Nevertheless, even in human affairs, such a
thing as 'righteous anger' is not unknown when some, at least, of
the more unworthy elements are purged, and we catch a glimpse
of a fiery zeal for the right which may be perfectly compatible
with pure love.

Those who object to the conception of the wrath of God should
realize that what is meant is not some irrational passion bursting
forth uncontrollably, but a burning zeal for the right coupled
with a perfect hatred for everything that is evil. It may be that
wrath is not a perfect word to describe such an attitude, but no
better one has been suggested, and we must refuse to accept
alternatives which do not give expression to the truth in question.
Perhaps there is a certain anthropomorphism involved in the use
of the term wrath, but it must not be forgotten that 'A false
anthropomorphism is to be laid to the charge not of those who
maintain that there is, in the biblical sense of the word, such a thing
as the wrath of God. It is rather to be laid to the charge of those
who encourage the idea that God is like an easy, good-natured,
benevolent man.'[1] We sometimes find among men a love which is
untempered by a sterner side, and this we call not love but

---

[1] L. Pullan, *The Atonement*, London, 1907, p. 194. Cf. Emil Brunner: 'If we
understand it properly it has nothing whatever to do with primitiveness, with
naïve anthropomorphism. On the contrary, it is the necessary expression of
God, taking himself and us seriously. He takes us so seriously that our changed
attitude with regard to him produces a change in his attitude towards us. . . .
The term "God's wrath" therefore means that the breach of communion,
which has been made from our side, means also a breach for God. It means that
our guilt is guilt in his sight too, that our separation from him is a reality for him
too, that his holy will, encountering resistance, becomes in itself resistance:
"God resisteth the haughty." God's law must not be broken; if we do break it,
it will break us' (*The Scandal of Christianity*, pp. 77f.).

sentimentality. It is not such that the Bible thinks of when it speaks of the love of God, but rather of a love which is so jealous for the good of the loved one that it blazes out in fiery wrath against everything that is evil. D. M. Baillie gives expression to this when he speaks of God's wrath as being 'identical with the consuming fire of inexorable divine love in relation to our sins'.[1]

Now if there is such a divine hostility to evil it is obvious that something must be done about it if man, sinner as he is, is ever to be accepted before God. Sometimes the Scripture directs attention to the cause of the hostility and speaks of sin being remitted or purged, but sometimes also it points us to the hostility itself, and speaks of its removal in the terms we have been discussing in this chapter. Thus we have the concept of propitiation brought in to help us understand how this comes about and the evidence that the Scripture means what it says when it uses this term is so strong that, as we saw earlier, S. R. Driver can speak of propitiation as one of the three main categories used in the New Testament to interpret the death of Christ.[2] From a slightly different point of view Denney says: 'If the propitiatory death of Jesus is eliminated from the love of God, it might be unfair to say that the love of God is robbed of all meaning, but it is certainly robbed of its apostolic meaning'.[3] The writers of the New Testament know nothing of a love which does not react in the very strongest of terms against every form of sin.

---

[1] *God Was In Christ*, London, 1948, p. 189. Similarly T. H. Hughes speaks of 'the urge or chafing of love' (*The Atonement*, London, 1949, p. xxv), and Dr. Maldwyn Hughes refers to the divine anger as 'nothing else than unquenched and quenchless holy love'(*What is the Atonement?* London, n.d., p. 56).

[2] See p. 125.

[3] *The Death of Christ*, London, 1950, p. 152; and similarly Heinrich Vogel says: 'whoever thinks he can smile at God's wrath will never praise him eternally for his grace' (*The Iron Ration of a Christian*, London, 1941, p. 102). P. T. Forsyth often gives expression to such a thought, as when he says of the love of God: 'It has been detached from the idea of propitiation with which the Apostles identify it (1 Jn. iv. 10), and regarded as an infinite dilation of human affection (where the real revelation is held to be). Judgment is viewed but as a device of the Father instead of a constituent of His Fatherhood as holy. Little wonder then that love has gone thin in the expansion and lost power. It has ceased in the process to be understood as Holy Love' (*The Justification of God*, London, 1948, pp. 85f.).

It is the combination of the deep love for the sinner and the reaction against sin which brings about the situation in which the Bible refers to propitiation. Since God would not leave man to suffer all the consequences of his sin, Christ suffered, and as J. C. Lambert puts it, 'While springing from the Divine love, the death of Christ is represented in the Epistles not less clearly as *a propitiation for sin* . . . any interpretation of the mass of NT evidence seems difficult and forced which does not recognize that, in the view of these writers, Christ's death was really our death in a vicarious and propitiatory sense'.[1] This statement stresses once more the fact that propitiation is thought of as springing from the love of God. Among the heathen, propitiation was thought of as an activity whereby the worshipper was able himself to provide that which would induce a change of mind in the deity. In plain language he bribed his god to be favourable to him. When the term was taken over into the Bible these unworthy and crude ideas were abandoned, and only the central truth expressed by the term was retained, namely that propitiation signifies the averting of wrath by the offering of a gift. But in both Old Testament and New the thought is plain that the gift which secures the propitiation is from God Himself,[2] He provides the way whereby men may come to Him. Thus the use of the concept of propitiation witnesses to two great realities, the one, the reality and the seriousness of the divine reaction against sin, and the other, the reality and the greatness of the divine love which provided the gift which should avert the wrath from men.

Those who seek to reduce the concept of propitiation to a mere expiation do not, in general, face the questions which expiation raises, such as 'Why should sin be expiated?' 'What would be the consequences to man if there were no expiation?' 'Would the hand of God be in those consequences?' It seems evident on the Scriptural view that if sin is not expiated, if men 'die in their sins', then they have the divine displeasure to face, and this is but another way of saying that the wrath of God abides upon them.

[1] HDCG, I, p. 433.

[2] See, for example, Lv. xvii. 11; Rom. iii. 25. For the implication cf. J. G. Simpson: 'All that we can now say is that, when it is the Eternal Son who offers Himself without spot to the Eternal Father, the ethical objection to a propitiatory sacrifice vanishes' (*What is the Gospel?* London, 1914, p. 192).

It seems that expiation is necessary in order to avert the wrath of God, so that nothing seems to be gained by abandoning the concept of propitiation.

Then there is the question of the meaning to be given to expiation. As commonly used the term seems to signify the removal of sin or guilt, but neither of these is a *thing* which can be objectively removed. Expiation can be given an intelligible meaning only when we move into the realm of personal relations. Sin has altered the relations between God and man, and expiation cannot be understood apart from the effects of the expiatory act on these relations. Unless we are prepared to say that in expiation all that happens is a subjective change in man, it would seem that we are committed to the view that expiation has a Godward aspect so that God now treats the sinner differently from before. Instead of God's severity the sinner experiences God's grace, which is only another way of saying that propitiation has taken place. If we give expiation a fully personal meaning it seems then that we are brought back to propitiation; if we do not it is difficult to see how we are to understand the term. Certainly propitiation, when carefully safeguarded, is a more intelligible concept than an impersonal expiation.

If we are to retain the Christian conception of God with its insistence on the divine activity in the affairs of men, and the divine abhorrence of sin, it seems necessary to retain some such conception as propitiation. Certainly we must retain the idea of the wrath of God, for as Edwyn Bevan has pointed out, the idea that God cannot be angry is neither Hebrew nor Christian, but something borrowed from Greek philosophy.[1] But not only is the Hebrew and Christian idea of a God who can be wrathful different from the Greek philosophic view. It is a superior idea. Granted that it contains an element of anthropomorphic imagery, it yet

---

[1] 'Greek philosophy had long ago repudiated emphatically the conception common to primitive and popular Greek religion and to the Old Testament. Anger was a weak and discreditable emotion, it taught, in men, and to attribute such an emotion to a divine being was absurd and blasphemous. Deity, every novice in Greek philosophy knew as an axiom, must be *apathes*, without disturbing emotions of any kind. The idea of the divine anger was not something which penetrated into Christianity from its pagan environment: it was something which the Church maintained in the face of adverse pagan criticism' (*Symbolism and Belief*, London, 1938, p. 210).

points to a reality within the divine being which gives point and force to moral sanctions.[1]

Then, too, unless we give a real content to the wrath of God, unless we hold that men really deserve to have God visit upon them the painful consequences of their wrongdoing, we empty God's forgiveness of its meaning.[2] For if there is no ill desert, God ought to overlook sin. We can think of forgiveness as something real only when we hold that sin has betrayed us into a situation where we deserve to have God inflict upon us the most serious consequences, and that it is upon such a situation that God's grace supervenes. When the logic of the situation demands that He should take action against the sinner, and He yet takes action for him, then and then alone can we speak of grace. But there is no room for grace if there is no suggestion of dire consequences merited by sin.

One final point is that the process of propitiation envisaged in the Bible is one which involves an element of substitution. In both Old and New Testaments the means of propitiation is the offering up of a gift, the gift of a life yielded up to death by God's own appointment. The Scripture is clear that the wrath of God is visited upon sinners or else that the Son of God dies for them. Either sinners are punished for their misdoings or else there takes place what Hodgson calls 'that self-punishment which combines the activities of punishing and forgiving'.[3] Either we die or He dies. But 'God commendeth His own love toward us, in that, while we were yet sinners, Christ died for us' (Rom. v. 8).

---

[1] From a somewhat different angle Hodgson says: 'We cannot draw a breath or lift a finger except by our use of that share of His power which He has entrusted to us for our earthly life. How can we be sure, when we use it to sin with, that He continues holy, that He is still there in unsullied perfection, able, when we come to a better frame of mind and repent of our sin, to welcome us back to share in His life of goodness? . . . The wrath of God and divine punishment are essential elements in a doctrine which is to face the facts of evil and retain a fundamental optimism. The belief that God has sworn in His wrath that men who do certain things shall not enter into His rest enables the Church to open its worship each day with the words, "Come, let us sing unto the Lord, let us heartily rejoice in the strength of our salvation" ' (*The Doctrine of the Atonement*, London, 1951, p. 60).

[2] Cf. Bevan, *op. cit.*, p. 246.

[3] *Op. cit.*, p. 79.

CHAPTER VI

RECONCILIATION

I. INTRODUCTION

T. H. HUGHES lays it down 'that in the New Testament the basic idea of the Atonement is that of reconciliation',[1] an idea which must be based upon the general climate of New Testament thinking rather than upon specific references, for when we consult a concordance to find reconciliation passages we discover that they are few, though important. The conception is explicit in two notable Pauline passages, Rom. v. 10f. and 2 Cor. v. 18–20, in both of which we find the verb καταλλάσσω and the noun καταλλαγή. The verb is found nowhere else in the New Testament and the noun only in Rom. xi. 15 where the rejection of the Jews is 'the reconciliation of the world'. Reconciliation through the death of Christ is alluded to by the use of the verb ἀποκαταλλάσσω in Eph. ii. 16 and in Col. i. 20f. Other words from this word group occur in the New Testament, but they are not applied to the atonement.

However, it is clear that the concept of reconciliation is sometimes present when the actual word itself does not occur, for example when 'making peace' is spoken of, and this opens up for us the whole New Testament conception of peace with God. Other conceptions may also be held to be linked with that of reconciliation. For example, Vincent Taylor treats of freedom, sonship, fellowship with God and sanctification under the heading of reconciliation.[2] But it scarcely seems as though all these conceptions are to be considered as properly part of the idea of reconciliation, and we shall confine ourselves in this treatment to those passages which speak of reconciliation and of peace.

[1] *The Atonement*, London, 1949, p. 312. Similarly, Vincent Taylor: 'The best New Testament word to describe the purpose of the Atonement is *Reconciliation*' (*The Atonement in New Testament Teaching*, London, 1946, p. 191).

[2] In his work *Forgiveness and Reconciliation*, London, 1946, pp. 70f.

We examine first of all καταλλάσσω and its cognates. This word group derives ultimately from ἄλλος. Thus the basic significance of ἀλλάσσω would be either to change (make other) or to exchange (provide an other), a good example of the first meaning being found in Acts vi. 14, while in Rom. i. 23 we have the second use.[1] This basic meaning is modified and confirmed in the various compounds. For example, ἀντάλλαγμα is used of the price for which a thing is purchased, or more generally for an equivalent or substitute, a meaning we see in Mk. viii. 37, 'for what shall a man give ἀντάλλαγμα (in exchange for) his life?' So ἀπαλλάσσω signifies 'to make other through removal' (as in Acts xix. 12).[2]

The exact significance of the preposition in καταλλάσσω is not easy to determine (though cf. W. F. Howard quoted below), but the basic idea of changing remains. The word was in use for the process of money-changing where one set of coins was exchanged for an equivalent set. Other uses of a more metaphorical sort also arose, and the one which is of particular interest to us is that the word came to signify 'to make other a state of enmity', 'to exchange enmity for friendship'. The noun καταλλαγή has meaning corresponding to that of the verb, 'exchange', 'reconciliation', the latter being its New Testament significance.

For the rest διαλλάσσω is very similar in meaning to καταλλάσσω, but as it is not used in the New Testament of the atonement it hardly concerns us. ἀποκαταλλάσσω is not found before the New Testament where it occurs in Ephesians and Colossians,[3] Epistles in which καταλλάσσω is not found. The meaning is much the same as that of the last-mentioned verb, but probably with an intensification. Thus W. F. Howard says it means '*to effect a thorough change* (perfective κατά) *back, reconcile*'.[4]

---

[1] Cf. with this Ps. cv. 20 καὶ ἠλλάξαντο τὴν δόξαν αὐτῶν ἐν ὁμοιώματι μόσχου κ.τ.λ.

[2] Other uses of course, arise from this, a common one being 'to free' as in Heb. ii. 15.

[3] Büchsel thinks Paul may have coined the word (TWNT, I, p. 259).

[4] *Grammar*, II, p. 298.

II. THE καταλλάσσω WORD GROUP IN THE SEPTUAGINT

καταλλάσσω is found once in the canonical Scriptures of the Old Testament, namely Je. xxxi (xlviii). 39, where the MT reads 'ekh hattah but where the LXX appears to mean 'How is it changed!' The passage does not help us much.

The noun καταλλαγή occurs in Is. ix. 5 where it is doubtful whether the LXX can be derived from the MT for the former seems to mean 'For they will recompense for every robe obtained by deceit, and (every) garment with compensation (μετὰ καταλλαγῆς).' Although the passage is difficult it seems clear that καταλλαγή is used in its older sense of something given in exchange, an equivalent or substitute.

ἀποκαταλλάσσω does not occur in the LXX and the use of the other words in this word group does not appear to help us greatly, with one exception, namely the use of διαλλάσσω in 1 Sa. xxix. 4, where the Philistine lords say of David, 'wherewith will this man be reconciled to his master?' The point here is that David is spoken of as being reconciled, although the enmity to be removed is not his, but Saul's, and this has its importance for an understanding of passages wherein man is said to be reconciled to God.

III. RECONCILIATION IN JUDAISM

According to Strack-Billerbeck, 'In Rabbinic writings the two verbs ritstsah and piyyeṣ are especially used for καταλλάσσειν'.[1] Both these verbs speak of the removal of enmity, the first having the idea of causing to be pleasant, and the second of calming. Thus both imply a previous enmity, and sometimes there is an explicit reference to 'wrath', or similar evidence of ill-feeling in the context.

Reconciliation is sometimes between men, but often this is part of the process of reconciliation with God. Thus R. Jose used a parable: 'A man lent his neighbour a maneh and fixed a time for payment in the presence of the king. When the time arrived he did not pay him, and he went to excuse himself to the king. The king, however, said to him: The wrong done to me I excuse you, but go and obtain forgiveness

---

[1] Vol. III, p. 519.

from your neighbour'.[1] The application of the parable is not far
to seek, and it is typical of the teaching of the Rabbis that a
man must be reconciled with his fellow if he would expect to
be reconciled with his God. The responsibility of reconciliation is,
of course, with the person doing the wrong; but sometimes we
hear of the wronged one taking the initiative in an attempt to
heal the breach.[2]

God is thought of as angry with men because of sin, and reconciliation accordingly becomes necessary. A number of midrashes
speak of reconciliation after the episode of the Golden Calf. For
example, a saying of R. Isaac is recorded: 'Moses reconciled God
with Israel through the second Tables'. It goes on to put forward
the curious explanation that Moses pretended to be angry with
the people, causing God to say that they both could not be angry
with them, and thus He became reconciled to them.[3] In another
place we are told that, when he found that God's wrath was
towards the people because of the calf, 'Moses instantly rose and
sought mercy from Him, begging Him to be reconciled with
them'. But God only put away part of His wrath, and when the
tabernacle was built Moses is depicted as wondering whether this
would do away with the remainder of the wrath. '. . . is He
reconciled with them and will He display towards them the
Attribute of Mercy?' The answer is that He is reconciled. A little
later in the same section this is given in the words of R. Berekiah,
the priest, speaking in the name of R. Judah son of R. Simon:
'The Holy One, blessed be He, said to Moses: "Formerly there
was hostility between Me and My children, there was contention

---

[1] b R.H. 17b (Soncino trans., p. 70). So also Ber. 31b: 'R. Eleazar said: From
this we learn that one who suspects his neighbour of a fault which he has not
committed must beg his pardon; nay more, he must bless him' (Soncino trans.,
p. 192).

[2] Yoma 87a has much to say about the duty of being reconciled and praises
R. Zera for giving opportunities to any who had wronged him to effect
reconciliation: 'When R. Zera had any complaint against any man he would
repeatedly pass by him, showing himself to him, so that he may come forth to
pacify him' (Soncino trans., p. 435). The passage then goes on to speak of Abba
taking the initiative in seeking reconciliation with a man who had wronged
him.

[3] Dt. R. iii. 15 (Soncino trans. p. 84).

between Me and My children. Now, however, that this Tabernacle has been made there will be love between Me and My
children, there will be peace between Me and My children".
This explains the text, "*For He will speak peace unto His people*",
namely to Israel, because they have made the Tabernacle'.[1]

Such passages as the ones we have so far quoted would perhaps
leave the impression that the Rabbis dwelt on the wrath of God
in a very anthropomorphic fashion, and it is true that they sometimes did. But there are many passages reflecting a nobler view
of God. Thus we read a saying of R. Judah on the verse 'She
(i.e. Jerusalem) is become as a widow' that, '(The verse implies)
blessings "*as a widow*"; not a real widow, but a woman whose
husband has gone to a country beyond the sea (fully) intending to
return to her'.[2] Here we find the thought that the disciplines of
suffering imposed upon the nation are but temporary, and that
God will shortly cause them to cease. So also we read: 'Come and
see how different from the character of one of flesh and blood is
the action of the Holy One, blessed be He. As to the character of
one of flesh and blood, if one angers his fellow it is doubtful
whether he (the latter) will be pacified or not by him. And even
if you would say, he can be pacified, it is doubtful whether he will
be pacified by mere words. But with the Holy One, blessed be
He, if a man commits a sin in secret, He is pacified by mere
words'.[3] This must not, of course, be interpreted as meaning that
right inward dispositions are not necessary, but the saying is a
strong affirmation of the merciful nature of God.

Sometimes the thought of reconciliation takes on a cosmic
aspect as in Col. i. 20. Thus, 'R. Safra on concluding his prayer
added the following: May it be Thy will, O Lord our God, to
establish peace among the celestial family, and among the earthly
family, and among the disciples who occupy themselves with
Thy Torah'.[4] Sometimes this is given a different twist, as when
we read that God 'made peace (*hishlim*) between His works and
His creatures. How so? He caused the fire to be at peace with

---

[1] All these citations are from Nu. R. xii. 1 (Soncino trans. pp. 448f.).

[2] b Taan 20a (Soncino trans. p. 99).

[3] b Yoma 86b (Soncino trans. p. 429).

[4] b Ber. 16b–17a (Soncino trans. p. 99).

Abraham our father; He caused the sword to be at peace with Isaac; He caused the angel to be at peace with Jacob.'[1] Here God is thought of as making peace; but sometimes Israel is thought of in this way, as in Gn. R. lxvi. 2, Cant. R. vii. 1 where that nation's acceptance of the Law is thought of as the means of making peace with God and thus preventing the destruction of the world.

We may notice here that Josephus makes use of the verb καταλλάσσω on three occasions. Twice he uses it of human reconciliations, namely when the woman says to David: 'Be first reconciled to your own son and let your anger toward him cease'.[2] and when the Levite of Jdg. xix went after his concubine 'redressed her grievances and was reconciled to her.'[3] The third occasion tells of Samuel who 'all night long set himself to entreat God to be reconciled to Saul and not wroth with him'.[4] This verb also occurs three times in 2 Maccabees, namely 2 Macc. i. 5, vii. 33, viii. 29, in each case in the passive with God as subject, e.g. '. . . and if for rebuke and chastening our living Lord hath been angered a little while, yet shall he again be reconciled with his own servants'. There is discussion as to whether God can be said to be reconciled to men in the New Testament references, but there can be no doubt as to the position in Maccabees.

The noun καταλλαγή is found in 2 Macc. v. 20 with reference to the restoration of the temple worship, 'and (the place) which was forsaken in the wrath of the Almighty was, at the reconciliation of the great Sovereign, restored again with all glory'. Here again we see the noun used to signify reconciliation, and the mention of the divine wrath makes it clear that God is thought of as being reconciled, and not simply men.

Thus we see that among the Jews there was the thought that God was angry when men sinned, and that this situation demanded an act of reconciliaton. They do not hesitate to speak of

[1] Cant. R. iii. 11. 1 (Soncino trans. p. 171).

[2] *Ant.* vii. 184 (Loeb edn. v, p. 459).

[3] *Ant.* v. 137 (Loeb edn. v, p. 65).

[4] *Ant.* vi. 143 (Loeb edn. v, p. 239). Cf. Büchsel: 'When God allows it to come about that He gives up His wrath and is gracious again, then one calls this a καταλλαγῆναι of God' (TWNT, I, p. 254.).

God being reconciled to men, this being the removal of His just wrath. As regards method of reconciling God there is divergence; but the best Rabbinic thought had risen to the concept of God Himself bringing about the reconciliation, and in men they looked for repentance and a readiness to be reconciled to other men.

IV. THE RECONCILIATION TERMINOLOGY
IN THE NEW TESTAMENT

The chief difficulty to be solved in the New Testament use of reconcile, reconciliation, etc., is whether, in the process of reconciliation, God can be said to be reconciled to man, or whether the process is one in which man only is reconciled. As we have seen the Old Testament says little in set terms about the matter (though it often speaks of the wrath of God and of its removal, and this is nothing else than the reconciliation of God). The idea that God is reconciled to man is seen in the Rabbinic writings, in the apocrypha and in authors like Josephus. Yet all this amounts only to demonstrating that it was quite usual in early times to think of God's being reconciled to man, and that καταλλάσσω and its cognates (or their equivalents) were used of the reconciliation of God. The New Testament must be allowed to speak for itself, and when it does so we are immediately struck by the fact that God is never said in so many words to be reconciled to man. Almost always He is the subject of the verb and is said to reconcile man to Himself. This manner of speaking reminds us that the process of reconciliation originates with God, and that it is only by the outworking of His love that man can be brought into right relationships with his Maker, but it is not of itself conclusive. The argument from silence is always precarious, and doubly so, when, as here, there are few passages in question.

Under the general heading of reconciliation there are various sections to consider, for the New Testament speaks of ideas such as those of making peace, fellowship, etc., which may well be held to be parts of the same conception as that denoted by καταλλάσσω, and we have already noted that Vincent Taylor discusses a wide range of topics under the heading of 'reconciliation'. But for our purpose it will suffice to consider the thoughts of enmity, of making peace and those behind such words as καταλλάσσω.

a. ἐχθρός and ἔχθρα

The thought that men are enemies of God is undeniably to be discerned in the New Testament, as for example in Rom. v. 10, 'While we were enemies, we were reconciled to God', or Col. i. 21, 'And you, being in time past alienated and enemies in your mind in your evil works', or again, Jas. iv. 4, 'Whosoever therefore would be a friend of the world maketh himself an enemy of God', and there are other passages. There is no disputing the fact that Scripture regards man as constituting himself God's enemy by the fact of his sin. But in view of the fact that the New Testament strongly insists on the all-pervading love of God it seems to many today that God cannot be thought of as regarding man with hostility. In other words, in view of the love of God, it is said that when man is spoken of as God's enemy that must be understood as meaning that man is hostile to God with a one-sided hostility, a hostility which meets with nothing but love in return.

The usage of ἐχθρός and ἔχθρα in the New Testament does not furnish a completely final argument, although there are some points which should carry weight. Thus there is the repeated injunction to 'love your enemies' (Mt. v. 44; Lk. vi. 27, 35), or, again, Paul's 'if thine enemy hunger, feed him; if he thirst, give him to drink' (Rom. xii. 20) which indicate that the attitude of the Christian in the face of hostility is to be one characterized by love; he may not respond with vindictiveness. It is impossible to think that the attitude of God will be less worthy than that He requires from His people. Indeed we are assured in Rom. v. 8-10 that God loves men, even while they are sinners and enemies.

But that does not mean that God will remain inactive in the face of sin. After all it is possible for a Christian to be righteously angry and still retain an attitude of love, and we cannot think that this is impossible with God. This being so we cannot overlook the fact that ἐχθρός in general denotes a mutual hostility (although it can be used when the hostility is on one side only). We see something of this in such a passage as Gal. iv. 16, 'So then am I become your enemy, because I tell you the truth?', where Paul speaks of himself as the enemy, although the hostility immediately in mind is on the side of the Galatians.[1] This sort of usage prepares us for

---

[1] A similar conclusion might perhaps be drawn from 2 Thes. iii. 15.

Rom. xi. 28, where the Jews are said to be 'enemies for your sake', an expression which most scholars hold to indicate that they are being treated as enemies by God. The general context seems to demand such a meaning, especially the 'for your sake (δι' ὑμᾶς)' and the parallelism with ἀγαπητοί which must be taken in the sense of 'beloved of God'. C. Anderson Scott thinks that too much weight should not be attached to 'grammatical symmetry' and understands the passage to mean, 'Seen in the light of the gospel, still hostile to God for your sakes: but in the light of election still beloved for the fathers' sakes'.[1] But this does not seem to do justice to the apostle's thought. Throughout the chapter he is arguing that salvation has come to the Gentiles only because Israel fell away from being true to her vocation as God's people (see verses 11, 12, 15, 19, etc.). He does not mince his words when he speaks of God's attitude to Israel, for he thinks of the nation as being cast away (verse 15), he likens them to branches broken off (verses 17, 19, etc.), he says 'God spared not the natural branches' (verse 21), and he directs attention to God's action toward Israel as a striking example of 'severity' (verse 22). Moreover, if there were only a hostility of the nation without a corresponding reaction on God's part, it is difficult to see how this could avail to bring salvation to the Gentiles. The whole tenor of the chapter, as well as the specific points of language noted above, indicates that the nation is thought of as the object of God's hostility in verse 28, and most scholars accept this point of view.

In 1 Cor. xv. 25f. it is said that 'he must reign till he hath put all his enemies under his feet', so that God is not regarded as passive in opposition to His enemies. The same may be true of Lk. xix. 27, though this verse must be used with caution as it occurs in a parable. Again, in Acts xiii. 10, Elymas is shown as the 'enemy of all righteousness'. But God does not remain passive, for it is due to 'the hand of the Lord' that his subsequent blindness occurs. Similarly Paul speaks of 'perdition' as the end of certain 'enemies of the cross of Christ' (Phil. iii. 18f.), and James says that God 'resisteth the proud' (Jas. iv. 6).

Thus a consideration of the passages in which the term 'enemy' occurs indicates that God takes action against those who are His

---

[1] *Christianity According to St. Paul*, Cambridge, 1927, pp. 77f.

enemies. It is admitted that the usage of the New Testament is not such as to give us a complete and final proof that God may rightly be said to be hostile to His enemies, but the evidence we have points in that direction.

With regard to ἔχθρα, a state of enmity usually denotes a reciprocal hostility as in Lk. xxiii. 12 where Herod and Pilate had been 'at enmity between themselves'. On the other hand, when we read in Rom. viii. 7 that 'the mind of the flesh is enmity against God; for it is not subject to the law of God, neither can it be', it seems that a hostility from the side of man only is meant, although the following 'they that are in the flesh cannot please God' indicates that even here the divine reaction is not being overlooked. For the rest 'enmities' is one item in a list of 'the works of the flesh' in Gal. v. 20 and does not help us much, unless we assume that what can be referred to as a 'work of the flesh' cannot under any circumstances be referred to God, a proposition which is negatived by the fact that in the same verse 'wraths' (θυμοί) also occurs, and the thought of 'the wrath of God' is quite scriptural. ἔχθρα also occurs in Jas. iv. 4, 'Ye adulteresses, know ye not that the friendship of the world is enmity with God?' in a context which implies the divine reaction against those who are His enemies (cf. verses 6, 9–10). It is also found in Eph. ii. 15f., in the first of which verses it refers to the mutual enmity between Jew and Gentile, while in the second the same enmity may be in view, but the thought seems to be extended so as to include the enmity between man and God. Whichever way it be understood the enmity is slain through the cross. Foerster's comment on this verse, 'Enmity with one another and enmity against God (not enmity from the side of God as Gal. iii. 10, but against God as Rom. viii. 7)'[1] sums up much in this discussion. The passages in which ἔχθρα occurs may not prove a divine enmity against men but other passages in the Bible do.

For the fact seems to be that the question of whether, prior to the effecting of reconciliation, God is to be conceived of as in some sense hostile to man must be determined from the general scriptural position, and not from those passages in which ἐχθρός or ἔχθρα are found. And it is surely not without significance

[1] TWNT, II, p. 815.

that it is only in the Scriptures that we find this thought of an enmity caused by sin. It is not always noted that sinful man is not hostile to God. He is quite content to get along amiably with his Maker, and does not, in point of fact, regard his sin as a just cause for enmity. He himself is not greatly concerned about the trifle of wrongdoing that is in him, and he cannot see why God should be. Now if Jones says that Smith is his enemy, but Smith says 'No, I am peaceable!' then we must decide that there is enmity from the side of Jones, even though the term 'enemy' is fastened on Smith. So when sinful man is content to let bygones be bygones, but nevertheless God (through the mouth of His servants) speaks of an enmity, it is hard to see how it can be maintained that there is no enmity from the side of God. The point is that it is God's demand for holiness which causes the enmity, and not a conscious hostility on the part of man towards God.

It is important to be clear on the point that there is, on the scriptural view, a definite hostility on the part of God to everything that is evil. Throughout both Old and New Testaments we come across a multiplicity of passages speaking of 'the wrath of God', of the divine activity in punishing evil, of the demand for the follower of God to 'hate evil', and many similar things. Thus, quite apart from details of interpretation of particular passages, there is strong and consistent teaching to the effect that God is active in His opposition to all that is evil. Nor will it do, as some in this age seem inclined to do, to differentiate between God and the punishment of wrong. Some would see in 'the wrath' a semi-personalized entity separate from God, and not truly expressive of Him. Others, again, think of wrath as the working out of an impersonal law of retribution, and there are other ways of avoiding the scriptural position. But all such shifts seem incompatible with a genuine belief in the sovereignty and immanence of God. If God really made the universe a moral universe in which punishment follows sin, then He cannot be exempted from responsibility when it does so. We may choose to call the result the outworking of the wrath of God as the scriptural writers do, or we may prefer some other way of putting it, but the important thing is that we do not overlook the *fact*.

Scripture is insistent that God reacts in the strongest possible way to men's sin.[1]

We insist that this does not compromise the conception of the love of God. We are not forced to choose between a God of wrath and a God who loves; rather, the wrath is the obverse side of the love. Gifford has an apposite remark, namely, 'Human love here offers a true analogy: the more a father loves his son, the more he hates *in him* the drunkard, the liar, or the traitor'.[2] If this be quite possible in a human father with all his failings we cannot account it incredible in God whose wrath must be held to lack those imperfections which mar the human emotion of righteous anger at its purest.

Nor must it be overlooked that the very fact that Christ had to die to reconcile men to God is a witness in itself to the hostility from the divine side, especially since His death is a death which avails for us. 'One died for all', says St. Paul, 'therefore all died' (2 Cor. v. 14). But why should all die? Surely this points to a divine hostility, manifested in the sentence of death. As A. Schlatter puts it, 'As Paul saw in the death of Christ the death prepared for him he recognized that he has God against him. The God who condemns to death treats man as His adversary whom He withstands'.[3]

We conclude then that the biblical teaching on ἐχθρός and ἔχθρα taken in conjunction with the wider biblical teaching on the

---

[1] Cf. C. Ryder Smith: 'The concept of wrath, even when it is regarded as the sequel of justice, seems to revolt the mind of today, but it is doubtful whether any theist can escape it. When a theist looks at the world, is he not bound at least to say: "God has made the world in such a way that if men and nations sin, misery befalls them?" . . .Where a modern theist says that God has so made the world that if men sin, they suffer, the Biblical writers speak of "the wrath of God". It is true that, at first sight, there is the difference that the former attributes indirect action to God and the latter direct action, but it is very doubtful whether such a distinction exists for omnipotence, and, in any case, is there any ultimate difference between the two? Both ascribe a certain responsibility to God' (*The Bible Doctrine of Salvation*, London, 1941, p. 157).

[2] *Romans*, p. 114. He understands 'enemies' in Rom. v. 10 of God's enemies and he says: 'By God's enemies are here meant those who lie under His wrath, and they are reconciled to Him, when that wrath is removed in the remission of sins' (*Ibid.*).

[3] *Paulus der Bote Jesu*, Stuttgart, 1934, p. 565.

wrath of God indicates that there is a very real hostility on the part of God to all that is evil, and that this hostility is not incompatible with a deep love of God for sinners.

b. καταλλάσσω and καταλλαγή

One of the most important passages under this heading is Rom. v. 8–11, where we are reminded of the love of God shown in the cross, of our being justified in Christ's blood and saved from the wrath through Him, and then, 'For if, while we were enemies, we were reconciled to God through the death of his Son, much more being reconciled, shall we be saved by his life; and not only so, but we also rejoice in God through our Lord Jesus Christ, through whom we have now received the reconciliation'.

Here let us notice first of all that there is an aspect of reconciliation which is outside man, an objective element; for we are said to have received the reconciliation, which, therefore, is in some sense independent of us. Obviously reconciliation must be personal to be effective, and we must enter into a state of being reconciled; but, nevertheless, there is a sense in which a reconciliation can be said to be proffered to us. In other words the New Testament view is that reconciliation was wrought on the cross before there was anything in man's heart to correspond.[1] There is an objective aspect to reconciliation, and this may well be held to imply that there is a sense in which God can be said to be reconciled to man. As Denney puts it: 'Reduced to its simplest expression, what an objective atonement means is that, but for Christ and His passion, God would not be to us what He is'. He goes on to indicate the seriousness of rejecting this position by saying, 'The alternative is to say that quite independently of any value which Christ and His passion have for God, God would still

---

[1] Cf. Denney: 'Unless we can preach a finished work of Christ in relation to sin, a καταλλαγή or reconciliation or peace which has been achieved independently of us at an infinite cost . . . we have no real gospel for sinful men at all' (The Death of Christ, London, 1950, p. 86). Similarly Forsyth: 'Reconciliation was finished in Christ's death. Paul did not preach a gradual reconciliation. He preached what the old divines used to call the finished work. . . . He preached something done once for all—a reconciliation which is the base of every soul's reconcilement, not an invitation only' (The Work of Christ, London, 1948, p. 86).

be to us what He is. But this is really to put Christ out of Christianity altogether'.[1]

Then there is the term ἐχθρός which St. Paul applies to men in their state prior to reconciliation (Rom. v. 10). It may be granted that in this context the major idea conveyed by ἐχθρός is that men were hostile to God, for the apostle is trying to show us the greatness of the love of God and he insists that even when men were hostile to God He effected reconciliation. But this does not mean that we have exhausted the meaning of the term ἐχθρός. As we saw in the previous section, it is a word which may well be held to imply a severe reaction on the part of God to man's sin. While it is true, of course, that the usage in other passages does not determine the meaning in this, it does show us that there is scriptural warrant for thinking of an opposition of God to sin and sinners which can be referred to by the use of ἐχθρός. As Vincent Taylor says, 'We must conclude that in Rom. v. 10 ἐχθρός describes, not only the hostile attitude of men, but also their character in the eyes of God. He sees them as enemies; and yet He reconciles them to Himself'.[2]

Seen, then, in the wider context of the New Testament thought, Rom. v. 8-11 may be said to indicate a reconciliation in which there is a Godward as well as a manward aspect. The narrower context of the particular chapter also favours this idea, for the words about reconciliation are immediately preceded by a reference to 'the wrath' from which men are saved through Christ,[3] a thought which is typically Pauline, and which we saw in Chapter Five is developed in the first three chapters of the Epistle.

In addition to the context, the meaning of the verses in question points in the same direction. Thus we are said to be reconciled by the death of Christ, and this seems to indicate a Godward rather than a manward aspect of the atonement. As Liddon says, 'Christ's death removed God's enmity against man, and man's enmity

---

[1] *The Christian Doctrine of Reconciliation*, London, 1917, p. 239.

[2] *Forgiveness and Reconciliation*, London, 1946, p. 75.

[3] Cf. Godet on Romans: 'The enmity must above all belong to Him to whom wrath is attributed; and the blood of Christ . . . did not flow in the first place to work a change in our dispositions Godward, but to bring about a change in God's conduct to ourselves' (i, p. 330).

against God only ceased, as a moral consequence of faith. καταλλαγέντες and καταλλάγημεν must, therefore, be understood to express, not merely the reconciliation of the moral nature of the Christian with God, but the new relation of God to man in Christ which made this possible'.[1] While it is quite true that when a man comes to a position of faith in Jesus there is a change of heart and outlook, such that his enmity to God is done away, and while it is also true that the display of divine love which we see on the cross is a powerful force in bringing him to this position of faith, yet it is difficult to think that Paul is trying to express either of these truths in this passage. If he had wished to say something like that he had a splendid opening when he spoke of God commending His own love to us (verse 8). But his point in making this statement is not to lead on to the thought of this love inducing men to lay aside their enmity, but rather to stress that it was 'while we were yet sinners' that 'Christ died for us'. From there he goes on to speak of justification, of being saved from wrath, of being reconciled while still enemies. It is not that the apostle is indifferent to the new life, for he goes on to mention it as a consequence of reconciliation—'much more, being reconciled, shall we be saved by his life'. Being saved by or in His life is surely another way of putting what Paul says in 2 Cor. iv. 10f., '. . . that the life also of Jesus may be manifested in our body. For we which live are alway delivered unto death for Jesus' sake, that the life also of Jesus may be manifested in our mortal flesh'. Thus there is a change in man such that, instead of living his own fleshly life, he now shows Christ living in him. But this seems to be the consequence of reconciliation and not reconciliation itself. We are not helped here by the fact that the English terms for reconciliation, etc., do not seem to denote exactly the same things as their Greek counterparts. If, in English, we speak of God and man being reconciled, we necessarily think of a reconciliation in which right relationships now exist on both sides, and perhaps the same is true with regard to the Greek terms when reconciliation is thought of as being fully consummated. But it is possible to use the Greek terms to denote the fact that God has dealt with the obstacle to fellowship, and that He now proffers reconciliation to man. Thus Paul can speak of

---

[1] *Romans*, pp. 100f.

man 'receiving the reconciliation',[1] which implies that reconciliation is a boon given by God. It is not denied that it is also possible to think of reconciliation as something calling for man's co-operation, for 'Be ye reconciled' is also a word of St. Paul. All that is being insisted upon is that the Greek and the English words do not have quite the same usage, so that the Greek can be used of a more one-sided process than the English, and it is suggested that there is more than a hint at a largely one-sided process in Rom. v. 9–11.

The other great passage on reconciliation is 2 Cor. v. 17ff., 'Wherefore if any man is in Christ, he is a new creature: the old things are passed away; behold, they are become new. But all things are of God, who reconciled us to himself through Christ, and gave unto us the ministry of reconciliation; to wit, that God was in Christ reconciling the world unto himself, not reckoning unto them their trespasses, and having committed unto us the word of reconciliation.

'We are ambassadors therefore on behalf of Christ, as though God were intreating by us: we beseech you on behalf of Christ, be ye reconciled to God. Him who knew no sin he made to be sin on our behalf; that we might become the righteousness of God in him. And working together with him we intreat also that ye receive not the grace of God in vain'.

Here we have no mention of wrath in the context as we have in the Romans passage,[2] and the context has much to say about the

---

[1] Cf. Denney: 'It is very unfortunate that the English word reconcile (and also the German *versöhnen*, which is usually taken as its equivalent) diverges seriously, though in a way of which it is easy to be unconscious, from the Greek καταλλάσσειν. We cannot say in English, God reconciled us to Himself, without conceiving the persons referred to as being actually at peace with God, as having laid aside all fear, distrust, and love of evil, and entered, in point of fact, into relations of peace and friendship with God. But καταλλάσσειν, as describing the work of God, or καταλλαγή, as describing its immediate result, do not necessarily carry us so far. The work of reconciliation, in the sense of the New Testament, is a work which is *finished*, and which we must conceive to be finished, *before the gospel is preached*' (*The Death of Christ*, London, 1911, p. 103).

[2] Yet Strachan can say this wrath 'must be in the background, if we are to see, in these verses, as I think we must, Paul's expression of what he regarded as the essential meaning of the Cross of Christ' (*2 Corinthians*, MNTC, p. 116).

new life in Christ, which indicates the close connection between reconciliation and the resultant Christian victorious living. It is thought by some to point to reconciliation as essentially an activity within man, but this seems to be going too far, and to be neglecting some of the points that Paul is making.

First of all let us notice that the process the apostle has in mind is one which is wrought by God. 'All things', he tells us, 'are of God, who reconciled us'; 'God was in Christ reconciling the world unto himself', 'him . . . he made to be sin on our behalf'. Though it is true that there is an aspect in which men may be exhorted to be reconciled to God, yet there is no question that Paul is thinking of something God has done for men, and not of some merely human activity.

In verse 19, moreover, reconciliation is explained as 'not reckoning unto them their trespasses'. This is in keeping with much in the Scriptures which assures us that the obstacle to fellowship between God and man is sin, so that if there is to be peace between the two something must be done about that sin. It can be alleged, of course, that it is necessary for man to forsake his sin and that, when he does this, there is reconciliation with God. Thus C. Anderson Scott equates reconciliation with 'the flooding of human hearts with the love of God, the disappearance of hostility, the joyful acceptance of forgiveness',[1] and similarly C. Ryder Smith, in discussing the idea of the wrath of God, says, 'but here (i.e. Rom. iii. 23–26), as always, it is taken for granted that, if man repents, the "wrath" of God died'.[2] There is of course truth in these statements; for if a man truly repents, has his heart filled with the love of God, finds his hostility to God disappear and accepts forgiveness gladly, then he is certainly reconciled to God.

But it is difficult to believe either that this is the whole story or that this is St. Paul's meaning in the passage which we are considering. Such statements come perilously close to leaving Christ out of reconciliation,[3] and it is the activity of Christ that

---

[1] *Christianity According to St. Paul*, Cambridge, 1927, p. 84. He adds: 'This is not all that Paul has to say about the "Atonement", but it is the heart of it'.

[2] *The Bible Doctrine of Salvation*, London, 1941, p. 260.

[3] R. Travers Herford, speaking not of reconciliation in particular, but of Christianity in general, says: 'Paul grasped the fact that the Christian religion
[continued on p. 203]

Paul is especially concerned to stress, and in particular the necessity of His death. For although in these verses the apostle does not specifically mention the death of the Lord, there is not the slightest doubt that he has it in mind. For it is only through this death that man's trespasses are put away on Paul's view, and thus the cross is vividly present to his mind in verses 19, 21. Nor does he conceive of the activity of Christ as being confined to making such a display of the love of God as will arouse in men's breasts appropriate feelings of gratitude, love and repentance so that they forsake sin and in this way are reconciled. When Paul speaks of Christ being 'made sin' for us it seems clear, at least, that he conceived of the death of the Lord as availing in an objective manner to put away man's sin.[1]

It is common in these days to assert that Paul here means nothing more than that Christ entered into a perfect sympathy with sinners, much in the same manner as a loving mother feels deeply for her erring son. Such analogies are often drawn out to show that the mother may have a more intense suffering than the son, that she may loathe the sin more than he does in his imperfect penitence, and so on. But, true as all this is, it does not seem that this is what Paul is saying. Rather the verse is to be understood along with Gal. iii. 13 which speaks of Christ becoming 'a curse' for us, as indicating that He bore to the full the consequences

[1] Cf. Forsyth: 'The greatest passage which says that God was in Christ reconciling says in the same breath that it was by Christ being made sin for us. The reconciliation is attached to Christ's death, and to that as an expiation' (*The Cruciality of the Cross*, London, 1948, p. 68). J. Scott Lidgett says: 'Christ enters into our sin, takes it upon Himself, is wrapped in it. He stands for us and with us, as though a sinner, and in that capacity He dies on our behalf' (*The Spiritual Principle of the Atonement*, London, 1898, p. 42).

was founded on a Person, not an idea' (*Judaism in the New Testament Period*, London, 1948, p. 227). The comment has relevance to the point we are discussing, for the Christian view of reconciliation is not simply an Idea, such that if a man repents all will be well; it concerns a *Person*. And the characteristic Christian thought is that reconciliation is wrought by Christ, and is to be found only in Him. 'God's reconciliation rested upon this, that on His Eternal Son, who knew no sin in His experience . . . sin's judgment fell' (P. T. Forsyth, *The Work of Christ*, London, 1948, p. 82).

of sin.[1] When He was made sin that we might become 'the righteousness of God', then in some way He took upon Him our sin and we bear it no more. As Denney puts it, 'Christ died for us, died that death of ours which is the wages of sin. In His death, all sinless as He was, God's condemnation of our sin came upon Him; a divine sentence was executed upon the sin of the world.'[2] Or to quote a more recent writer, the verse means that 'He made Him die that death which is the wages of sin, as our substitute'.[3] Such also is the interpretation of Schrenk: 'Because the Christ is substitutionarily ἁμαρτία for us, may we be δικαιοσύνη ἐν αὐτῷ'.[4] Such interpretations are much nearer to the thought of Paul than those which minimize the force of the passage.

Arising out of all this is what Paul calls 'the word of reconciliation', the message to men that they must 'be reconciled to God'. This stresses that there is the need for man to respond to the divine grace, that reconciliation is not something which is carried through independently of men's reaction. While it is true that, in some sense, reconciliation can be thought of as something offered to man on the basis of Christ's work, yet it cannot be thought of as availing in the case of any individual man until he himself has become reconciled to God. But if there is anything in what we have been saying the need for this action on the part of the sinner should not blind us to the fact that the really important part of reconciliation is in the action of God and not in the sinner's response. Because God has made Christ sin for us, because God is not reckoning to men their trespasses, therefore there is a word of reconciliation, a message of good news that can and must be proclaimed to men. Well may Paul exhort his readers to 'receive

---

[1] H. Wheeler Robinson also takes these two verses together saying of the idea of Christ becoming a curse for us in Gal. iii. 13: 'This is one of the clearest indications that St. Paul conceived the death of Christ as both substitutionary and penal, its parallel being that of 2 Cor. v. 21, where the Sinless is said to be made sin in our behalf, that we might obtain acquittal and become actually righteous' (*Redemption and Revelation*, London, 1942, p. 271).

[2] *Studies in Theology*, London, 1895, p. 112.

[3] A. B. Macaulay, *The Death of Jesus*, London, 1938, p. 174.

[4] TWNT, II, p. 212. Similarly L. S. Thornton says of this verse and Gal. iii. 13: 'Whatever these mysterious phrases may mean, they certainly put our Lord in the place of sinners' (*The Common Life in the Body of Christ*, London, 1950).

not the grace of God in vain'. But it is 'the grace of God' and not merely some subjective change in their own hearts of which he is speaking.[1]

Apart from these two passages καταλλάσσω occurs only in 1 Cor. vii. 11 where St. Paul charges those married 'That the wife depart not from her husband (but and if she depart, let her remain unmarried or else be reconciled to her husband)'. It is surely of significance that while the wife is envisaged as the party actively seeking the reconciliation she is exhorted to 'be reconciled' indicating a change from her side as well as his.[2]

The noun καταλλαγή is found also in Rom. xi. 15, 'For if the casting away of them (i.e. the Jews) is the reconciling of the world', but this does not help us greatly. Paul is here developing an argument that it is because the Jews were temporarily rejected that reconciliation came to the Gentiles, but he does not indicate in what manner this reconciliation was effected. So for our understanding of the term, we are dependent upon the passages already considered.

c. ἀποκαταλλάσσω

Under this heading two passages fall to be considered, namely Eph. ii. 11ff. and Col. i. 19ff. The former begins with the enmity between Jew and Gentile, when the Gentiles were 'separate from Christ, alienated from the commonwealth of Israel, and strangers from the covenants of the promise, having no hope and without God in the world'. But the coming of Christ has altered all that. He 'made both one, and brake down the middle wall of partition, having abolished in his flesh the enmity, even the law of commandments contained in ordinances; that he might create in himself of the twain one new man, so making peace'. From this point the apostle goes straight on to consider the change wrought by Christ in the relationship of men to God, and says that He

---

[1] Cf. the passages quoted on p. 203, n. 1. From verses 19, 21 Büchsel thinks that 'the reconciliation includes also justification within itself' (TWNT, 1, p. 258).

[2] Büchsel comments: 'Were the woman in such a case to remain completely passive, there would arise no new union, no new reconciliation between her and her husband' (TWNT, 1, p. 256). Pearson understands 'be reconciled' here as 'appease and get the favour of her husband' (*On the Creed* 365, Oxford, 1890, p. 644).

'might reconcile them both in one body unto God through the cross, having slain the enmity thereby'. The upshot of it all is that the Gentiles 'are no more strangers and sojourners, but . . . fellow-citizens with the saints, and of the household of God'.

This passage strongly insists on the divine initiative in the process of reconciliation; indeed the whole process is described from the point of view of Christ, and men are not spoken of as doing anything in the matter. They were 'far off', they are 'made nigh' and all is the work of Christ. There is nothing here like the 'Be ye reconciled' of 2 Cor. v, although it may fairly be said that such an aspect of the subject is implied. But the point is that it is the divine initiative and the divine effort that is in view; the human response is not so much as mentioned.

This might accord well with the contention that, in reconciliation, God does not need to be reconciled. But in fact the passage does not indicate this. The fact that all is of God is freely admitted, but that does not carry with it the thought that there is no divine reaction against sin to be dealt with. It is quite possible that there should be such a thing as 'the wrath of God' against sinful men, and that God Himself should provide the means whereby this wrath is turned away and not poured out upon men, so that the mere fact that it is to God that the reconciliation is due does not decide the point as to just what the process of reconciliation is.

Everything depends on what we are to understand by 'the enmity'. If it is man's enmity against God only, then there is no Godward aspect of reconciliation in mind; but if it includes the thought that God reacts severely against sinners, then such an aspect cannot be dismissed. There is nothing in the immediate context which determines the point. The argument flows on evenly whatever interpretation of 'the enmity' we adopt. But if we pay attention to the wider thought of the Epistle (confining ourselves to this one writing since there are some who do not think it Pauline), we cannot overlook the strenuous divine reaction to evil. All men are thought of as 'by nature children of wrath' (Eph. ii. 3). Again, the writer says 'Let no man deceive you with empty words: for because of these things cometh the wrath of God upon the sons of disobedience' (v. 6). Masters are urged to forbear threatening on the grounds that they themselves have a Master in heaven 'and there is no respect of persons with him'

(vi. 9). Certain persons, namely, fornicators, the unclean and the covetous, are expressly said to be excluded from the kingdom of God (v. 5). Even the enthusiasm with which the writer speaks of salvation seems to be partly because he has in mind what men are saved from, as well as the new state into which they are saved. Taking the Epistle as a whole it seems clear that the author thought of God as hostile to evil. Therefore we can believe that an element in his thought of reconciliation is that this hostility is removed for them that are 'in Christ Jesus'.

This seems to be supported by the statement in ii. 17f. that Christ 'came and preached peace (εὐηγγελίσατο εἰρήνην) . . . for through him we both have our access in one Spirit unto the Father'. The good tidings must surely be that God has made a way of access, that He has removed the barrier which separated sinners from Himself. Therefore the idea that all men have to do is to realize that He loves them and will receive them seems inadequate to explain the passage. It looks as if the writer is referring to a new situation called into being by the death on the cross, so that, as a consequence of that death, there is good news of a completely novel situation in which they need not fear to draw near to God for the enmity has been 'slain'.

Again, it may not be without significance that the writer is led into his discussion of reconciliation by a consideration of the enmity between Jew and Gentile, and this was an enmity on both sides. This is not conclusive, but as far as it goes it points to a reconciliation affecting both parties.

Thus, surveying all the evidence, it would seem that grounds are not wanting for thinking that in this passage the writer is thinking of the removal of the divine wrath against sin as the effect of the death on the cross, and of peace being made between God and man accordingly. Admittedly a final proof of this is lacking, but it is contended that this is the most natural way of reading the available evidence.

The other passage where we find ἀποκαταλλάσσω used is Col. i. 19ff. which tells us that it was the Father's good pleasure through him 'to reconcile all things unto himself, having made peace through the blood of his cross'. The argument goes on: 'And you, being in time past alienated and enemies in your mind in your evil works, yet now hath he reconciled (or as B and Hil. read, you have been reconciled) in the body of his flesh through death, etc.'

Once more we notice the stress on the activity of God; it was His good pleasure that reconciliation should be effected, and the emphasis throughout the passage is on what He has done, and not on any puny effort of man.

Then we notice that each time reconciliation is mentioned we have a reference to the means. The first time 'having made peace through the blood of his cross' is added; the second time reconciliation is said to be 'in the body of his flesh through death'. Thus it is clear that reconciliation is closely tied up with the death of the Lord, and the implication is that this death really did something in the way of removing barriers. Once more it would seem that such explanations as that the death is an indication that God loves men and that if they turn to Him all will be well are inadequate as summaries of the thought of the writer. It is difficult to escape the impression that what Paul is teaching us is that the death of Christ did something quite apart from the stimulus it has on the feelings and actions of man.

It is sometimes argued that the statement of the nature of the enmity indicates that reconciliation takes place only from the manward side. Men are said to have been 'alienated and enemies in their mind in their evil works'. This, it is said, shows that reconciliation means the alteration of this state of affairs and the substitution of a better state of mind and of better works. But this seems to be going beyond the evidence. It is not disputed that the hostility in men's minds and actions is a serious affair, nor that it must be removed before there can be completely harmonious relations between God and men; but it can be maintained that this exhausts the concept of reconciliation only by holding that God's reaction to all this is not serious. That this is not the thought of the writer of the Epistle is shown by his mention of 'the wrath of God' coming 'upon the sons of disobedience' (Col. iii. 6), his statement 'For he that doeth wrong shall receive again for the wrong that he hath done; and there is no respect of persons' (Col. iii. 25), and the possibility of failing to attain 'the prize' (Col. ii. 18). These general considerations and the fact that the passage under discussion seems to imply that sinners are in no good case because of the attitude of a holy God to their sin indicate to the present writer that the cross was thought by St. Paul to be the veritable means whereby sin was put away and reconciliation thereby effected.

That man's response to this is important is undoubted, and that that response leads to a thoroughgoing reformation of man is clear. But the point is that it is man's response to something that God has done for him; it is not in itself the process of reconciliation.

Thus it seems clear that there are certain ideas running through the passages where the various reconciliation words are used in the New Testament. There is the common thought that it is the sin of man which represents the barrier to communion, and this must be dealt with if reconciliation is to take place. It is this which gives point to the idea that God can be said to be reconciled to man, for it is manifestly impossible for God to regard man in quite the same way before the barrier is removed as He does after that takes place. At the same time the reconciliation is always God's work, and in several ways we have the truth stressed that it is the love of God that is the dominant factor in bringing reconciliation about.

There is support for the idea that the reconciliation includes an aspect of reconciliation of God in the usage of διαλλάσσω, a word closely allied in meaning to καταλλάσσω. We have noted that this word was used in the LXX of David's being reconciled, when it was Saul's enmity which was to be removed, and therefore we would have expected the text to say that Saul was to be reconciled rather than David. We have exactly the same usage in Mt. v. 23f., 'If therefore thou art offering thy gift at the altar, and there rememberest that thy brother hath aught against thee, leave there thy gift before the altar, and go thy way, first be reconciled to thy brother . . .'. Here again we see the one taking the initiative spoken of as being reconciled, and this usage seems to be established for καταλλάσσω by 1 Cor. vii. 11. Thus the linguistic usage gives us ground for thinking that when reconciliation is applied to the relations between God and men it will signify, in part, that God is reconciled as well as man. Moreover, as Handley Moule says, καταλλαγή and its cognates 'habitually point to the winning rather the pardon of an offended king, than the consent of the rebel to yield to his kindness'.[1] Similarly Crawford long ago pointed out

[1] *Outlines of Christian Doctrine*, London, 1892, p. 79.

14

that καταλλάσσω and διαλλάσσω are used in the biblical writings 'to signify the removal of enmity, not from the *offending*, but from the *offended* party'; and again he says 'when one party is said "to be reconciled to another" or "to reconcile himself to another", the *latter*, and not the former, according to the Hellenistic idiom, is the party whose friendship and favour are conciliated'.[1]

d. Making Peace

The actual expression 'making peace' does not occur very often in the New Testament, but a common idea is that believers have peace with God. Since this is not thought of as applying to natural man (cf. Eph. ii. 3 'by nature children of wrath'), it may fairly be held to imply the thought of making peace.

It will be worth our while to notice a little of the content of the term εἰρήνη (peace). Among the Greeks it was used primarily to denote that state of rest which results from cessation of hostilities, peace in opposition to war. But in the LXX the term receives an extension of meaning. This is due to its being used as the regular word to translate the Hebrew *shalom*,[2] a word of wider meaning than εἰρήνη in profane Greek writings. *Shalom* can be used to denote the state of rest when there is no war, and it is used in this way in about thirty-eight of its 236 occurrences in the Old Testament. But this cannot be regarded as the word's essential meaning, it being better regarded as part of a wider conception of general well-being. Because such well-being is promoted in times when there is no war, and indeed such times may be regarded as an integral part of the general well-being, the term *shalom* was felt to be not inappropriately used to describe the condition of absence of strife. But that should not blind us to the fact that the essential

---

[1] *The Atonement*, Edinburgh, 1871, p. 67. Cf. also Pearson: 'In the language of the Scripture to reconcile a man to God, is in our vulgar language to reconcile God to man' (*Op. cit.*, 364, p. 643).

[2] εἰρήνη is found 282 times in the LXX, the Hebrew being *shalom* 192 times (including three verses marked with a query in H & R), while 76 times either there is no Hebrew or it is doubtful whether εἰρήνη is based on the present text. For the rest it translates *beṭaḥ* nine times (two queries), *shqṭ* and *shlwh* once each, while H & R include one passage each (queried each time) under *ḥlq*, *lqḥ* and *tsḥ*. From these figures it is plain that *shalom* is the Old Testament equivalent of εἰρήνη.

meaning of the word is to be sought elsewhere. BDB find it in the thought of 'completeness, soundness, welfare' and so 'peace'. G. von Rad thinks that 'The groundmeaning of the word is "well-being" and indeed with a manifest emphasis on the material side'.[1] E. de W. Burton says *shalom* 'has as its fundamental idea "soundness", "prosperity", "well-being".[2] There can be no doubt that the word conveyed to the Hebrews the thought of well-being in the widest of senses.

A full examination of such a rich and many-sided concept would take up more space than we have at our disposal, and we content ourselves with noticing one or two of the more important points in connection with the usage. *Shalom* is often thought of as emphasizing material aspects as we may see from such passages as Lv. xxvi. 5ff. But sometimes we detect a more spiritual note, as when the psalmist says, 'Mercy and truth are met together; righteousness and peace have kissed each other' (Ps. lxxxv. 10). So too the prophet says 'the work of righteousness shall be peace; and the effect of righteousness quietness and confidence for ever' (Is. xxxii. 17).[3] In such passages we must feel that more than material prosperity is in mind, that *shalom* in fact has an ethical content. This we might also deduce from the fact that sometimes *shalom* is ascribed to the Lord, as in Jb. xxv. 2, 'He maketh peace in his high places', or in 1 Ki. ii. 33 where it is said that unto David and his house 'shall there be peace for ever from the Lord'. In line with this is the name 'Jehovah-shalom', 'the Lord is peace', (Jdg. vi. 24) and the implications of the 'covenant of peace' which we meet in a number of passages and where it is clear that the peace is thought of as coming from the Lord (Nu. xxv. 12; Is. liv. 10; Ezk. xxxiv. 25, xxxvii. 26; Mal. ii. 5). Thus, while we may not say that the New Testament conception of peace with God is to be discerned in the Old Testament, yet we can see how the way was being prepared with the thought of a peace which includes an ethical content, and which takes its origin from God.

As εἰρήνη was used so regularly to translate *shalom*, it was inevitable that it should pick up some of the wide meaning

---

[1] TWNT, II, p. 400.
[2] *Galatians* (I.C.C.), p. 425.
[3] For similar thoughts see Is. xxvi. 2, 3; Ps. cxix. 165; Pr. xii. 20; Je. xxxiii. 6; Zc. viii. 19; Mal. ii. 6; etc.

associated with the Hebrew term. The reader of the LXX must have come to see, from the variety of contexts in which the word was used, that εἰρήνη denoted more than a cessation from hostility. In particular he was bound to see that the word often denotes a blessing which comes from God (Nu. vi. 26; Is. xlv. 7; Zc. viii. 12), and that it frequently has an ethical content (Ps. xxxiii. 14; Is. xxxii. 17; Zc. viii. 12; Mal. ii. 6, etc.).

During the period between the two Testaments this usage continues, and other elements are imported into it. We have already noted that the Rabbis think of an enmity between God and man and of various ways in which reconciliation is effected.[1] The Zadokite fragment speaks of the Lord striving with all flesh (i. 2), but not much can be made of this, for the words are 'based almost verbally on Je. xxv. 31'.[2] The Old Testament has the idea of the Lord having a controversy with men, and of reconciliation, inasmuch as punishment does not always come upon them. But the point is that this reconciliation is not indicated by the use of *shalom* (or εἰρήνη), and in this respect the Zadokite fragment has the Old Testament usage. In the Testaments of the twelve Patriarchs we find εἰρήνη used in connection with the judgment of God, as in Test. Lev. xviii where judgment is executed for a period (verse 2), but later 'there shall be peace in all the earth' (verse 4). Peace is thought of as coming from God, and there is an interesting passage where 'the angel of peace' makes his appearance. The patriarch Dan says, 'Draw near unto God and unto the angel that intercedeth for you, for he is a mediator between God and man, and for the peace of Israel he shall stand up against the kingdom of the enemy' (Test. Dan vi. 2). Here there is a conflict between God and man, or at any rate God and Satan, with evil in man very much the point at issue. But, although peace is used of the successful outcome, it seems rather in the sense of 'well-being, prosperity' than of a state of peace between God and man.

Somewhat similar, though closer to the thought of a state of peace between God and man, is the usage in the Ethiopic Enoch.

---

[1] See pp. 189ff.

[2] Charles, *Apocrypha and Pseudepigrapha*, II, p. 799. The citations following are from this translation.

Here we find the thoughts of peace and judgment connected:

'And the earth shall be wholly rent in sunder,
And all that is upon the earth shall perish,
And there shall be a judgment upon all (men).

But with the righteous He will make peace,
And will protect the elect,
And mercy shall be upon them' (En. xvii. 8).

Similarly peace seems closely allied to forgiveness: 'And ye shall have no peace nor forgiveness of sin' (En. xii. 5), 'And there shall be forgiveness of sins, and every mercy and peace and forbearance' (En. v. 6 and cf. En. v. 4, xvi. 4).

In Josephus there seems little to help us. He uses εἰρήνη of Abraham's returning in peace after recapturing Lot and the Sodomites (Ant. i. 179), which is quite a common usage. There is probably an ethical content when he refers to the Essenes as 'ministers of peace' (Bell. ii. 135), and he has an interesting passage in which he refers to Saul's having peace of soul (Ant. vi. 211), but as the peace referred to is rest from demons probably not much can be made of the reference. Philo once says that God is peace: 'Know then, good friend, that God alone is the real veritable peace' (De. Som. ii. 253, Loeb trans.), and again, he thinks of God as the only source of peace, speaking of God 'Whose voice granted to Phinehas the highest of blessings, peace—a gift which no human being can bestow' (Vit. Mos. i. 304, Loeb trans.). When he says that 'the results of continence are stability and peace' (Jos. 57, Loeb trans.) he seems to be giving εἰρήνη an ethical content.

Thus in these various Jewish writings there seems to be a tendency to retain something of the wider meaning given to εἰρήνη in the LXX. In particular we notice that peace is often regarded as coming from God, and that the ethical note is not seldom struck. Those writers who use it in connection with the judgment of God upon sin are getting near to the New Testament idea of peace following upon God's dealing with sin.

A striking feature of the New Testament use of εἰρήνη is the frequency with which it is associated, directly or indirectly, with

God. It is a difficult word to classify, as one group of meanings shades off into another, and there must always be a large subjective element in any classification adopted. But it may be said that of the ninety-two times the word occurs, fifteen refer to peace as opposed to war, personal strife, or confusion, while in all the others it is possible to see implied the thought that God is the giver. Peace is specifically connected with the Father or the Son about forty times, including the salutations in the Epistles.

Particularly important from our present point of view are those passages which directly associate peace with God. First of all there are those which indicate a tranquillity in the believer. But this is not a rest thought of as the possession of all men; it is a specifically Christian peace. As Burton says, it is a 'Tranquillity of mind, which comes from the assurance of being reconciled with God and under His care'.[1] A good example of this usage is Jn. xiv. 27 where Jesus says, 'Peace I leave with you; my peace I give unto you: not as the world giveth, give I unto you'; for here the peace is expressly associated with the speaker—it is 'His' peace—and also it is expressly differentiated from the peace which the world gives. Similar is the Lord's statement a little later, 'These things have I spoken unto you, that in me ye may have peace. In the world ye have tribulation: but be of good cheer; I have overcome the world' (Jn. xvi. 33). Here again peace is associated with Christ, and it is contrasted with the tribulation that is the world's gift. The peace spoken of seems to rest on the fact that Christ has overcome the world. So again in Rom. viii. 6, St. Paul says: 'For the mind of the flesh is death; but the mind of the spirit is life and peace'; and his subsequent reference to the mind of the flesh as enmity with God enables us to say with confidence that the peace he is thinking of is one in which that enmity has been overcome, it is a peace which results from the work of Christ for man.[2]

So completely is the idea accepted that peace comes from God that He can be referred to as 'the God of peace', an expression

---

[1] *Op. cit.*, p. 426.

[2] Other passages in which peace signifies a tranquillity of mind or soul, and which we should understand as a result of the work of Christ for man in accordance with the accepted Christian position include Rom. xiv. 17, xv. 13; Gal. v. 22; Eph. vi. 23; 2 Thes. iii. 16; 2 Pet. iii. 14.

which implies that the bringing about of this peace is a characteristic feature of His activity. A particularly instructive example is Rom. xvi. 20, 'And the God of peace shall bruise Satan under your feet shortly', for here, in the very sentence in which He is designated 'God of peace' that same God is pictured in the warlike activity of bruising Satan. Nothing could more graphically illustrate the fact that peace in the New Testament is not simply the absence of war. It is a much more positive concept, and one which, as here, may be compatible with struggle. It stands for spiritual well-being at the highest level, a prosperity of soul resulting from being in right relationship with God,[1] and God may be thought of as bringing about this relationship by His victory over Satan. This thought of God as the God of peace in connection with the atoning work of Christ is to be discerned also in the great benediction at the end of the Epistle to the Hebrews, where the writer refers to 'the God of peace, who brought again from the dead the great shepherd of the sheep with the blood of the eternal covenant, even our Lord Jesus' (Heb. xiii. 20). From such passages it seems clear that the giving of peace is thought of as a distinctive divine activity, and that it is associated with the atoning death of Christ. The passages in question do not say in so many words that we have peace because Christ died, but it is hard to see how this inference can be avoided. (Cf. the references to 'the God of peace' in Rom. xv. 33; 2 Cor. xiii. 11; Phil. iv. 9; 1 Thes. v. 23, and 'The Lord of peace' in 2 Thes. iii. 16).

There are a few passages wherein peace seems to be nearly identical with salvation. Thus in his speech in the house of Cornelius Peter refers to 'the word which he sent unto the children of Israel, preaching good tidings of peace by Jesus Christ (εὐαγγελιζόμενος εἰρήνην διὰ 'Ιησοῦ Χριστοῦ)' (Acts x. 36). It is very difficult to distinguish here between εἰρήνη and εὐαγγέλιον, and the content of the εἰρήνη in question must be that the enmity caused by sin has been done away with in Christ. It is not otherwise with Rom. v. 1, where 'peace with God through our Lord Jesus Christ' is mentioned in the closest of connections with justification by faith,

---

[1] P. T. Forsyth speaks of 'peace—by which he (i.e. Paul) meant not calm but the life-confidence of reconciliation and co-operation with God' (*Positive Preaching and the Modern Mind*, London, 1949, p. 111).

and where εἰρήνη seems to include more than simply tranquillity of mind. So also in Eph. vi. 15 we find a reference to 'the gospel of peace', where the meaning seems to be that the tidings are to be proclaimed that peace in the fullest sense is the result of God's activity in Christ. But in this connection the most important passage is Eph. ii. 14f. in which we find Christ designated as 'our peace', He is referred to as 'making peace', and as preaching 'peace to you that were far off, and peace to them that were nigh'. The passage is not without its difficulties, for the writer seems to be speaking first of the enmity between Jew and Gentile, and this does not drop entirely out of his thought, but at the same time the thought of the deeper enmity between sinful man and God comes in.[1] Christ, by His atoning death, has done away with the enmity, bringing about a comprehensive peace, which includes complete wholeness spiritually, and right relations with God issuing in right relations with man. So completely is Christ identified with this process of making peace that He can be said to be 'our peace'. Nothing could convey more definitely the thought that the peace in question is not of man's doing, but comes as a divine gift (cf. also Gal. vi. 16; Phil. iv. 7; Col. iii. 15).

It is this thought of a broadly-conceived peace which comes from God which is of importance in connection with the present inquiry. The New Testament does not regard man in his natural condition as at peace with God. Rather, so long as he is outside Christ, he is at enmity with God 'because the mind of the flesh is enmity against God; for it is not subject to the law of God, neither indeed can it be: and they that are in the flesh cannot please God' (Rom. viii. 7f.). It is unnecessary to labour the point, for it is the common New Testament view of man untouched by the gospel. But it is also the characteristic New Testament teaching that God did not allow matters to rest there. In the person of

---

[1] Cf. Foerster: 'One will not rightly evaluate the passage if one does not see that the law plays a double role, it divides the heathen from the commonwealth of Israel, and Israel from God. Through the law enmity between Jew and heathen stands opposed, and enmity of man and God. Therefore verse 14, αὐτὸς γὰρ ἐστιν ἡ εἰρήνη ἡμῶν, is to be taken in a comprehensive sense: when Christ abolished the law He did away with the double disorder in mankind, that with one another and that against God. εἰρήνη denotes peace with God and peace among mankind, and therewith a comprehensive "order"; a salvation of all relationships' (TWNT, II, pp. 413f.).

Jesus Christ He intervened and brought about a new state of affairs which may be designated 'peace'. It includes a great deal more than a cessation of hostility, as we have seen; but it does include this. Indeed, it may be regarded as fundamental to the other blessings included in the conception that there is no longer enmity between God and man, that a state of peace exists between God and His creation, and that accordingly His will to bless operates unhindered.

We have seen that there are some passages in which this thought of peace is connected explicitly with the atonement wrought by Christ, and such a connection must be postulated for an understanding of the passages where it is not expressed. For, on the one hand, nothing that man can do can effect this result. And, on the other, something must be done if a state of peace is to come about. The Scripture insists upon the seriousness of sin as separating man from God, and never gives countenance to any such thought as that man will one day simply drift into the kingdom of God, forgiven because God is like that. It is only because God in Christ took the initiative that peace could possibly come into existence.

V. THE NEW TESTAMENT CONCEPT OF RECONCILIATION

Such is the evidence upon which we must base our doctrine, and the conclusions which have in fact been drawn from it are diverse. On the one hand we find many who insist that the Scriptures which speak of God reconciling man to Himself are the significant ones, and that reconciliation takes place when man recognizes his sinfulness and the greatness of God's love. On the other hand there are those who insist upon the objective nature of the atonement, and stress the demands of the holiness of God, of the righteousness of God, and who refuse to dismiss from the consideration of this subject the passages which speak, for example, of the wrath of God.

Perhaps none have argued more fervently for the former position than Dr. Oman, who is insistent that God does not need to be reconciled to us. 'To be reconciled is to be forgiven, and to be forgiven is to be reconciled, yet Christ's whole manifestation of the Father depends on putting reconciliation first in our thoughts. We are not reconciled when, upon conditions, God has forgiven us, but we are forgiven when we know that He is waiting to be gracious. No word of religious insight says we need to beseech God to be reconciled to us'.[1] The same writer puts emphasis upon reconciliation as a factor in life here and now, as reconciliation to one's lot. 'As enmity against God is primarily enmity against the lives He has appointed for us, because we insist on using them for other ends than His, so reconciliation to God is primarily reconciliation to our lives by seeking in them only His ends. Its immediate significance is *reconciliation to the discipline He appoints and the duty He demands*. It is thus, in the first place at least, concerned with this life, not another, being the promise of sitting in the heavenly places amid the tumult of the present hour and not of sitting in a remote heaven in a passionless eternity' (italics Oman's).[2] He defines reconciliation: 'Reconciliation to God may be defined as a recognition of God's gracious relation to us through blessedness in our use of the world, our dealings with our fellow-men and our loyalty to His Kingdom'.[3]

We admire the learning and sincerity with which Dr. Oman argues his case, and agree that his contention that God's grace is primary in the manner of reconciliation is essentially right. But when full allowance has been made for all this we must beg leave to doubt whether justice is being done to all the scriptural teaching on the subject, and in particular to that aspect of reconciliation which connects it with the death of the Son of God. On Dr. Oman's view it is hard to see why Christ need have died at all, for all that is necessary is 'a recognition of God's gracious relation to us'. But the Scripture seems insistent that on Calvary something was done which has effects quite outside man. In other words all those passages which indicate an objective atonement cry out for explanation, and on the view we are considering they find none.[4]

---

[1] *Grace and Personality*, p. 217.

[2] *Op. cit.*, pp. 118f.

[3] *Op. cit.*, p. 121.

[4] Vincent Taylor objects to 'the view that reconciliation depends upon man's humble acceptance of the revelation of God made in Christ', saying: 'The real gravamen of the charge is that the attempt to say what the love of Christ does, as distinct from what it reveals, is largely abandoned. Attention is concentrated upon the psychology of man's response to that which, happily he has observed, rather than upon a work of God in Christ which is wrought on his behalf' (*Forgiveness and Reconciliation*, London, 1946, p. 108).

In the last resort everything depends upon the situation we conceive to result as a consequence of man's sin. If all that sin means is
that man has wandered away from God, but that he may one day
wander back again with nothing to consider other than his own
situation and desires, then such views as the one we have been
considering are adequate. But if man has come under condemnation so that the sentence of God is against him, then more is
required than repentance if man's rightful relationship to God is to
be restored. If God's attitude to sin is expressed in condemnation
then God's attitude is involved in reconciliation, for reconciliation cannot come about independently of that condemnation.[1]

Our next point might be introduced by a quotation from James
Denney, who makes it clear that reconciliation of the type we
have been advocating does not carry with it the rider that it was
won in the face of God's opposition; rather, it comes from Him
and is entirely due to His desire to bless us. Denney says: 'He is
not reconciled in the sense that something is won from Him for
us against His will, but in the sense that His will to bless us is
realized, as it was not before, on the basis of what Christ has done,
and of our appropriation of it'.[2] James Stewart notices this
statement and comments: 'But is this not using the language of
reconciliation in two distinct meanings? Surely what happens on
God's side is so essentially different from what happens on man's
side that to apply the one term to both can only cause confusion.'[3]
To the present writer it seems that, paradoxically, there is truth in
both these statements. Denney's statement seems to be correct, for
as we have endeavoured to make clear in the foregoing sections,
reconciliation in the Scripture seems to depend on more than
man's response to God's gracious invitation. Reconciliation
matters to God as well as to man, and, as Denney says, 'His will
to bless us is realized, as it was not before'. Nevertheless one must
sympathize with Stewart's difficulty, and it is possible that it
brings to a head much of the objection to such a view of reconciliation as that advocated by Denney. Denney does not say that

---

[1] 'The thing that has to be dealt with, that has to be overcome, in the work of
reconciliation, is not man's distrust of God, but God's condemnation of man'
(J. Denney, *Studies in Theology*, p. 103).
[2] *The Christian Doctrine of Reconciliation*, London, 1917, p. 238.
[3] *A Man in Christ*, London, 1947, pp. 221f.

reconciliation means the same thing to God as it does to man, and this would probably be admitted to be the truth by most folk who hold views similar to his. Certainly the present writer is of the opinion that the change which takes place in man is not the same as the change in God. There are unworthy elements in man's most perfect action which are absent from anything that God does; and in any case the situations are different. Man has departed from God by his sin, and erected the barrier which separates the two. The fault for the estrangement lies wholly on man's side. Thus, when reconciliation takes place, there are elements of penitence on man's side, there is a complete change of attitude; and these have no parallel from God's side.

Moreover, there is the fact that reconciliation in the case of man comes about from outside. God was reconciling the world to Himself. But we cannot say that God was reconciled by any third party; rather He must be thought of as reconciling Himself. Even to say that Christ reconciled God does not give us the true picture; for it suggests a disharmony in the Godhead and also raises a doubt as to the constancy of God's love. But we must insist that God's love for us remained unchanged throughout the process of reconciliation. P. T. Forsyth draws a distinction between 'a change of feeling and a change of treatment', and he goes on to say, 'God's feeling toward us never needed to be changed. But God's treatment of us, God's practical relation to us—that had to change'.[1] The distinction is important. God's love never varied. But the atonement wrought by Christ means that men are no longer treated as enemies (as their sin deserves), but as friends. God has reconciled Himself.

Thus we may speak of God as being reconciled. It may be necessary, indeed it is necessary, to use the term carefully, when we apply it to God. But then does not this happen with all our language? We must face the position that whenever we talk about God we must do so in language devised to describe man, and accordingly there must be a certain reservation in what we say about Him. This applies to reconciliation as well as to other

---

[1] *The Work of Christ*, London, 1948, p. 105. In another place he says: 'The Cross means more change in God than in man. . . . Real and thorough religion is theocentric more than anthropocentric' (*The Justification of God*, London, 1948, p. 37).

terms. When we say that God can be thought of as reconciled to man, that does not mean that, with various imperfections, He alters completely His attitude to man. Rather it is our groping way of expressing our conviction that He reacts in the strongest possible way against sin in every shape and form, and that man comes under His condemnation accordingly; but that when reconciliation is effected, when peace is made between man and God, then that condemnation is removed and God looks on man no longer as the object of His holy and righteous wrath, but as the object of His love and His blessing.

We must not overlook the fact that the relationship between God and man is a mutual affair. Some write as though man were the only factor affecting the position. After they have said 'God is love' there is no longer need to pay attention to the Deity, and all their attention is focussed upon what man does.[1] Reconciliation becomes then the change in man's attitude to God and that is all. But as A. E. Garvie says: 'When it is said that man is reconciled to God, and not God to man, what is ignored is that the relation of God and man is mutual, and involves a moral reciprocity. We may once for all dismiss as contemptible the current caricatures of evangelical theology that it represents God as implacable and vindictive, when it simply insists that moral perfection cannot be indifferent to moral differences in man, and must condemn sin even as it approves righteousness. This condemnation must be conveyed to and approved by the conscience of the forgiven in the very act of forgiveness'.[2] It is impossible to bow God out of His universe, and to maintain that He is indifferent to the moral condition of His people. His love is consistent and does not alter; but we cannot reason from that that the expression of that love is

---

[1] Cf. W. Milligan's comment on sacrifice and reconciliation: 'The leading or central idea of sacrifice was not mere pardon of sin, or atonement, or the procuring of the Divine favour, by which the relation of only one of the two parties to the other—that of God to His creature—was affected; while the love of God, contemplated by faith, was simply left to work as a motive of gratitude upon the heart. The relation of both parties to one another was involved in the Sacrifice itself. That act expressed all that was implied alike for God and Israel in the restoration of the covenant. It brought both back into a state of mutual reconciliation and fellowship' (*The Resurrection of Our Lord*, London, 1884, p. 276).

[2] *A Handbook of Christian Apologetics*, London, 1913, p. 121.

always the same. Love may be likened to a flame; it may give warmth and light, or it may sear and burn without changing its own essential nature. When men continue in sins all that they can see of a holy God is that aspect that they call the wrath of God. But when the Son of God Himself has borne that aspect, then men may know the warmth of His love. We do not impugn the consistency of God, but we insist that the relation between God and man is a mutual one, and that this must be borne in mind in estimating the biblical doctrine of reconciliation.[1]

A further point is that no true reconciliation can take place unless the cause of the estrangement is truly faced and dealt with. If it is ignored or glossed over, then a species of uneasy truce may result, but there can be no real restoration of fellowship, no true reconciliation. As Dr. H. Maldwyn Hughes says: 'there can be no reconciliation between persons by ignoring the deep-seated ground of offence. This must be eradicated and destroyed if the reconciliation is to be complete and lasting. If God and man are to be reconciled, it cannot be by the simple expedient of ignoring sin, but only by overcoming it'.[2] It is the consistent teaching of Scripture that man could not overcome the cause of the enmity. The barrier which the sin of man had erected the wit of man could not find means to remove. But in the death of Him who was 'made sin' for man the cause of the enmity was squarely faced and removed. Therefore a complete reconciliation results, so that man turns to God in repentance and trust, and God looks on man with favour and not in wrath.

We maintain, therefore, that there is no good reason for rejecting the conclusion to which the biblical evidence points,

---

[1] Cf. P. T. Forsyth: 'Our reconciliation is between person and person. It is not between an order or a process on the one hand and a person on the other. Therefore a real and deep change of the relation between the two means a change on both sides. That is surely clear if we are dealing with living persons. . . . Any reconciliation which only means change on one side is not a real reconciliation at all' (The Work of Christ, London, 1948, p. 75). Or H. Maldwyn Hughes: 'What the Atonement achieves is a change in the relation of persons, and no such change can be brought to pass without both parties being affected. Reconciliation is necessarily twofold . . . when God reconciles us to Himself, our relation to Him, and His relation to us are both put on a new basis' (What is the Atonement? London, n.d., pp. 20f.).

[2] Op. cit., p. 146.

namely, that reconciliation includes what we must call a change
on the part of God as well as on the part of man, since the wrath
of God is no longer directed towards man. We may well sum up
the position in the words of D. W. Simon, who says: 'Taking the
Pauline language in its natural sense, there is no evading the
recognition of three points—*first*, that a change—call it by any
name that may be liked—was brought about in the relation of
man to God; *secondly*, that this change was due to the intervention
of Christ; and, *thirdly*, that God Himself was the originator of
what may be anthropomorphically termed the plan or method,
by which the change in Himself and in man was brought about
and justified'.[1]

VI. RECONCILIATION AND SUBSTITUTION

Throughout this discussion substitution has been very much in
the background, for the very good reason that reconciliation has
in itself no very close connection with substitution. Reconciliation has to do with the bringing about of harmonious relations
where these did not exist before, and the metaphor directs
attention to an estrangement and to the overcoming of that
estrangement. The metaphor in itself is concerned only with
these things.

But in the particular manner in which the estrangement is
overcome it is possible that substitution may occur. In the particular case of the atonement the root cause of the estrangement is
man's sin; so long as that sin is there harmony with God is
impossible. Accordingly reconciliation proceeds by doing away
with sin, and the method of doing this was by the atoning death of
Christ. Whatever may be the case with other acts of reconciliation
Scripture is clear that the reconciliation between God and man
could be brought about only by the death of the Son of God.
Accordingly we may discern a substitutionary element, for as
Büchsel says 'The reconciliation comes into existence through the
death of Jesus (Rom. v. 10), which here obviously not only
benefits us, (being) a revelation of the love of God (Rom. v. 8),
but is a substitution for us (2 Cor. v. 20, 14f.).'[2]

---

[1] *The Redemption of Man*, London, 1906, pp. 271f.
[2] TWNT, I, p. 258.

JUSTIFICATION (1)

I. INTRODUCTION

THE first impression one receives on turning to the subject of justification after dealing with the conceptions already treated is of the abundance of the material to be considered. We have noted that propitiation, although an important conception, is alluded to with reference to the atonement only four times in all in the New Testament. Similarly reconciliation, in which some modern scholars are inclined to see the essential New Testament teaching with regard to the atonement, occurs only in five passages, all of them Pauline. By contrast, he who would expound justification is confronted with eighty-one occurrences of the adjective δίκαιος, ninety-two of the noun δικαιοσύνη, two of the noun δικαίωσις, thirty-nine of the verb δικαιόω, ten of the noun δικαίωμα, and five of the adverb δικαίως. On examination much of this may prove to have little relevance to the atonement, but it remains that the bare enumeration of the number of passages to be considered indicates that we are here dealing with a conception of great importance for the evaluation of the atonement. The tendency in some quarters to disparage the importance of justification in comparison with one or other of the alternative ways of looking at God's great work for men is not one which is reflected in our sources. Particularly is this true of St. Paul who uses the conception so frequently that we are compelled to think that for him it was a dominant idea.

The derivation of the root from which these words are derived is shrouded in obscurity. A number of suggestions have been made. One which has attracted a good deal of support is that which sees the basic idea in custom, habit, from which it is thought the conception of conformity to established law might well evolve. Again, some have thought that the root derives from δικεῖν, and that smiting with the judge's staff is the original idea. Another suggestion derives the idea from the throwing of the sacred lot; and there are others. The whole subject is so obscure that no suggested derivation can be said to be secure or even probable.

What does emerge from the discussion is that the two meanings of 'custom' and 'right' seem to go back as far as we can trace the words. Accordingly, if our endeavour is simply to find out what the word group meant in New Testament times, the search for the original root meaning is largely academic; for centuries these two ideas had been conveyed by the words in question. At least this is clear for δίκη, which is possibly the basic word of the group, though it is not possible to authenticate it for all the members. But as used in the first century there does seem to be a flavour of 'rightness', of 'justness' about these words. They do not indicate something arbitrary, but something in conformity with some standard of right. The righteous man is one who is adjudged right by such a standard, and righteousness indicates a state of having attained to the standard in question.

It is necessary to say a word or two more about the verb δικαιόω which in the New Testament is translated 'to justify' but which has been understood in more ways than one. Since verbs in -όω commonly express a causative idea it is urged by some that δικαιόω must mean 'to make righteous'. But it is to be noted in the first place that verbs of this class denoting moral qualities do not have the causative meaning (e.g. ἀξιόω means 'to deem worthy' not 'to make worthy' and similarly with ὁμοιόω ὁσιόω, etc.), and in the second, that in any case the meaning of a word is to be determined in the last resort by the way people used it. We cannot at this distance in time say that, since a verb is formed in such and such a fashion, therefore the Greeks must have understood it to mean so and so; all that we can do is to note how they did in fact use it, and deduce from that what it meant to them. And by this test δικαιόω certainly does not mean 'to make righteous'. In Greek literature generally it seems to mean 'to hold as right', 'to deem right', and thence 'to claim or demand as a right', and 'to do a man right or justice', which latter was commonly taken to mean 'to punish for wickedness' so that, interestingly enough, in many profane contexts the thought is of chastisement, in striking contrast with the use in the Bible. Neither the word structure nor the use of the verb outside the

Bible, then, gives countenance to the idea that 'to make righteous' is the meaning we are to understand.[1]

II. LAW AND JUDGMENT IN THE OLD TESTAMENT

There is a wealth of material awaiting the student of justification in the LXX, for δίκαιος and its cognates occur hundreds of times, and in this treatment it will not be possible to notice even all the important passages. But even if we were to take every occurrence of each of these words and examine it we should not exhaust the material; for the thoughts of right, righteousness, justification and the like are inextricably bound up with other concepts like those of judgment, pleading at law, law itself, and so on. It does not seem possible to overlook such concepts even in a short treatment of the subject for they have the effect of putting justification in its context. It is necessary to realize that justification is not an isolated concept which can be studied *in vacuo*, but part of the general Old Testament view of God and the world which sees in law and all its ramifications a means of understanding the divine ordering of all things. To the Hebrew mind God was a God of law. Herklots even goes as far as to say 'He was *law*'.[2]

The importance of this is seen in such a question as that asked by Abraham: 'Shall not the Judge of all the earth do right?' (Gn. xviii. 25). Here God is designated by the legal term 'Judge'; at the same time the question expresses the certainty that He would act in accordance with moral law. The gods of the heathen could not be depended upon in this way; they reacted in the most capricious fashion. It might be said, indeed, that this difference in the conception of the nature of God was the basic reason for the superiority of Israelite religion to that of the nations round about. Yahweh's actions were always in accordance with ethical laws, and He demanded of His people that they should similarly act in accordance with these laws. If they did not, then this same ethical nature

---

[1] Godet goes so far as to say: 'As to δικαιόω, there is not an example in the whole of classic literature where it signifies: *to make just*' (*Romans*, I, p. 157), and Morison (*Critical Exposition of Romans Third*, London, 1866, pp. 179, 183) and Plummer (*St. Luke*, I.C.C., p. 208) have similar statements.

[2] *A Fresh Approach to the New Testament*, London, 1950, p. 18 (Herklots's italics), and cf. the remark of P. T. Forsyth: 'The holy law is not the creation of God but His nature' (*The Atonement in Modern Religious Thought. A Theological Symposium*, London, 1903, p. 69).

of Yahweh demanded that He should punish them. The wrath of God was inevitably extended towards all sin, and the Hebrew could depend upon this also. Thus Jeremiah says, 'Yea, the stork in the heaven knoweth her appointed times; and the turtle and the swallow and the crane observe the time of their coming; but my people know not the judgement (*mshpt*) of the Lord' (Je. viii. 7, R.V. mg.). Judgment is as natural to the Lord as the movements of the birds are to them.

That judgment is connected with justification is attested by the large number of passages which connect one or other of the judgment words with one of the words of the righteousness group. Thus the two conceptions are very closely linked in the prayer of the psalmist: 'Enter not into judgement with thy servant; for in thy sight shall no man living be justified' (Ps. cxliii. 2); and a decisive passage occurs in Deuteronomy: 'If there be a controversy between men, and they come unto judgement, and the judges judge them; then they shall justify the righteous, and condemn the wicked' (Dt. xxv. 1). There is an air of the law-court about Is. l. 8: 'He is near that justifieth me; who will contend (*yaribh*) with me? let us stand up together: who is mine adversary?' From another point of view we are told that 'the thoughts of the righteous are judgement (*mishpat*)' (Pr. xii. 5). Similar passages could be adduced in great numbers, and even then the whole story would not have been told, for passages like Zc. viii. 16f. clearly regard judgment as an integral part of righteousness, although none of the righteousness words actually occurs in the passage. From such considerations as these it is obvious that the whole question of righteousness is bound up with legal conceptions, and some study of the latter must accordingly be attempted.

The word which leaps to the mind when one speaks of law in the Old Testament is *torah*, which BDB define as 'direction, instruction, law'. Whether we take this word to denote primarily 'law' or, as probably most modern scholars would take it, as 'instruction', it is not in dispute that its content is closely associated with Yahweh. Thus in more than eighty of the 220 places in which the word occurs it is expressly said to be His ('the law of Yahweh', 'my law', 'thy law', etc.), sixteen times it is ascribed to Moses, which, in view of the uniform scriptural view that Moses received the law from God, amounts to much the same thing, and in most other places it seems to be implied that the *torah* is from the Lord. In fact I have been able to find only seventeen places where it seems clear that the word is used of something other than of a law from God.[1]

Striking also is the association of words from the root *hqq* with Yahweh, who is spoken of as 'our lawgiver' (Is. xxxiii. 22), a significant appellation. There are two words for 'statute', *hoq* being connected with Yahweh in eighty-seven of its 127 occurrences and *huqqah* in no less than ninety-six out of 104. It is clear that Yahweh was thought of as a God with a deep interest in law. Perhaps we might single out as specially interesting, passages in which the phenomena of nature are said to be governed by a statute of the Lord who makes 'a statute for the rain' (Jb. xxviii. 26) and an 'everlasting statute' (Je. v. 22) which governs the limits of the sea. From such ordinances as these Jeremiah is able to reason to the continuing mercy of the Lord towards Israel (Je. xxxi. 36) which seems to imply that law is of the very essence of the Lord's working. Law is not simply a demand which He makes on Israel; it is the essential way in which He Himself administers His universe and He can be relied upon to act according to law.

Very much to the point is the use of the root *shpt*. The verb *shaphat* is used of divine activity over sixty times. Especially interesting is the use of the participle to denote the Lord as Judge, as for example Ps. l. 6, 'And the heavens shall declare his righteousness; for God is judge himself'. The concluding part of Jephthah's message to the children of Ammon, 'the Lord, the Judge, be judge this day between the children of Israel and the children of Ammon' (Jdg. xi. 27), might be held to imply that the Lord was thought of as Judge over all peoples and not simply over Israel: at any rate it extends His judicial functions beyond the bounds of His own people. *mishpat* occurs about 180 times in connection with Yahweh, frequently in the sense of 'laws', in which connection it differs little from the law words we have already

---

[1] It is often pointed out that *torah* is used of priestly instruction, and passages like Je. ii. 8, xviii. 18; Ezk. vii. 26; Ho. iv. 6; Hg. ii. 11; Mal. ii. 6, 7, 8, 9, are pointed out. But I have not thought it worth while to go deeply into these passages, for even though a priestly *torah* seems to have been recognized, it was held to be due, not to the priests themselves, but to the Lord, as we see from Ho. iv. 6 and the Malachi passage.

considered.[1] It is also used in a more general sense, sometimes in conjunction with the righteousness words as in Ps. xxxvi. 6, 'Thy righteousness is like the mountains of God; thy judgements are a great deep'; or again in Je. ix. 24, 'I am the Lord which exercise lovingkindness, judgement, and righteousness, in the earth: for in these things I delight, saith the Lord', where judgment and righteousness seem to be part of the essential nature of the Lord.

In line with this He is often pictured as engaging in legal action as in the impressive opening to Is. xli. 1, 'Keep silence before me, O islands; and let the peoples renew their strength: let them come near; then let them speak: let us come near together to judgement'. Such passages certainly have a strongly figurative aspect, but it seems also that they indicate that Yahweh is ready to deal with people on the basis of law and equity. It is in accordance with this outlook that Job can desire to plead, as in a court, before the Lord (Jb. xxiii. 3, 4), and Jeremiah can say 'Righteous are thou, O Lord, when I plead with thee: yet would I reason the cause with thee (R.V. mg. "speak judgements")' (Je. xii. 1). Although we sometimes come across statements like 'For he is not a man, as I am, that I should answer him, that we should come together in judgement' (Jb. ix. 32), yet these are but ways of making plain the immense gulf between God and man, and do not interfere with the principle that God's ways are not completely unpredictable, for He delights in law and judgment. This interest in law is to be discerned also in the fact that He requires judgment in men as we see from many passages (e.g. Ps. xxxiii. 5; Pr. xxi. 3; Is. v. 7, lvi. 1), and also in the repeated prediction of an eschatological judgment (e.g. Is. xxxii. 1; Je. xxiii. 5, xxxiii. 15). This latter point reminds us that judgment is not thought of as a temporary accommodation to man's present position, but it endures to the end of time.

There are some interesting passages in which the shephaṭim of the Lord are referred to, as when Yahweh says, 'I will lay my hand upon Egypt, and bring forth my hosts, my people the children of Israel, out of the land of Egypt by great judgements'

---

[1] Snaith distinguishes between torah and mishpaṭ. 'They are different in that torah, at this early state, meant an original pronouncement, whilst mishpaṭ meant a decision according to precedent. But both are equally the word of God' (The Distinctive Ideas of the Old Testament, London, 1944, p. 75).

(Ex. vii. 4), where the mighty power of the Lord is not thought of as a display of power as such but as an exercise of judgment. All is in accordance with law.

This idea is sometimes brought out by words from the root *ykh* as in Mi. iv. 3 'and he shall judge between many peoples, and shall reprove strong nations afar off', or Is. xi. 4 (cf. the 'daysman' of Jb. ix. 33). Or again *dyn* is used in this connection as in Ps. vii. 8f., a beautifully trustful appeal to the Lord as Judge, an appeal based on the fact that the Judge is 'the righteous God'. It is because the nature of God is such as to vindicate righteousness that the psalmist can be so confident.

Sometimes we find the very atmosphere of the lawcourt, as when Isaiah says: 'The Lord standeth up to plead, and standeth to judge the peoples. The Lord will enter into judgement with the elders of his people, etc.' (Is. iii. 13). This is clear, too, in Ps. ix. 7f.: 'But the Lord sitteth for ever: He hath prepared his throne for judgement. And he shall judge the world in righteousness, he shall minister judgement to the peoples in uprightness'. Such passages argue a congruity of the divine method with legal processes, and perhaps we could come to the same conclusion from a consideration of the passages where this verb indicates that the Lord requires men to exercise judgment as part of their service of Him.

The legal aspect of Yahweh's dealings with men is stressed by the use of *ribh*, which means 'strive, contend' and thence 'conduct a lawsuit'. It is often used of disputes between men, as between Jacob and Laban (Gn. xxxi. 36), or between Nehemiah and his fellow-countrymen (Ne. v. 7, xiii. 11, 17, 25). When applied to the dealings of Yahweh with men it is used both of His intervention on their behalf and of His bringing accusations against them. Under the former heading we might note David's ejaculation, 'Blessed be the Lord, that hath pleaded the cause of my reproach from the hand of Nabal' (1 Sa. xxv. 39); or the word of the Lord to Jeremiah concerning the oppressed Israelites, 'Their redeemer is strong; the Lord of hosts is his name: he shall throughly plead their cause' (Je. l. 34); or again, a very good example is the saying of the servant in Is. l. 8, 'He is near that justifieth me; who will contend with me? let us stand up together: who is mine adversary?', for here we have an unmistakable connection between the legal process and justification.

On the other hand we notice the statement in Jeremiah, 'Wherefore I will yet plead with you, saith the Lord, and with your children's children will I plead' (Je. ii. 9), and the passage goes on to give the grounds of Yahweh's indictment of the nation. Later in the same chapter we have 'Wherefore will ye plead with me? ye all have transgressed against me, saith the Lord' (verse 29), where again the essential rightness of the Lord's ways is implied. There can be no possible hope of a plea succeeding when it is attended by sin. Because God's pleading is always concerning sin in man there is often a note of condemnation in the use of this verb as the helplessness of sinful man in the face of a God whose laws are perfectly righteous is emphasized. 'Woe to him that striveth (or pleadeth) with his maker!' (Is. xlv. 9) cries the prophet; but even here there is a note of hope for again he gives the word of God as 'For I will not contend for ever, neither will I be always wroth' (Is. lvii. 16), a saying which indicates the close connection between Yahweh's pleading and His wrath, and which also indicates something of His mercy.

From the same stem we get the noun *ribh* 'strife, dispute', used especially in the sense 'controversy, dispute at law'. It is used in two senses in the same way as the verb, namely, in controversies where Yahweh takes the side of men, vindicating them, and in controversies where He opposes them, condemning their sin. Very majestic is the legal scene depicted by Micah: 'Hear ye now what the Lord saith: Arise, contend thou before the mountains, and let the hills hear thy voice. Hear, O ye mountains, the Lord's controversy, and ye enduring foundations of the earth: for the Lord hath a controversy with his people, and he will plead with Israel' (Mi. vi. 1f.). Here the controversy is between the Lord and His people; but sometimes it is with the heathen (as in Is. xli. 21), or with the whole earth, 'A noise shall come even to the end of the earth; for the Lord hath a controversy with the nations, he will plead with all flesh' (Je. xxv. 31). Even allowing for the element of imagery which undoubtedly inheres in such passages the conclusion seems to be established that the Lord deals with the peoples, and especially with His own people, according to law. He has laid down righteous statutes, and by these will men be judged.

Nor is the story complete when we have considered the technical legal terms. There are verbs like *shlm* which have in themselves no necessary forensic significance and which, in their sense of 'requite, reward, recompense', yet convey a not very different meaning. Thus when Adoni-bezek says, 'as I have done, so God hath requited me' (Jdg. i. 7), he is clearly implying that he has been judged by God and dealt with accordingly. This thought is carried farther by Jeremiah, who tells us that 'the Lord is a God of recompences (*'el gemuloth*), he shall surely requite' (Je. li. 56), for here the idea of recompensing for evil is carried into the very nature of God, which is possibly the case also with 2 Sa. iii. 39, although it is likely that this verse is to be taken as a prayer with R.V. The general principle is stated in Ps. lxii. 12, 'For thou renderest to every man according to his work', and many passages could be cited showing how this operates, both in rewarding the good, and punishing the evil.

Other words could be dealt with such as *pqd* which is often used in the sense of visiting with a view to requiting, or *gml* which has been quoted once above, but there seems little point in multiplying examples. Enough has been said to show that the concept of law is a far-reaching one in the Old Testament.

But we cannot leave this section without noting that covenant is a legal conception and, as we noted in the chapter on that subject, is the characteristic way of viewing the relationship between God and His people. It was that which gave Israel its legal standing in the eyes of God. A legal basis is inherent in the very nature of covenant (cf. Jos. xxiv. 25), and often this comes to the surface, for example in 1 Ch. xvi. 17 (=Ps. cv. 10), 'And confirmed the same unto Jacob for a statute, to Israel for an everlasting covenant' where the parallelism makes 'statute' very nearly the same thing as 'covenant'. Or, again, Jeremiah applies the concept of law in nature to illustrate covenant: 'Thus saith the Lord: If my covenant of day and night stand not, if I have not appointed the ordinances of heaven and earth; then will I also cast away the seed of Jacob, etc.' (Je. xxxiii. 25f.). Here the orderly movement of day and night is spoken of as itself due to a covenant with the Lord, thus equating covenant and law; then this is applied to show the permanence of the covenant with the nation.

From this brief examination it seems quite clear that the Old Testament consistently thinks of a God who works by the method of law. This is not the conception of one or two writers but is found everywhere in the Old Testament, and is attested by a variety of conceptions, many of them taken straight from forensic practices. Among the heathen the deity was thought of as above all law, with nothing but the dictates of his own desires to limit him. Accordingly his behaviour was completely unpredictable, and while he made demands on his worshippers for obedience and service, there were few if any ethical implications of this service and none of a logically necessary kind. Far otherwise was it with the God of the Hebrews. The Old Testament does not conceive of anything outside Him which could direct His actions, and we must be on our guard against the thought of a law which was over Him. But Yahweh was thought of as essentially righteous in His nature, as incorporating the law of righteousness within His essential Being. Accordingly He works by a method which may be called law—He inevitably punishes evil-doing and rewards righteousness. He himself acts righteously, and He demands that His people do the same. This is the consistent teaching of the Old Testament. As Quell says, 'That God lays down the right and as a righteous God is bound to right means for Old Testament piety with all its variation, a proposition which may not be surrendered'.[1] Thus, as we approach the question of the use of justification in the Old Testament, we are not dealing with an isolated conception which appears briefly now and then, but with an idea of law which runs through and through the ancient Scriptures.

III. THE δίκαιος WORD GROUP IN THE SEPTUAGINT

It must be borne in mind that in both Hebrew and Greek 'justification' and words like 'righteous', 'righteousness', etc., come from the same root (which fact in itself shows the essentially forensic meaning of the word group), so that our net must be widely cast. So frequent are these words that it will not be possible in a brief examination to do more than glance at a few passages. But we trust that these are representative.

a. Justification
The basic significance of the Hebrew root tsdq, from which the righteousness and justification words take their origin, has been the

[1] TWNT, II, p. 178.

cause of much discussion, the derivations receiving most support being those which see the essential idea in the notions of hardness and straightness. We cannot here enter into a discussion of the merits of the various suggestions put forward, and can only lay it down that such considerations as those adduced by Snaith[1] seem to indicate that the latter is the idea to be preferred, and that the word group points us to the thought of a standard. '*Tsedeq*, with its kindred words, signifies that standard which God maintains in this world. It is the norm by which all must be judged. What this norm is, depends entirely upon the Nature of God'.[2] If this is so, then the idea of righteousness is conformity to God's standard, and justification will be a process in which this conformity is either attained, or declared to be attained.

When we turn to those passages where the verb 'to justify' occurs, there can be no doubt that the meaning is to declare rather than to make righteous. Thus in Dt. xxv. 1 we find a direction that the judges 'shall justify the righteous, and condemn the wicked', where the forensic background is unmistakable and the verb can only mean 'to declare righteous' or 'to acquit'. The same usage is seen in Ex. xxiii. 7, 'I will not justify the wicked', and in Is. v. 23 with its woe to them that 'justify the wicked for reward', while the legal content of the term is brought out from another angle when we read, 'let them bring forth their witnesses that they may be justified' (Is. xliii. 9), where legal proof based on the testimony of witnesses is the ground for justification.

These are typical passages, and although there are places where the forensic note is not so strong they do not invalidate our conviction that the basic idea is one of acquittal. Both in Hebrew and Greek the verb in question is capable of being used in a variety of non-legal contexts, quite like our verb 'to judge'. But again, like this verb, the Hebrew and Greek verbs in question remind us of processes of law, and take their essential meaning from those processes of law. That a declaratory process rather than a making righteous is meant is clear from the fact that the verb is applied to Jehovah (Ps. li. 4), for it is an impossible thought that He should be 'made righteous' in any sense other than 'made righteous before men' or 'declared righteous'.

[1] *Op. cit.*, pp. 72ff.
[2] *Op. cit.*, p. 77.

Finally, let us notice the important words of the psalmist: 'enter not into judgement with thy servant: for in thy sight shall no man living be justified' (Ps. cxliii. 2). Here we are face to face with the ultimate question in religion, and the conclusion is that it is impossible for any man to have confidence in his standing before God on the grounds of his deeds.

b. The righteousness of men

When we turn to the noun and the adjective from this root we find the same essentially forensic significance. The righteous are those acquitted at the bar of God's justice, and righteousness is the standing of those so acquitted. Thus Skinner explains his view that in the Old Testament 'the forensic element preponderates' in the idea of righteousness by saying: 'what is meant is that questions of right and wrong were habitually regarded from a legal point of view as matters to be settled by a judge, and that this point of view is emphasized in the words derived from *tsdq*. This, indeed, is characteristic of the Hebrew conception of righteousness in all its developments: whether it be a moral quality or a religious status, it is apt to be looked on as in itself controvertible and incomplete until it has been confirmed by what is equivalent to a judicial sentence'.[1] The Hebrew concept is not grasped by making a facile equation with the Greek δικαιοσύνη or the English 'righteousness'; it is not an ethical term, but a religious. It takes its origin in the forensic sphere and makes its home in the law of God.

The forensic background to the concept is seen clearly in such a passage as Is. v. 23, which pronounces a woe upon them that 'take away the righteousness of the righteous from him', for obviously a moral quality cannot be taken away from a man. What is meant is that wicked judges will, for the sake of gain, give the verdict to the wrong party, thus depriving the innocent of the status of acquittal which is his due. This is the sin which is described in Pr. xvii. 15 as 'condemning the just' (or righteous), while in Pr. xxiv. 23f., saying to the wicked 'Thou art righteous' is apparently an illustration of the saying, 'It is not good to have respect to persons in judgment'. An instructive passage along similar lines is Dt. xvi. 18-20, where words from the *tsdq* root ('just', 'righteous')

---

[1] HDB, IV, p. 273.

are freely intermingled with legal terms ('judges', 'judgement', etc.).

Such intermingling is far from being rare, and indeed 'to do judgement and justice' is by way of being a stock Old Testament phrase, while we also find references like that to 'violent perverting of judgement and justice' in Ec. v. 8. In the same category we must place Amos's impassioned plea, 'Let judgement run down as waters, and righteousness as a mighty stream' (Am. v. 24).

The forensic use of words from this root is often found in the book of Job, as when the patriarch says: 'Behold now, I have ordered my cause; I know that I shall be justified' (Jb. xiii. 18), where he can mean only that he will be declared righteous, as by a judge giving sentence in a lawsuit. So, also, when the Lord says to Job, 'Wilt thou also disannul my judgement? wilt thou condemn me, that thou mayest be righteous?' (Jb. xl. 8), the forensic note of the passage and the opposition of condemning to being right-eous shows that 'righteous' here means something very like 'declared righteous legally'. It is this which gives us the back-ground against which we must understand the question thrice repeated with slight changes: 'How should man be just with God?' (Jb. ix. 2, and see xv. 14, xxv. 4). In each case it is standing with the Lord that is in question, and the implication is that man is completely unable of himself to attain such right standing.

It is, of course, true that 'righteous' comes to have an ethical meaning and in many passages this is to be stressed. But this meaning develops naturally out of the forensic idea and we need not doubt that the legal idea is the basic one.

c. The righteousness of God

The Old Testament consistently thinks of Jehovah as a just (or righteous) God, and for example He is depicted often as a Judge: 'the heavens shall declare his righteousness: for God is judge him-self' (Ps. l. 6); 'he cometh to judge the earth: he shall judge the world with righteousness' (Ps. xcvi. 13); 'the Lord of hosts shall be exalted in judgement' (Is. v. 16), and many another passage. It is clear that the men of the Old Testament delighted to view God in His capacity as Judge.

An interesting insight into the way these men viewed their God is to be found in an expression in the Song of Deborah. With reference to recalling the great deliverance wrought by the Lord the singer says: 'there shall they rehearse the righteous acts (mg. righteousnesses) of the Lord' (Jdg. v. 11). The actions in question were displays of power, but the thing which appealed to the Hebrew mind was that they were not simply displays of power, but evidence of the righteous nature of their God. 'The righteous Lord loveth righteousness' (Ps. xi. 7). Nor is this regarded as a temporary manifestation, but as a permanent element in God, for the prophet gives the word of the Lord as: 'my righteousness shall not be abolished . . . my righteousness shall be for ever' (Is. li. 6, 8).

Implied in the thought that God is the righteous Judge is the idea that He demands right living on the part of men, and this is expressed so often in the Old Testament that it is superfluous to make quotations to prove it. It is fundamental that the Lord has set His law before men and that He expects them to walk therein.

A very interesting feature of Old Testament teaching on the righteousness of God is the fact that it is often linked up with salvation, as when the psalmist says: 'The Lord hath made known his salvation: his righteousness hath he openly showed' (Ps. xcviii. 2), or when the prophet gives the words of the Lord: 'my salvation shall be for ever, and my righteousness shall not be abolished' (Is. li. 6). This connection is met with sufficiently often for us to think that it is not accidental; righteousness included a salvation aspect. But it is always a salvation in accordance with ethical laws, a salvation which accords with righteousness. It is a deliverance of the people of God, who are proper objects of such deliverance just because they are the people of God. In passing we note that this is not the same as the New Testament teaching on the righteousness of God. There we have the different thought that 'the righteousness of God' brings salvation (and salvation in a fuller sense) to sinners.[1]

d. Imputed Righteousness

In view of the importance of the concept of imputed righteousness for New Testament doctrine we must notice its occurrence in the Old Testament, although it cannot be thought of as a leading Old Testament idea. It is found in the case of Abram, who 'believed in the Lord; and he counted it to him for righteousness'

---

[1] See below, pp. 252ff.

(Gn. xv. 6); and Phinehas: 'Then stood up Phinehas, and executed judgement: and so the plague was stayed. And that was counted unto him for righteousness unto all generations for evermore' (Ps. cvi. 30f.). In both cases the meaning would seem to be that the men are brought into right relationship with God: they are given the status of being 'right' with Him. In the case of Phinehas there is an action that is applauded, but the motive was important, as we see from Nu. xxv. 11: 'he was zealous for my sake among them'. These two examples, and especially that of Abram, are important as showing that men might be reckoned as righteous before God on grounds other than that of having lived meritorious lives.

IV. THE PLACE OF FAITH

Since we can hardly think of the New Testament doctrine of justification without adding 'by faith', it is worth our while to inquire whether this has roots in the Old Testament, or whether it was a completely new thought in New Testament times. Certainly Paul did not think he was enunciating an entirely novel doctrine, for he speaks of Abraham as being justified in the same way as Christians of his own day, namely, by faith; and indeed he used the example of that patriarch as a means of showing to men of his day that God has always worked on the principle that men are justified by faith.

First of all we must notice that there is no formal statement of the doctrine in the Old Testament, and if we look for a complete enunciation of this truth we shall be disappointed. For that we must wait until New Testament days. But the essence of the doctrine is there nevertheless. If we understand justification by faith to include this at least, that man is ultimately accepted in the sight of God, not on the grounds of what he himself has accomplished, but on account of the divine mercy shown in forgiving love, there are many passages which may be cited. So, too, if we are seeking an indication that the proper attitude on the part of man is trust in God and not in his own deeds we shall not have far to look.

Thus, as regards acceptance on the grounds of the divine mercy, we might notice Is. lv, where in the first verse we find God's gift represented as completely unearned: 'Ho every one that thirsteth, come ye to the waters, and he that hath no money; come ye, buy, and eat; yea, come, buy wine and milk without money and without price'. When we come to verses 6 and 7 men are clearly accepted on the grounds of God's mercy and not of their deeds: 'Seek ye the Lord while he may be found: call ye upon him while he is near: let the wicked forsake his way, and the unright-eous man his thoughts: and let him return unto the Lord, and he will have mercy upon him; and to our God, for he will abundantly pardon'. Again, Micah can say: 'Who is a God like unto thee, that pardoneth iniquity, and passeth by the transgres-sion of the remnant of his heritage? he retaineth not his anger for ever, because he delighteth in mercy. He will turn again, he will have compassion upon us; he will subdue our iniquities; and thou wilt cast all their sins into the depths of the sea' (Mi. vii. 18f.), while his next verse, 'Thou wilt perform the truth to Jacob, and the mercy to Abraham, which thou hast sworn unto our fathers from the days of old', takes us back to the patriarchal age quite in the manner of St. Paul, as though he would say: 'God deals with men in mercy and has always dealt with them so'.

These are great passages and express great thoughts. We might continue for long without exhausting the supply of such, for the mercy of God is one of the leading conceptions of the Old Testa-ment. It is integral to Israel's faith that the Lord is a God of mercy —'his compassions fail not; they are new every morning' (La. iii. 22f.). Accordingly this merciful nature of God is recognized as man's only hope wherever men are occupied with a profound sense of sin. 'If thou, Lord, shouldest mark iniquities, O Lord, who shall stand? But there is forgiveness with thee . . . . I wait for the Lord, my soul doth wait, and in his word do I hope' (Ps. cxxx. 3–5). So is it with the prayer of Dn. ix, where the sin of the people is stressed (verses 5ff.), but where there is nevertheless an atmo-sphere of hope, for 'to the Lord our God belong mercies and forgivenesses' (verse 9), and 'we do not present our supplications before thee for our righteousnesses, but for thy great mercies' (verse 18).

This conception almost carries with it the other point that man's right attitude to God is one of trust, for if acceptance is due to God's mercy then man obviously cannot rely on what he himself does, and must rest his faith elsewhere. It is this which underlies Hab. ii. 4, 'the just shall live by his faith'. The Hebrew word 'emunah, as Gifford notes,[1] usually conveys the thought of fidelity rather than trust, of 'the faith which may be relied on, rather than the faith which relies'. But, for a Hebrew, faithfulness under difficult circumstances could arise only from reliance on Jehovah, so that the two thoughts are not really so far apart, and we may feel that the Greek versions are justified when they render the word by πίστις, and the English versions when they translate 'faith'. But, however we translate, the thought of the verse is that the righteous will live by his constant reliance on God.

Be that as it may, there is no lack of passages indicating the importance of trust in the Lord. Thus the psalmist sings: 'I have trusted in thy mercy; my heart shall rejoice in thy salvation' (Ps. xiii. 5), while nothing could more fully express the attitude of humble dependence upon God than the words of another psalm: 'Our soul waiteth for the Lord: he is our help and our shield. For our heart shall rejoice in him; because we have trusted in his holy name. Let thy mercy, O Lord, be upon us, according as we hope in thee' (Ps. xxxiii. 20-22). There are many similar passages in the Psalms, but the conception is by no means confined to them. Thus Nehemiah thinks of Abraham's acceptance with God and says: 'Thou . . . foundest his heart faithful before thee' (Ne. ix. 8), while the prophet expresses his confidence in the words: 'Behold, God is my salvation; I will trust, and not be afraid: for the Lord Jehovah is my strength and my song; he also is become my salvation' (Is. xii. 2). Again we find passages like 'Thou wilt keep him in perfect peace, whose mind is stayed on thee; because he trusteth in thee. Trust ye in the Lord for ever: for in the Lord Jehovah is everlasting strength' (Is. xxvi. 3f.). This too is a list which might be continued almost indefinitely, for trust in the Lord is evident throughout the Old Testament. But enough has been said to indicate the position, and we close this section by drawing attention to the fact that this attitude of trust is connected now and then with one or other of the words from the tsdq group, as in Ps. lxiv. 10: 'The righteous shall be glad in the Lord, and shall trust in him,' or Ps. xxxi. 1: 'In thee, O Lord, do I put my trust; let me never be ashamed: deliver me in thy righteousness'.

---

[1] *Romans*, p. 62.

V. JUSTIFICATION AND FAITH IN JUDAISM

The forensic meaning which we have seen to lie at the basis of justification in the Old Testament is, if anything, intensified in the Rabbinic writings. There is a lively interest in the whole subject, and it is everywhere assumed that being righteous means being accepted with God because acquitted by His judgment.

The judgment of God is thought of in several ways. There is the conception of a judgment being worked out now, and thus we are told that 'on New Year's Day all that come into the world pass before Him like legions of soldiers',[1] while the thought is quite common that every year on New Year's Day God weighs the merits and demerits of men, assigning rewards and punishments, but that He then gives them until the day of atonement to repent of their misdoings before His decree becomes unalterable.[2] But upon them who do not repent He visits His wrath, and thus we get the conception of temporal punishments.

But the judgment in the world to come is more important, and there are many references to it. 1 Enoch i–v is taken up with a description of this judgment, and there is a well-known passage in Wisdom which describes how the righteous only 'seemed to have died…For even if in the sight of men they be punished, their hope is full of immortality; and having borne a little chastening, they shall receive great good. … But the ungodly shall be requited, etc.' (Wisdom iii. 2–10, R.V.), and again: 'They shall come, when their sins are reckoned up, with coward fear' (iv. 20, R.V.). This final judgment will be with complete justice: 'Thou hast judged well, Thou hast condemned well, well provided Gehenna for the wicked, and Paradise for the righteous'.[3]

The very nature of this judgment presupposes that man is able to acquire merit in the sight of God by his own efforts, and we find this assumed throughout the Rabbinical literature. If we may take a typical statement:

'When R. Eliezer fell ill, his disciples went in to visit him. They said to him: "Master, teach us the paths of life so that we may through them win the life of the future world." He said to them:

[1] Mishna, R.H. i. 2.
[2] See for example b R.H. 17a, b.
[3] b Erub. 19a (Soncino trans. p. 129).

"Be solicitous for the honour of your colleagues, and keep your children from meditation, and set them between the knees of scholars and when you pray know before whom you are standing and in this way you will win the future world".[1]

As R. Eliezer is dated c. A.D. 90 we have a statement of the Jewish view not far removed from New Testament times, and it shows us clearly that the Judaism of that time took it as an axiom that man is able to acquire merit in God's eyes, the only question being how it was to be done. Many answers are given to this question, and in general we may say that, ultimately, good deeds rest on some law of God, merit being acquired by keeping His commandments, the study of the Torah and the doing of almsdeeds being mentioned especially often.

Every good deed was thought of as having a certain quantum of merit attached to its performance, while similarly every evil deed incurred a corresponding portion of demerit. The final judgment represented a weighing up of the merits and demerits acquired by a man during the course of his lifetime, and this is often represented as a weighing in the scales. If the good deeds outweighed the bad, then the man was adjudged righteous, and entered into blessedness, whereas, if the bad deeds predominated, Gehenna was his portion. This is very important for our study, because the writers of the various books of the New Testament were for the most part pious Jews, and we should be clear that first-century Judaism thought of the righteous not so much as those possessed of certain moral qualities, as of those who obtained the verdict at the tribunal of God. 'Righteous' was a forensic term.[2] Of course it is possible that the Christian writers repudiated this as they did much of the Jewish system but we shall require evidence for this, and cannot merely assume it.

Certain consequences follow from the Jewish system. One of them is that there is no place for assurance. No matter how well a man may have lived, it is always possible for him to slip into some bad sin which will outweigh all his merits. Hence the dictum of Hillel: 'Trust not in thyself until the day of thy death.'[3] Also man

---

[1] b Ber. 28b (Soncino trans. p. 173).
[2] On this point see SB, IV, pp. 3–19.
[3] Ab. ii. 5.

does not know the precise amount of merit attached to each good deed, and so cannot know where he stands. Berakhoth 28b gives us a moving picture of an aged Rabbi who, although a good man, was facing death with alarm, not knowing whether he was bound for Paradise or Gehenna. Such uncertainty seems inevitable if the Rabbinic presuppositions are taken seriously, and it forms a striking contrast with the Christian's assurance of salvation.

Also it leaves little place for the mercy of God. It is true that the Rabbinic writings delight to dwell on the mercy of the Lord, but they leave little room for this mercy to operate. It has some scope, as for example when a man's merits and demerits are equal, and God presses down the merit side of the scales, but on the wider view man ultimately decides his own eternal destiny by his own deeds, and the function of God is that of a just Judge.

Finally we must mention briefly that Judaism attached importance to faith. But the faith meant was rather a species of intellectual belief than what Christianity knows as faith, and it was regarded as itself one of the many meritorious works, so that he who exercised it acquired merit before God. There is nothing in Judaism to match the enthusiastic allegiance to, and committal of oneself to, a person, which means so much for the Christian idea of faith.

JUSTIFICATION (2)

I. NEW TESTAMENT TEACHING

IT IS important that we should approach the subject of justification in the New Testament by way of the Old Testament and later Jewish writings. Many have fallen into serious error by taking it for granted that everyone knows what 'righteous' and 'righteousness' mean, even if there may be room for a little discussion on 'justification'. It is not at all certain that in the Scriptures righteousness bears the same meaning as it has come to have in western civilization of the twentieth century, or that it had in profane Greek of the first. The words of this group were associated in non-biblical Greek with ethical conduct; for example, δικαιοσύνη was one of the four cardinal virtues, and the adjective δίκαιος denoted the sort of conduct associated with this virtue.

But while it is true to say that the New Testament inculcates the very highest ethical standards, and that these standards may sometimes be indicated by words from the righteousness word group, yet the characteristic meaning of the word group is to be derived from Hebrew rather than Greek roots. We have seen that in the Old Testament the righteous man is the one who is accepted before God, the one who secures the verdict of acquittal, and that this sort of thinking was developed and elaborated by the Rabbis with their picture of a great assize when all men would be tried before God, and some be accepted as righteous, while others would be condemned as wicked. It is from minds steeped in this way of regarding righteousness that the New Testament terminology is derived. Basically the righteous man is the one who is accepted before God, the one who conforms to His way. Now if a man is accepted, is truly accepted before God, he finds himself in such a relationship to the heavenly Father, the fount of all love and holiness and purity, that he can never be the same man again. In Scriptural language, he is born again, and the new life he now lives is one in which ethical qualities have a prominent place.

This being so there is room for confusion between the qualities denoted respectively by the Hebrew and the Greek ways of looking at the terms in question. It may be true that, ultimately, the Christian comes to practise what is involved in the Greek understanding of δικαιοσύνη, but his starting point is the Hebrew idea, and the New Testament can scarcely be understood until that is realized.

a. δίκαιος

Schrenk begins his treatment of δίκαιος in the New Testament by underlining the distinction from the usual Greek usage upon which we have been insisting. 'The New Testament δίκαιος is separated by a deep gulf from the Greek ethical ideal, from the contemplative method which isolates man in his deeds as self-sufficient'. Later he says: 'In substance the New Testament δίκαιος is broadly determined by the Old Testament'.[1] This is borne out by an examination of the passages in which the term occurs.

It is possible to get a wrong impression if we make our beginning with the statements of Pilate's wife, of Pilate himself, or of the centurion at the cross, all of whom refer to Jesus as 'righteous' (Mt. xxvii. 19, 24; Lk. xxiii. 47). In such passages we discern an element akin to the Greek conception of righteousness. But these are not the typical New Testament statements, and we go astray if we take our standard from them, and then proceed to force other passages into this mould. Rather must we begin with passages like Mt. xxv. 31f. which pictures a great assize in the typical Jewish fashion and refers to those who are acquitted as 'the righteous' (see particularly the culmination of the scene, 'these shall go away into eternal punishment: but the righteous into eternal life'). So is it with the introduction to the story of the Pharisee and the Publican in Lk. xviii. 9, 'And he spake also this parable unto certain which trusted in themselves that they were righteous', and with the Jewish spies, sent forth to trap Jesus into an unwary statement, who 'feigned themselves to be righteous', and in this character commended the Lord for teaching the way of God truly (Lk. xx. 20f.). In both these incidents the Jewish colouring is unmistakable, and it would be a violence of exegesis to interpret 'righteous' in other than the usual Jewish sense. (Cf. also Mk. ii. 17; Lk. xiv. 14, xv. 7, etc.)

[1] TWNT, II, pp. 189, 190.

It is clear that the Hebraic idea of the righteous as those accepted by God is to be found in the New Testament. But that is not to say that there is no advance on the Old Testament conception, for in the New Testament the requirements if a man is to be adjudged righteous are different from those accepted in Judaism. Whereas, for the ordinary first century Jew, the righteous man was the one who had performed many meritorious deeds, for the Christian he was one with faith in Christ Jesus. Thus St. Paul can quote from Habakkuk, 'the righteous shall live by faith', but he is not merely repeating an idea accepted generally in his day, for he has transformed the conception of faith, and conceives of it as a warm personal trust in Jesus as a living Saviour. A man becomes righteous, acceptable with God, when he has such a faith. We find similar citations of the passage from Habakkuk in Gal. iii. 11; Heb. x. 38, and in each case faith is understood in a Christian sense. The same thought is expressed in a different form in Rom. v. 19, 'through the obedience of the one shall the many be made righteous', where again 'righteous' is a term signifying those accepted by God, and the grounds of this acceptance are given in terms of the work of Christ. It hardly needs to be pointed out that faith on the part of the recipient of the divine gift is implied here, just as the activity of Christ is implied in the passages we have just been considering where salvation is linked with faith.

It may be freely admitted that we do not find this expressed uniformly throughout the New Testament. St. Matthew's Gospel, for example, is more closely identified with the Jewish conception than are the Epistles of St. Paul. But it is no part of our purpose to trace the growth of Christian doctrine. We are concerned, rather, to show what this conception means in its definitive Christian form. When we approach the New Testament with this in view we find, in the first place, that δίκαιος is characteristically used to denote those accepted with God, and in the second, that men are accepted with Him, i.e. are righteous, only on the grounds of their faith and of the work of Christ.

When we have grasped the fact that the righteous are those accepted by God, some of the controversy concerning imputed and imparted righteousness seems beside the point. What difference does it make whether we impute or impart a *status*? Denney has well said on this matter: 'the distinction of imputed and infused righteousness is unreal. The man who believes in Christ the propitiation—who stakes his whole being on sin-bearing love as the last reality in the universe—is not fictitiously regarded as right with God; he is actually right with God, and God treats him as such. He is in the right attitude to God the Redeemer, the attitude which has the promise and potency of all rightness or righteousness in it, and it only introduces intellectual and moral confusion to make artificial distinctions at this point.'[1] Those who come relying trustfully on the work of Christ for their acceptance with God are accepted as righteous, and if we bear in mind the essentially forensic nature of the term 'righteous' there seems little need to dwell unduly on imparted or imputed righteousness. By the same token it may be possible to cavil at Denney's inclusion of a reference to 'the promise and potency of all rightness or righteousness', for men are justified on Paul's view not on account of any merit of their own, potential or actual, but only on account of Christ's work and of their faith.

The adjective δίκαιος is applied to God in five passages, namely Jn. xvii. 25; Rom. iii. 26; 2 Tim. iv. 8; 1 Jn. i. 9; Rev. xvi. 5. In the first of these the reference is quite general, 'O righteous Father, the world knew thee not'; but in the last of them the meaning clearly has to do with the process of judging, 'Righteous art thou, which art and which wast, thou Holy One, because thou didst thus judge'. Here there can be no doubt but that God is shown to be righteous by the process of just judgment, and this accords with the expression 'the Lord, the righteous judge' in 2 Tim. iv. 8. In the Johannine passage God is spoken of as 'faithful and righteous to forgive us our sins', which we may well understand as indicating that God's forgiveness is in accordance with the laws of His holy nature. The remaining passage is that in which St. Paul says that the propitiatory death of Jesus was 'for the shewing of (God's) righteousness at this present season: that he might himself be just, and the justifier of him that hath faith in

---

[1] *The Christian Doctrine of Reconciliation*, London, 1917, pp. 164f. Again he says: 'When He pronounces the sinner δίκαιος, he *is* δίκαιος. Before he saw Christ and believed in Him he was all wrong with God: God could do nothing but condemn him. Now, in virtue of his faith, he is all right with God, and there is henceforth no condemnation for him. Nor in all this is there anything unreal, anything akin to legal fiction' (*Op. cit.*, p. 292).

Jesus'. This is a critical passage for St. Paul's view of justification, and it is clear that we must understand that God is δίκαιος in the very act whereby He justifies sinners, namely in the atonement wrought on Calvary. We have seen that in the Old Testament God is thought of as acting in accordance with the eternal law of righteousness which is part of His very being, and it would seem that it is this which Paul is here affirming. The act of forgiveness is not one in which God treats the moral obligation as of comparatively little account, or in which His love triumphs over His righteousness. God acts righteously and Paul sees this in the very act of forgiveness. Nor is this altogether an isolated thought. Throughout the New Testament we may discern the underlying thought that God is not capricious, but that He always acts in accordance with His holy nature, and sometimes this comes to the surface, as, for example, when Paul writes to the Thessalonians: 'it is a righteous thing with God to recompense affliction to them that afflict you, and to you that are afflicted rest with us' (2 Thes. i. 6f.). It is much more congenial to the modern mind to dwell on the love of God than to think of His righteousness, but we must bear both aspects in mind if we are to be true to the Scriptures. The New Testament regards the righteousness of God as something far too important to be ignored or glossed over. Even the act of forgiveness which might be thought of as an act of mercy was seen to be also an act in accordance with righteousness.

b. δικαιοσύνη

There are many passages in the New Testament where the use of δικαιοσύνη is akin to that of Judaism. Thus, when our Lord says, 'except your righteousness shall exceed that of the scribes and Pharisees, ye shall in no wise enter into the kingdom of heaven' (Mt. v. 20),[1] it is quite clear that righteousness is a concept common to Judaism and the new religion. But at the same time it must be recognized that there is a radical novelty here. Granted

---

[1] The connection of righteousness with law, quite in the manner of Judaism, might be inferred from statements about sin such as: 'Where there is no law, neither is there transgression' (Rom. iv. 15), or 'sin is lawlessness' (1 Jn. iii. 4). On the latter E. A. Knox remarks: 'St. John does not define sin as transgression of a definite command, issuing from authority and revocable by authority, but as lawlessness, antagonism to that principle of law which is of the very essence of the nature of God' (*Glad Tidings of Reconciliation*, London, 1916, p. 127n.).

the premises of the Pharisees, it is difficult to see how their righteousness could be exceeded, but there is no doubt that Jesus did not grant their premises. He was not thinking as they were of the accumulation of merit by the performance of law-works, of punctilious conformity with the letter of the law. For Jesus, with His emphasis on the spirit rather than the letter, righteousness took on a new meaning; so that, while there is undoubted continuity with Judaism, there is also a new departure. This is typical of the New Testament conception of righteousness; it cannot be completely understood apart from its Hebraic ancestry, and it cannot be completely explained by that Hebraic ancestry.

This combination of the traditional Hebraic usage with a resounding novelty associated with the divine activity makes it difficult to hold the idea, advocated by some, that the essence of the New Testament idea of righteousness is to be found in kinship with mercy. It is pointed out, for example, that in Mt. vi. 1 some texts read δικαιοσύνην and others ἐλεημοσύνην, and it is inferred that in New Testament times righteousness was held to include a large element of mercy, with which in fact it is nearly identical, the forensic idea being merely incidental. This is reinforced by an appeal to the association of salvation with righteousness in Is. xl–lxvi, and by such facts as the use of both δικαιοσύνη and ἔλεος to translate ḥesed in the LXX. But, as we have seen, in the Old Testament the forensic idea is basic and the association with mercy incidental, and nobody who has taken the trouble to examine closely the ninety-two examples of the use of δικαιοσύνη in the New Testament will doubt that the forensic use is primary there also. It is true that δικαιοσύνη, especially as applied to the dealings of God with man, includes an element of mercy. But the primary conception is undoubtedly forensic; and when, for example, St. Paul speaks of the righteousness which is by faith, he is not thinking in terms of mercy in men, but of their legal standing before God. Righteousness seems to stand occasionally in opposition to mercy, as in Tit. iii. 5, 'not by works done in righteousness, which we did ourselves, but according to his mercy he saved us', although it is true that it is human righteousness that is being contrasted with the divine mercy.

The whole idea of righteousness has been modified for New Testament writers because Jesus Christ has come into the world.

'He that doeth righteousness is righteous, even as he is righteous' (1 Jn. iii. 7) brings the very conception of righteousness into the closest of relationships to the life of the incarnate Lord. This again is a thought which recurs, and may be detected underlying many passages where it is not explicit. For the early Christians all things were made new, their standards of righteousness included, because the Son of God had come into the world. Accordingly, there are many passages which exhort believers to lives of righteousness, and it is just as characteristic of the New Testament that righteousness in the ethical sense should be a distinguishing mark of those who are Christ's, as it is that not their righteousness brings them salvation, but the righteousness of God. (Compare the aim of an upright life in Phil. iii. 10ff. with the express disclaimer of the value of any 'righteousness of mine own' in verse 9.)

But although there is this clamant demand for right living, and although the righteousness terminology is used in part to express it, yet it remains true that this is not the characteristic nor distinctive use of this terminology. We have seen that, in the Old Testament and in Judaism, there is a forensic basis for this word group, and we must feel that this forensic background is of importance for the New Testament writers.

We see this in such a passage as Rom. ix. 30–32: 'What shall we say then? That the Gentiles, which followed not after righteousness, attained to righteousness, even the righteousness which is of faith: but Israel, following after a law of righteousness, did not arrive at that law. Wherefore? Because they sought it not by faith, but as it were by works. They stumbled at the stone of stumbling.' The forensic idea is very strong here. The apostle is saying that the Gentiles did not seek before God that righteous standing which the Jews sought by the way of works of merit. Nevertheless they attained to righteousness, namely the righteousness that is of faith. The Jews who were very anxious to establish themselves as righteous before God failed to do so because they came by the way of law works instead of by that of faith, which is the way God has appointed. What is quite clear here is that righteousness is being used to denote a standing, a status, a verdict of acquittal, and not an ethical quality. In that righteousness plainly means here acceptance with God, 'rightness' before Him, we can see the Hebraic background; but in that this acceptance is not to be found in any works of merit, but only by the way of faith, we see the distinctively Christian contribution. The further reference to the 'stone of stumbling' is also integral to the Christian idea, for faith is not something grounded on mere subjectivism, but is something which operates on the basis of what Christ did on Calvary. The divine activity mediated to believers by their faith is essential to the Pauline conception of righteousness.

The point which is stressed over and over again is that this righteousness is not a matter of human merit, not a work of law. Paul was no stranger to the righteousness of the law, and he tells us that he had been 'blameless' regarding it. But his contact with Jesus Christ had changed his ideas. His aim now was 'that I may gain Christ, and be found in him, not having a righteousness of mine own, even that which is of the law, but that which is through faith in Christ, the righteousness which is of God by faith' (Phil. iii. 6-9). Here he expressly disclaims the righteousness which is of the law, and elsewhere his words are, if possible, even stronger, as in Gal. ii. 21, 'if righteousness is through the law, then Christ died for nought' (which seems to imply that righteousness not only is not, but cannot be, through the law);[1] or Rom. iv. 14f., 'For if they which are of the law be heirs, faith is made void, and the promise is made of none effect; for the law worketh wrath' (which again means that if men may attain righteousness by law works then the revelation in Christ is useless); or Rom. x. 4, 'For Christ is the end of the law unto righteousness to every one that believeth' (which makes it clear that there can be no way of law for the believer). It is hardly necessary to pursue the point further, for it can hardly be disputed that for St. Paul it was absolutely basic that no righteousness of human origin could avail in the sight of God.

We have already noticed that he speaks of righteousness as something which can be said to come from God, and this again is a point which means much to him. It is not peculiar to him, and we find it, for example, underlying the beatitude, 'Blessed are they that hunger and thirst after righteousness: for they shall be filled' (Mt. v. 6), where it is plain that the people in mind are those who

---

[1] As Burton says, 'The argument of the sentence is from a Christian point of view a *reductio ad absurdum*' (*Galatians*, I.C.C., p. 141).

have realized that their own efforts do not, and cannot, produce righteousness before God, and it is He Himself who will fulfil their longing.[1] So again when men are exhorted 'Seek ye first his kingdom and his righteousness' (Mt. vi. 33), righteousness just as much as the kingdom must be regarded as a gift to be sought from God. Similarly, when in Heb. xi. 7 we read that Noah 'became heir of the righteousness which is according to faith', it seems that righteousness is being regarded as a gift from God.

But it is in the writings of St. Paul that this thought receives its fullest expression. He speaks of grace reigning 'through righteousness unto eternal life through Jesus Christ our Lord' (Rom. v. 21), where righteousness means very nearly the gift of eternal life, and the thought of our dependence on God is implied also in the Pauline use of the expression 'the righteousness of God'. Much has been written about this expression, and in particular controversy has raged about whether it should be understood as referring to a quality of God's own nature, or whether it is a way of referring to the gift of righteousness bestowed upon believers. The considerations adduced by Sanday and Headlam[2] seem sufficient for concluding that both these aspects are involved. On the one hand, passages like Phil. iii. 9 leave us in no doubt that it is a righteousness of God which is the apostle's possession and whereby he is saved. On the other hand, we cannot overlook the fact that the New Testament consistently thinks of God as righteous, and there are not wanting passages where the expression ἡ δικαιοσύνη τοῦ θεοῦ must be thought of as indicating a divine quality (e.g. Rom. iii. 5, 25f.). It would be true to say, with Delitzsch, that this 'δικαιοσύνη is the harmony of God's actions with His law',[3] but this should not be understood in any static way. δικαιοσύνη is a dynamic term bringing home to us that all salvation owes its origin to God, we can be accounted as righteous only because of His activity. In the gospel, Paul says, there 'is revealed a righteousness of God' (Rom. i. 17), which makes it clear that the essential content of the gospel is closely related to the righteousness of God. This comes out

---

[1] On this verse Schrenk says: '. . . in opposition to the Jewish conception of merit the δικαιοσύνη is seen as a gift which God bestows on him who longs after Him' (TWNT, II, p. 200).

[2] *Romans* (I.C.C.), pp. 24f.   [3] *Hebrews*, II, p. 433.

again in Rom. iii. 21f.; 'But now apart from the law a righteousness of God hath been manifested . . . even the righteousness of
God through faith in Jesus Christ unto all them that believe'.
This righteousness is further defined by being brought into
relationship with the death of Christ, and in Rom. iii. 25f. it is
reiterated that the Lord's death was for the showing of God's righteousness. We are reminded of the conjunction of righteousness
with salvation in the Old Testament (especially in Is. xl–lxvi), but
the thought here goes further, and that in more directions than one.
Thus, whereas salvation in the Old Testament is concerned
largely, if not exclusively, with deliverance from temporal ills,
here it is concerned with expiation of sin.[1] St. Paul is dealing with
a more fundamental issue than were the men of the old covenant
when they used this terminology. Then, too, as we saw when we
were dealing with δικαιοσύνη in the LXX, there is a difference with
regard to the people being saved. In the Old Testament we have a
picture of God delivering the downtrodden and oppressed, but it
is always οἱ δίκαιοι who are thus delivered. St. Paul's thought
here is in marked contrast. He is thinking of men who were
utterly unable to achieve the status of being δίκαιοι. A little later
he speaks of God 'that justifieth the ungodly' (Rom. iv. 5), and
that is his thought here too. The righteousness of God with which
he is concerned is a righteousness which takes men in their sins,
alienated from the mind of God, subject to the wrath of God, and
justifies them.

Then there is another thought. It is not only that it is a righteous
thing that God should intervene to save His people; there is also
the thought that He saves in a manner which accords with right.
The very act wherein He delivers men is one in which He shows
Himself to be acting righteously. Paul says that God set forth
Christ 'to be a propitiation . . . to shew his righteousness, because
of the passing over of the sins done aforetime in the forbearance
of God; for the shewing, I say, of his righteousness at this present

---

[1] Cf. L. S. Thornton: 'The biblical doctrine of justification as exemplified
in deutero-Isaiah acquired in St. Paul's teaching a more specific meaning.
Through his act of expiation our Lord made it possible for God to declare us
"not guilty", thus releasing us from Law, Sin and ultimately Death' (*The Common Life in the Body of Christ*, London, 1950, p. 56 n. 2); and he adds that this
'includes a vindication of God's righteousness'.

season: that he might himself be just and the justifier of him that hath faith in Jesus'. Here the line of thought appears to be that the fact that God had not always punished sin with full severity in the past, but had 'passed over' such sin, gave rise to the danger that He might not appear to men to be completely righteous. But now, in the cross, He has forever removed that danger, and He has shown Himself completely righteous.

This is not always recognized and, for example, C. Ryder Smith writes: 'To put Paul's meaning in modern terms, he is saying: "God pleased to make man so that it was possible for him to sin; He also made man so that every sin should spread its evil infection through the mass of mankind; we have just seen the hideous result (Romans i. 18–iii. 18); God, who must have foreseen this, would not even be righteous if He did not find a way to save men from this; He has found such a way by sending His Son".'[1] But while there is truth in this, one cannot feel that it expresses Paul's essential meaning. 'How could God be righteous if He did not forgive?' is the question before Ryder Smith; but that which worried Paul was rather 'How could God be righteous if He did forgive?' Ryder Smith's paraphrase suggests that the end is all-important—it is the fact that men are saved that shows God to be righteous and the means are relatively unimportant. But Paul seems at this point of his argument to be more concerned with the means than the end. It is not salvation in general, but salvation by the way of the cross that shows God to be righteous.

Classical Protestantism has understood this to mean that Christ bore the penalty of our sin, and that God in this way showed that the eternal law of righteousness cannot be allowed to suffer disrepute.[2] Calvin puts it thus: 'As the law allowed no remission, and God did remit sins, there appeared to be a stain on divine

[1] The Bible Doctrine of Salvation, London, 1941, p. 260.

[2] Cf. J. Scott Lidgett: 'Thus for the apostle, the solemnity of the dealing with the Jewish law involved in the death of Christ lay in this, that though its form was Jewish, even governed by the text, "Cursed is every one that hangeth on a tree," yet that Jewish form was the special and peculiar expression of universal principles, and represented a demand and satisfaction so divine that they are the revelation of the means by which the righteousness of God wrought for the salvation not only of the Jew, but of the world' (The Spiritual Principle of the Atonement, London, 1898, p. 46).

justice. The exhibition of Christ as an atonement is what alone removes it.'[1] Or, to quote a later divine: 'the plan of salvation which the Bible reveals supposes that the justice of God which renders the punishment of sin necessary has been satisfied . . . the Scriptures recognize the truth that God is just, in the sense that He is determined by His moral excellence to punish all sin, and therefore that the satisfaction of Christ which secures the pardon of sinners is rendered to the justice of God. Its primary and principal design is . . . to satisfy the demands of justice; so that God can be just in justifying the ungodly'.[2] This kind of interpretation has been vigorously assailed, but it does appear to give the gist of the apostle's argument at this point. It may well be true to say that there is more to the atonement than this; or even that this does not give the essential meaning of the atonement. But, in view of the undoubtedly forensic colouring of the passage, and the general drift of Paul's argument, it does not seem that we can deny that he is here giving expression to the view that Christ bore the penalty for man's sin, and so showed the divine concern for law. This is admitted by such a theologian as Hastings Rashdall, although his own view of the atonement is so very different, for he says: 'St. Paul does not quite say why God could not remit the penalty of sin without the death of His Son. But it cannot be denied that those theologians who declare that this would be incompatible with God's justice—the justice which requires that somehow sin should be punished—or with the consistency which demands the infliction of the particular punishment which God had threatened, namely death—are only bringing out the latent presuppositions of St. Paul's thought'.[3]

It is objected to this interpretation that the bearing of penalty by one in the place of another is not really just, so that when Christ suffers for us it is not a matter of fulfilling legal requirements.

[1] Comm. in loc. (Owen's translation).
[2] Charles Hodge, Systematic Theology, London and Edinburgh, 1878, I, pp. 492f.
[3] The Idea of Atonement in Christian Theology, London, 1925, pp. 91f. The idea of bearing penalty is present in some passages where none of the δίκαιος words occurs, for example in Rom. viii. 3, on which Rashdall comments: 'What can this mean but that in the death of Christ the judgement pronounced against the sin of Adam and his posterity was satisfied?' (Op. cit., p. 93).

There is some force in this objection, and there would be more it we were dealing with a human law. But the fact is that we are not. The law in question is the law of God's holy nature, and that nature is merciful as well as just. Thus God's justice, while it is not capricious but works by the method of law, is a justice which finds a large place for mercy and is not hard, bare, and legalistic. At any rate, whether our legal categories can find a place for mercy or not, those of the Bible can and do. In the very passage we are considering there is a mention of the forbearance (ἀνοχή) of God which leads to the passing over of sins. Neither justice nor mercy must be whittled down; but neither must they be separated.

The forensic thought again seems to underlie passages such as Rom. v. 17 where righteousness is spoken of as a gift: 'much more shall they that receive the abundance of grace and of the gift of righteousness reign in life'. If righteousness is thought of as a gift, obviously it cannot be a quality of living; indeed, a standing before God seems the only interpretation adequate to the context. As G. O. Griffiths says: 'Certainly, if righteousness means "good works" it cannot be bestowed; but Paul's point is that this is not what it does mean: fundamentally it means *right relationship*, and it is this that God provides'.[1] So, too, when it is said that 'him who knew no sin he made to be sin on our behalf; that we might become the righteousness of God in him', there is clearly a forensic thought, although it is probably true that more than that is intended to be conveyed by the expression.[2] So is it in 1 Cor. i. 30, where Christ is said to be 'made unto us wisdom from God, and righteousness and sanctification and redemption'.

---

[1] *St. Paul's Gospel to the Romans*, Oxford, 1949, p. 108.

[2] Thus A. Schlatter: 'He makes His righteousness manifest in us; it forms us within and without, gives us a will and a destiny, makes us one with God's will and gives us a portion in His life' (*Paulus der Bote Jesu*, Stuttgart, 1934, pp. 568f.). The forensic meaning of the verse is well brought out by Rashdall when he says: 'This can hardly mean anything but that God treated the sinless Christ as if He were guilty, and inflicted upon Him the punishment which our sins had deserved; and that this infliction made it possible to treat the sinful as if they were actually righteous'. He regards this as one of 'a few passages which necessarily suggest the idea of substituted punishment or substituted sacrifice. But there they are, and St. Paul's argument is unintelligible without them' (*Op. cit.*, p. 94).

We come now to the question of imputation which has seemed to very many to be a necessary corollary of the forensic view. Traditional Protestantism has made much of the doctrine of imputed righteousness and has given it precision by saying that the merits of Christ are imputed to believers. Thus Calvin can say 'the Son of God, though spotlessly pure, took upon him the disgrace and ignominy of our iniquities, and in return clothed us with his purity'.[1] But in modern times this position has been strenuously opposed, and for example N. Snaith maintains that, if we hold to imputed righteousness, 'we have not emancipated ourselves from that very doctrine which Paul spent most of his life in combatting—namely, that salvation is by righteousness'; and he goes on to say: 'The fact of the matter is that God does not require righteousness at all, in any shape or shadow, as a condition of salvation. He requires faith'.[2]

It is very difficult to substantiate either extreme from Scripture. Against Snaith, righteousness is definitely said to be imputed to Abraham on the grounds of his faith (Rom. iv. 3), and the general principle is laid down that 'to him that worketh not, but believeth on him that justifieth the ungodly, his faith is reckoned for righteousness' (Rom. iv. 5). The chapter then goes on to deal further with the subject, culminating in the statement that 'it was not written for his sake alone, that it was reckoned unto him; but for our sake also, unto whom it shall be reckoned' (verses 23f.). In view of plain statements like these it seems impossible to hold that Paul found no place for the imputation of righteousness to believers. On the other hand he never says in so many words that the righteousness *of Christ* was imputed to believers, and it may fairly be doubted whether he had this in mind in his treatment of justification, although it may be held to be a corollary from his doctrine of identification of the believer with Christ.[3]

[1] *Institutes*, II, 16. 6 (trans. Beveridge I, p. 439).

[2] *Op. cit.*, p. 164.

[3] Cf. E. A. Knox: 'Why should he (i.e. Paul) not speak of an imputed righteousness, or of Christ's righteousness reckoned to him? If Christ lives in him, what should God see in him, of what should God take account in him, but of the living indwelling Christ in all His perfect righteousness?' (*The Glad Tidings of Reconciliation*, London, 1916, p. 74).

But, if our primary idea is correct, then the basic thought in righteousness is of a standing with God,[1] and we should think of a status conferred on men by God on the grounds of the atoning work of Christ. There is a sense in which it can be said to be imputed, for it is in no sense an ethical righteousness attained by the believer by the performance of good works, but rather a gift from without, from God. But it seems preferable to regard the idea of conferred status as primary, rather than to look at the whole subject through the comparatively few passages which speak of imputation.

Next we must notice that, while on the one hand St. Paul stresses the fact that righteousness is a forensic affair, on the other he insists strongly that it is attained only by faith, thus linking up the conception with the inner spiritual life of the believer. Both this inner experience and the outward status must be kept in mind. See Rom. iv. 11, 13, ix. 30, x. 6; Phil. iii. 9, etc.

Among the Jews there could be no justification until the day of judgment (for as long as ever a man lived it was always possible for him to sin and fall away from his momentary right standing). That justification has such a future aspect is recognized in such a passage as Gal. v. 5; but while this is not overlooked, it does not receive the emphasis in the Christian view. Rather the glorious truth insisted upon by St. Paul is that justification is a present experience. This comes out sometimes in specific expressions like the 'now' of Rom. iii. 21, or the frequent use of the present tense in alluding to justification. But it is not so much from isolated passages as from the general tenor of his teaching that we gather the importance of this truth. Because justification is an act of God rather than of man there is an assurance about it which means that it is not presumptuous to speak of being justified now. Justification is both present and future, but it is the present aspect which received emphasis in the New Testament.

---

[1] 'The righteousness which is the content of justification is, according to St. Paul, neither imputed nor imparted; it is a status conferred, not as had previously been believed, on the ground of merit, but on the ground of faith; and that faith was faith in God particularly as He was revealed in the sacrifice of Christ' (C. Anderson Scott, *Christianity According to St. Paul*, Cambridge, 1927, p. 97).

c. δικαιόω

We have seen that there is good ground for thinking that both δίκαιος and δικαιοσύνη are understood in the New Testament in terms of their forensic background. When we come to consider δικαιόω the forensic nature of the term is even clearer, and in point of fact it is difficult to explain any of the occurrences of the verb without recourse to the forensic.

The continuity with the Jewish usage is to be discerned in a number of passages. Thus Jesus said 'every idle word that men shall speak, they shall give account thereof in the day of judgment. For by thy words thou shalt be justified, and by thy words thou shalt be condemned' (Mt. xii. 36f.), where the general idea is clearly that of an assize such as the Jews conceived of at the day of judgment, and the opposition of καταδικασθήσῃ to δικαιωθήσῃ seems to put the matter beyond doubt. So is it in Acts xiii. 39 and Rom. iii. 4.

This last passage refers to God being justified, which is enough to show that the meaning of the word must be something like 'declare righteous', for it is impossible to think that the apostle (or, for that matter, the psalmist Paul is quoting) meant that God was to be 'made righteous'. He is affirming that in the process of judgment God's words would show that He is righteous. We have another reference to God's being justified in Lk. vii. 29, and one to Christ in 1 Tim. iii. 16. This little group of passages is very important, for it shows, at the very least, that the New Testament writers could understand δικαιόω as signifying 'to declare righteous' or 'to show as righteous'.

Equally conclusive are the passages wherein men are said to justify themselves, as in the case of the lawyer of Lk. x. 29, or the Pharisees of Lk. xvi. 15, of whom Jesus said: 'Ye are they that justify yourselves in the sight of men; but God knoweth your hearts: for that which is exalted among men is an abomination in the sight of God'. In this latter passage particularly it is quite plain that the justification in question is a declaring, or showing, to be just: the second half of the verse shows that there cannot be the thought of making righteous.

Not every one of the passages we have so far noted is forensic in the sense that it describes a court-room scene. It is obvious that a metaphorical element is quite common. But that should not blind us to the fact that, in each case, there is the implication of a judgment given and of a favourable verdict. The case is not unlike that of English verbs like 'to judge', 'to acquit', which are capable of being used in connection with matters far remote from law-courts, but which nevertheless are undeniably derived from legal practice and retain the essential part of their legal significance. So is it with δικαιόω. It may be used, it is used, in connection with matters where there is no formal giving of sentence in a law-court; but that does not alter the fact that the verb is essentially a forensic one in its biblical usage, and it denotes basically a sentence of acquittal. Thus it is that R. S. Franks can say: 'What St. Paul means by justification is simply the forgiveness of sins, expressed in legal terminology. Justification signifies the pronouncing of the sinner righteous before God'.[1]

This comes out clearly in such a passage as Rom. ii. 13, 'for not the hearers of a law are just before God, but the doers of a law shall be justified', and Paul goes on to speak of 'the day when God shall judge'. Here the apostle is evidently arguing in terms of current Jewish ideas, and we have already seen that that meant that the justified were those acquitted at the bar of God's justice. But quite apart from the fact that the words irresistibly recall Rabbinic conceptions, their plain meaning is that a certain class are those reckoned as righteous, those acquitted.[2] There is an ineluctable forensic element here. And this seems to be true whenever St. Paul uses the term. He has in his mind the thought of all men being tried before God, and by God; and the verb denotes the process whereby they are adjudged righteous or acceptable with God.

There are several places where St. Paul makes it quite clear that this status is not achieved by human effort, by works of law. 'We reckon therefore that a man is justified by faith apart from works of law' (Rom. iii. 28) comes as the climax of his argument in the

---

[1] *The Atonement*, London, 1934, p. 62. He goes on to say that justification 'proceeds upon no legal principle: it is purely an act of grace'.

[2] The apostle is, of course, dealing with a hypothetical case, and not laying down the way in which men in point of fact are justified. Elsewhere (Gal. ii. 21, iii. 11, etc.) he makes it quite clear that men cannot attain justification by their own efforts in keeping the law.

early part of Romans. His statements elsewhere are, if anything, even more emphatic. 'Knowing that a man is not justified by works of law, but only through faith in Jesus Christ, even we believed on Christ Jesus, that we might be justified by faith in Christ, and not by works of law: because by works of law shall no flesh be justified' (Gal. ii. 16, R.V. mg.). 'Now that no man is justified by law in the sight of God is evident' (Gal. iii. 11). Such statements rule out the remotest possibility of justification being wrought by merely human effort. St. Paul does not even speak of the works of the law, the Jewish law, but uses the anarthrous term 'law', law in general. No works of law can avail in the sight of God.

St. James takes up rather a different position when he expressly says that 'by works a man is justified, and not only by faith' (Jas. ii. 24), and when he uses the examples of Abraham and Rahab to reinforce his position. But it should be noted that he recognizes implicitly the place of faith; his polemic is directed not against faith as such, but against faith without works. He reiterates that that sort of faith is dead, 'faith, if it have not works, is dead in itself. . . . For as the body apart from the spirit is dead, even so faith apart from works is dead' (Jas. ii. 17, 26). Moreover the Epistle does not inculcate a demand for law works in the accepted sense; there is no thought of an accumulation of merit by the performance of deeds in accordance with the letter of the law. Rather there is a stress on love (ii. 8f.), humility (iv. 6f.) and kindred qualities. When we try to evaluate the teaching of the Epistle as a whole we see that the 'works' of James are very like 'the fruits of the Spirit' of Paul. While we must recognize that James has expressed his point of view in very un-Pauline language, yet the fact remains that he does not replace Paul's scheme of justification by another based on law-works. He does not mean by works what Paul means, and he does not mean by faith what Paul means. His demand is for a 'faith that worketh by love' (Gal. v. 6), if we may borrow a Pauline phrase, and his polemic is directed against those whose faith is revealed to be a hollow sham, by the absence of lives of service.

When St. James speaks of 'the implanted word, which is able to save your souls' (Jas. i. 21), he appears to be thinking of a divine activity operative in salvation, and this thought is brought out by St. Paul over and over again. This was part of the divine plan, for the Scripture foresaw 'that God would justify the Gentiles by faith', and so 'whom he called, them he also justified' (Gal. iii. 8; Rom. viii. 30). Again Paul can give a triumphant question and answer: 'Who shall lay anything to the charge of God's elect? It is God that justifieth' (Rom. viii. 33). It is of the very marrow of his thought that, not only is justification impossible by any works of law, by anything done in merely human strength, it can be effected only by an act of God; but gloriously, it *is* so effected. This justification is, of course, associated with the cross, for we are 'justified by his blood' (Rom. v. 9).

This thought of justification by divine action is not unlike that suggested by Jesus in the parable of the Pharisee and the Publican. The publican confesses his sinfulness and throws himself on the mercy of God. He relies wholly on God and produces no law works whatever. Jesus says, 'This man went down to his house justified' (Lk. xviii. 14).

It only remains for us to notice that, though justification is effected only by a divine action, it becomes operative in the lives of individuals only when they exercise faith. This is to be found in many passages, the principle being laid down in Rom. iv. 5: 'to him that worketh not, but believeth on him that justifieth the ungodly, his faith is reckoned for righteousness'. Faith, of course, is not merely an intellectual adherence to a set of propositions, but the response of the whole man to the divine act on Calvary, as he trustfully commits himself to his Creator, and rests in Him for time and for eternity. This whole doctrine represented a radical novelty in St. Paul's day, as G. O. Griffith reminds us: 'It is often said that to speak of "justification by faith" is to use language which, to the modern man, is meaningless. What is often forgotten is that such language was as meaningless to ancient man also, apart from the gospel which gave it significance'.[1] It is hardly fair to speak of the doctrine as one which was acceptable enough in the first century, but which cannot be accepted today, because our thought world is different; for the thought world of the first century was different also. But St. Paul made so much of this aspect of the gospel, even though the language was unfamiliar to

---

[1] *Op. cit.*, p. 106.

his hearers, because it seemed an aspect which was vital. We may or may not like imagery with forensic associations, but surely the heart of the Christian gospel is that no works of our hands will avail to make us acceptable before God, but that we are acceptable if we come in faith on the grounds of God's own action in Christ. And this great truth St. Paul delighted to express in the forensic language of justification.

d. Other words of the δίκαιος group

Of the other words in this word group δικαίωμα is used most often in the New Testament. Mostly it has the sense 'ordinance' as in the LXX, and we see, for example, almost the LXX usage in Lk. i. 6 where we read that Zacharias and Elizabeth were both 'walking in all the commandments and ordinances (ἐντολαῖς καὶ δικαιώμασι) of the Lord'. (Cf. also Rom. ii. 26; Heb. ix. 1, 10.) In all this connection with legal concepts is plain, and the forensic sense of the term clear.

But the word has many shades of meaning, and we find it used, for example, in Rev. xv. 4 of God, where RV reads 'all the nations shall come and worship before thee; for thy righteous acts have been made manifest'. But there is some doubt as to whether δικαίωμα can really mean 'a righteous act', even though many commentators give it this meaning here, or in Rev. xix. 8 or Rom. v. 18. Such a meaning is certainly not demanded by the context, and Charles' explanation seems preferable: 'δικαιώματα here means the judicial sentences of God in relation to the nations either in the way of mercy or condemnation'[1]. This is in accordance with the inherent meaning of the word itself, and also with the evidence adduced by Charles.

Of the other passages wherein δικαίωμα occurs, Rom. v. 16 says, 'for the judgment came of one unto condemnation, but the free gift came of many offences unto justification', where the opposition to κατάκριμα and the reference to judgment fix the sense of δικαίωμα as 'sentence of justification', or 'acquittal'. This probably settles the meaning of the word also in verse 18, although the structure of this latter verse with δικαιώματος answering to παραπτώματος leads some commentators to prefer the meaning 'righteous act' or the like. If the former be the correct

---

[1] Comm. *in loc.*

way of understanding the term, then St. Paul is referring to the Father's sentence of acquittal; if the latter, he has in mind the Son's act of expiation. While it would not be beyond the apostle to use the word in two such different senses within such a short compass it does not seem necessary to understand the passage in this way, and the reasons adduced by such commentators as Gifford, Godet, Sanday and Headlam and others seem sufficient for us to conclude that 'sentence of justification' is the meaning here, which interpretation is that adopted by Schrenk in the *Wörterbuch*.

This leaves us only with Rev. xix. 8 which the RV renders: 'And it was given unto her that she should array herself in fine linen, bright and pure: for the fine linen is the righteous acts of the saints'. Here, again, there are many who accept the meaning given to the word by the revisers; but in view of the fact that this is a meaning we have not been able to find elsewhere, it is probably better to understand the word in a way consonant with other New Testament passages of the sentence of justification which gives the saints their standing in the sight of God.

The noun δικαίωσις differs from δικαίωμα in being the act of justifying of which δικαίωμα is the concrete expression. It occurs twice only in the New Testament, namely Rom. iv. 25, v. 18. The former passage tells us that Jesus our Lord 'was delivered up for (διά) our trespasses, and was raised for (διά) our justification'. A good deal of ingenuity has been expended upon the two διά's, and some divergent results have been attained. But the position seems to be, as Gifford says, that διά with the accusative 'simply traces an effect to a cause, it marks the *existence* of a causal relation between them, without defining its particular character'.[1] Thus 'for our trespasses' may grammatically mean 'because we had trespassed', or 'to atone for our trespasses'; and similarly 'for our justification' is capable of two explanations, 'because our justification had been accomplished', or 'with a view to our justification'. There seems no conclusive reason that can be urged in favour of either way of taking justification, but possibly the former view is more in harmony with St. Paul's usual way of stating the fact of justification. But in any case if we adopt the latter view it must be in the sense that the resurrection is the completion of God's mighty act of justification,

[1] *Romans*, p. 109.

and not as though the resurrection were a justifying act quite apart from the death.[1]

Rom. v. 18, the other passage where we find the word, reads: 'So then as through one trespass the judgment came unto all men to condemnation; even so through one sentence of justification the free gift came unto all men to justification of life', the expression which concerns us here being εἰς δικαίωσιν ζωῆς. It is an unusual expression, and is probably to be understood of justification with a view to life. As Gifford says, 'the genitive expresses the effect or purpose: "*justification*" is unto, or in order to, "life" '.[2] The context (cf. verses 17, 21) shows that life is to be understood in an eschatological sense, and the passage thus indicates that justification issues in eternal life. Justification here corresponds to κατάκριμα, and thus there can be no doubt that it is a forensic term, meaning 'the act of acquitting'.

None of the other words from this root has great importance for our present inquiry. δικαιῶς occurs with the meaning 'justly' in Lk. xxiii. 41; 1 Pet. ii. 23 (the forensic sense being plain in the latter case), and with the meaning 'righteously' in 1 Cor. xv. 34; 1 Thes. ii. 10; Tit. ii. 12. δίκη is personified justice in Acts xxviii. 4, and it signifies 'punishment' in both its other occurrences, 2 Thes. i. 9; Jude 7. δικάστης means 'judge' in Acts vii. 27, 35, being cited from Ex. ii. 14 both times. δικαιοκρισία is found only in Rom. ii. 5 where we read of 'the day of wrath and revelation of the righteous judgment of God'. Here the wrath of God visited upon sinners is recognized as showing God's judgment to be righteous.

---

[1] See Godet *in loc.* for a fuller statement of the view adopted here, and in addition to Gifford, TWNT, II, p. 228, for the alternative view. *Inter alia* the latter says: 'Because death and resurrection continually occur in the closest connection, because the Crucified is that which He is only since He is at the same time the Risen One, Paul can say both: we are justified through the death of Jesus, and also: He is risen on account of our justification'.

L. S. Thornton comments on this passage: 'justifying faith is the faith of those "who believe on him that raised Jesus our Lord from the dead" in accordance with Scripture. . . . Once again our salvation depends, not only upon the substance of what is believed, but also upon the form in which it is believed. Unless our faith with regard to the resurrection of the Christ implies a miraculous work of God like that which is carefully stated in Romans iv. 17-22 our justification is in jeopardy' (*Op. cit.*, p. 278).

[2] Comm. *in loc.*

Thus in all this word group we may discern a close connection with the law court and with judgment generally. The forensic sense is sometimes very strong, and sometimes scarcely perceptible, which is what we would expect when we are dealing with so many occurrences of the words. But almost throughout we are able to detect the forensic undertone, and it is quite clear that many important passages will yield up their meaning only when we recognize that the imagery is being taken from processes of law. In particular we have reached the important conclusion that justification is in essence a matter of right status or standing in the sight of God, the status which shows that we are accepted with Him.

II. THE SIGNIFICANCE OF JUSTIFICATION

We have seen that the scriptural doctrine of justification includes a forensic element; but some theologians have made little of this in their final summing up, and some have excluded it altogether. Thus Oman objects to the category of law and says: 'We are justified because by faith we enter the world of a gracious God, out of which the old hard legal requirements, with the old hard boundaries of our personality and the old self-regarding claim of rights, have disappeared, a world which is the household of our Father where order and power and ultimate reality are of love and and not of law'.[1] This is finely said, and nobody, surely, would dispute the description of the new life we enter by faith. But whether this is a description of what the New Testament understands by justification is another matter. The consequences of the atonement are many, and the blessed state of the believer may be indicated in many ways, of which Oman's words point us to one, and that a very important one. But it is only by ignoring much scriptural evidence that this can be called justification, for, as the preceding examination should have made clear, justification is essentially a *legal* concept. It may well be that there are other spheres more important to Christianity than that of law, but that does not give us grounds for using the legal terminology to describe those other spheres. Justification is essentially concerned with the legal status of the believer, and we must leave descriptions of the new life for other categories.

[1] *Grace and Personality*, p. 206.

We might urge a similar objection against the position which says, 'To be justified, then, is not to have the consequences of sin condoned or even obliterated, but so to be reconciled to God in spite of sin, that we can face all evil with confident assurance of final victory over it, and by God's succour transform all its consequences, whether the evil be natural or moral, the outcome of our own sin, or from necessary fellowship with others in His family.'[1] Again we may say that there is truth in what is being said, and that it is a very real part of the Christian faith that believers are reconciled to God, and that they rely on Him to give them victory over evil. But this is not what the Bible means when it speaks of justification. There seems little point in transferring the name 'justification' from its proper sphere to some other which pleases the theologian better.

Similarly we protest against those views which see the essence of justification in the changed nature of the believer. W. Fearon Halliday comes near to this when he says: 'it has not always been seen that no man can be justified before God unless his nature is so changed that the assent of God is the assent to a reality'.[2] It is quite true that sanctification and justification should not be sundered, but rather kept in the closest of relations to one another; but that does not mean that we are to confuse the one with the other. If a man is truly justified by faith, then that faith will surely lead him in the power of God to a new life, and the one experience may well be held to imply the other. But that is not the same as saying that the two experiences are in essence the same. Though in practice they may go together, yet for purposes of discussion they may be considered separately, and justification is the name given in the Bible to the changed status, not the changed nature.

If we do not like the doctrine of justification it is more straight-forward to abandon it altogether, rather than to retain the name while applying it to something other than the scriptural doctrine. This is what Berdyaev has done, asserting that justification is both impossible and unnecessary. 'In reality grace can change man but not justify him, because it is the free action of divine power working upon human nature. For the rest, we may well ask is the

---

[1] Oman, *op. cit.*, p. 221.

[2] *Reconciliation and Reality*, London, 1919, p. 154.

justification of man necessary so far as God is concerned? It seems as if we are faced here with a juridical notion created by the limitations of human thought, which were incapable of accepting the divine truth of Christianity'.[1] Again he can say: 'The meaning of the coming of Christ into the world lies in a real transfiguration of human nature, in the formation of a new type of spiritual man. . . . In Christianity the central idea is that of transfiguration, not justification'.[2] But we can hold such views only if we give up altogether the attempt to ground our views on Scripture. There can be not the slightest doubt to any who has worked much with a concordance that justification is one of the very central truths of the New Testament. It is employed far more often than reconciliation and other ways of interpreting Calvary, and we may very fairly doubt, in view of the central place assigned by the New Testament to the death of Christ, whether even the change in man is thought of as often as justification. And even where the new life is thought of it is the consequence of the new standing before God which is justification. While we may welcome Berdyaev's reminder that the power of the divine love operative within man is an integral part of the Christian way, we must decline it as a substitute for justification.

Justification, then, is a conception which is deeply rooted in the Scriptures, and it witnesses to the importance of law in the divine economy. This witness cannot be set aside by a facile appeal to the antithesis between law and love, because it is the very Scriptures which tell us that God is love that stress the place of law. But indeed it may be doubted whether the antithesis is a valid one. While it is true that there is a legalism which is far removed from

---

[1] *Freedom and the Spirit*, London, 1944, p. 351. He goes on to say: 'Even in Orthodoxy the theology of the schools is infected with this idea of justification, although to a lesser degree than in Catholicism. Theological doctrine holds that man is saved by Christ and that he is reconciled to God by the sacrifice of Christ.

'But if we go into the matter more deeply we shall see that many are not saved *by* Christ but *in* Christ, in the new spiritual race which Christ began, in the new nature, and in the new spiritual life. Christ is above all the revelation of this new life, and of the kingdom of God. Justification and salvation are only secondary moments in the path of spiritual progress—a truth which Orthodoxy grasps more easily than Catholicism'.

[2] *Op. cit.*, p. 176.

love, and at times in the history of Christian doctrine it is some such legalism which has been posited of God, yet there is no inherent contradiction in affirming that God works by law and by love.[1] Indeed we cannot affirm that God is love in any meaningful sense unless we also say that God is law; for unless an element of law inheres in the divine nature we can have no guarantee that the love we see today will not be replaced by wrath tomorrow. It is perhaps a recognition of this truth, coupled with a realization of the legal significance of justification, which causes one so far removed from being a legalist as R. S. Franks to say: 'God's righteousness is His love considered as a law of conduct'.[2] So too, Denney says emphatically: 'It cannot be too often repeated that, if the universal element, or law, be eliminated from personal relations, there is nothing intelligible left: no reason, no morality, no religion, no sin or righteousness or forgiveness, nothing to appeal to mind or conscience.'[3]

Now, if God is thus a God of law, this has two consequences of importance to our present inquiry. The first is that He will require men to live in accordance with His law; the second that His forgiveness can be only such as is consonant with the law of His holy nature.

Concerning the first, Scripture insists over and over that God demands that men should live in accordance with the law which He sets before them. Moreover, it is part of the very nature of law as we know it that it attaches penalties to the breaking of the law, and in this respect the scriptural law is no exception. Again and

---

[1] Cf. Gustaf Aulen: 'The will of God, thus revealed in His Law, is nothing but the will of His Love. The Law no less than the Gospel is an expression of His Love' (*Church, Law and Society*, New York, 1948, p. 66). 'Law and Gospel belong together . . . they are only different sides of one and the same message' (*Op. cit.*, p. 100).

[2] *Op. cit.*, p. 152. H. Bushnell says: 'Consider and make due account then, of the fact, that the eternal law of right, which we cannot well deny is the basis of God's perfections, and of all law human and divine, is only another conception of the law of love' (*The Vicarious Sacrifice*, London, 1866, p. 252; and cf. pp. 187, 254).

[3] *The Death of Christ*, London, 1911, p. 277. So, too, H. Wheeler Robinson: 'The law of righteousness itself belongs to the divine nature' (*Redemption and Revelation*, London, 1942, p. 273).

again we are told that God views the breaking of the law with the gravest displeasure, that His wrath is extended towards the sinner, and that none can expect immunity, for there is no respect of persons with Him. It is quite in accordance with Rom. vi. 23 (and much other Scripture besides) when W. Milligan speaks of death as 'the first demand of the Divine law upon the sinner',[1] or when Westcott says, 'The particular act (i.e. of sin) calls for a proportionate reparation, the moral discipline of the debtor coinciding with the satisfaction due to the broken law.'[2] Modern man may have largely lost sight of it, but the Bible insists that sin is followed by punishment, and that that punishment is not only the temporal consequences of sin.

So we come to our second point, that God's forgiveness can be only such as is in accordance with the law of His own holy nature. We cannot expect God to make light of the moral demand when he deals with the situation posed by man's sin. It would be no answer to the needs of the situation for the Creator to say, 'It does not matter. I freely forgive'. P. T. Forsyth puts it strongly when he says that God 'could not trifle with His own holiness. He could will nothing against His holy nature, and He could not abolish the judgment bound up with it. Nothing in the compass of the divine nature could enable Him to abolish a moral law, the law of holiness. That would be tampering with His own soul. It had to be dealt with. Is the law of God more loose than the law of society? Can it be taken liberties with, played with, and put aside at the impulse even of love? How little we should come to think of God's love if that were possible. . . . God's holy law is His own holy nature. His love is under the condition of eternal respect. It is quite unchangeable.'[3] While we may be convinced from our knowledge of God as love that He will not leave man to be punished with the full rigour of the penalty prescribed, yet we

---

[1] *The Resurrection of Our Lord*, London, 1884, p. 140.

[2] *The Epistles of St. John*, p. 39.

[3] *The Work of Christ*, London, 1948, pp. 112f. He also says: 'The moral law differs from every other law in having a demand, and a universal demand, a claim upon us for ever. And that has to be made good and sound. It is a claim, because we are here in a moral and not a natural world. It is one thing to make good a gap and another thing to make good a claim. The claim must be met' (*Op. cit.*, p. 124). Cf. also Hodgson's remarks about punishment quoted on p. 185 footnote.

must hold that His forgiveness will be such as to uphold and not such as to set at nought the moral law.

It is in this context that we must understand the biblical teaching on justification. Justification in itself, as we have seen, is a legal term indicating the process of declaring righteous, but in itself it does not say how this is to be done. There is an element of the paradoxical in the New Testament idea of the way in which, in fact, men's justification is accomplished. For St. Paul can speak in Rom. iv. 5 of 'him that justifieth the ungodly' (that acquitteth the guilty as we might say). Nevertheless we are not to think of God as relaxing the moral law in order to accomplish this paradox, for it is categorically stated that He is δίκαιος in the very act of justification (Rom. iii. 26). This is a truth insisted upon over and over again by P. T. Forsyth who insists that justification is the justification of God as well as that of man, and indeed the justification of God before it can be the justification of man. 'We are bidden to recognize that God's demand on man takes the lead of man's demand on God. And both are overruled by God's demand on God, God's meeting His own demand. And we learn unwillingly that only God's justification of man gives the secret of man's justification of God.'[1] 'We can only understand any justification of man as it is grounded in this justification—this self-justification—of God. The sinner could only be saved by something that thus damned the sin'.[2]

This, then, is the significance of justification. It is not the only way of viewing the atoning work of Christ, and we must certainly give due consideration to other aspects if we are to have an adequate and balanced view of Christ's great work for us. But we cannot do without justification with its insistence that part of what was done on Calvary concerned the inflexible law which is at the very basis of the being of God. That law was honoured in the process whereby forgiveness was wrought.[3]

---

[1] *The Justification of God*, London, 1948, p. 40.

[2] *The Cruciality of the Cross*, London, 1948, pp. 102f., and cf.: 'God could only justify man before Him by justifying Himself and His holy law before men' (*The Work of Christ*, London, 1948, p. 136).

[3] The importance of the place of law in God's manner of working is not obscured by remembering that the New Testament emphasises that God is

[continued on p. 272]

III. JUSTIFICATION AND SUBSTITUTION

There is no inherent connection between justification and substitution, and there have been systems which included the one without the other. Thus Rabbinic Judaism, to name no other, was insistent that it is possible for a man to be justified before God because of his accumulation of merit, a form of justification in which there is no thought of substitution. But in the particular way in which Christ accomplished our justification it may well be held that there is a definitely substitutionary emphasis.

Among the older Protestant theologians this was almost taken for granted. Thus Calvin can say: 'Our acquittal is in this—that the guilt which made us liable to punishment was transferred to the head of the Son of God (Is. liii. 12). We must specially remember this substitution in order that we may not be all our lives in trepidation and anxiety, as if the just vengeance, which the Son of God transferred to himself, were still impending over us.'[1] From a slightly different point of view James Morison, in his *Critical Exposition of the Third Chapter of Paul's Epistle to the Romans* (a very thorough and scholarly work published in 1866), speaks of δικαιόω as referring to 'a judicial declaration of the reality of the substitutionary righteousness judicially found in the possession of believers'.[2] The very fact of man's justification was held by such theologians to imply a process of substitution.

In later times this emphasis was lost, especially as men came to think of the essence of the atonement as consisting in salvation from the power rather than the penalty of sin. It became almost axiomatic that substitution could have no part in a right understanding of atonement, and the real meaning of the cross was

[1] *Institutes*, II, 16. 5 (trans. Beveridge I, p. 439).

[2] *Op. cit.*, p. 198.

Father, for, as Scott Lidgett reminds us: 'Fatherhood is, by necessity, legislative and judicial. The very intensity of its desire to foster the true life of its children forces it to watch them with sleepless vigilance, to lay upon them those laws which promote that life, and to visit their departures from truth and goodness with stern fidelity. So far from true fatherhood being easy-going in these respects, its eye is more searching and its judgment more inflexibly righteous, than those of any judge less nearly concerned in the conduct of those who appear before him' (*Op. cit.*, p. 230).

sought elsewhere.[1] But more recently there are some writers who realize that this reaction is perhaps too extreme. Thus in 1948 F. W. Camfield wrote in the *Scottish Journal of Theology* that in the work of Christ 'we are met by the reality of substitution', and he goes on to affirm roundly 'Justification and substitution stand or fall together'.[2] Again, no less a person than Karl Barth suggests that we need to learn again what the Scriptures say about and mean by substitution,[3] and he can say: 'Yes, exactly in the depths of our misery He intercedes for us, and substitutes Himself for us, warding off the wages justly due us and suffering and making restitution what we could not suffer and where we could not make restitution.'[4]

These words last quoted look very much like an affirmation that there is a substitutionary process at work in the method of justification—the wages of our sin are averted by the substitution of the Christ, and He suffered what we could not suffer. This thought is to be found also in other writers. Thus H. Maurice Relton repeats over and over again that there is a substitutionary aspect to the atonement, and sums up much of his argument when he says: 'We have seen that there is a real element of substitution in the Calvary sacrifice. . . . We have suggested that it consists in His paying the debt in a final agony of dereliction; a spiritual death, which is sin's wages'.[5] But this is only another way of saying that the Christian method of justification is one which is substitutionary. This is affirmed also by H. Wheeler Robinson

[1] Sometimes it was admitted that the biblical conception of justification was substitutionary, and this aspect of it was rejected. Rashdall says: 'It is clearly St. Paul's conception that Christ has paid that penalty in order that man may not have to pay it. It is impossible to get rid of this idea of substitution, or vicarious punishment, from any faithful representation of St. Paul's doctrine' (*Op. cit.*, p. 92).

[2] Vol. I, p. 289. The full quotation is: 'Christ was crucified because man, confronted by the last things strove to push them out of his way. But here also we are met by the reality of substitution. Man in faith ceases to justify himself. He now looks to Christ as his justification. And his justification is no mere human experience, but an objective reality to which man's whole existence is related. Justification and substitution stand or fall together'.

[3] *God in Action*, p. 123.

[4] *Op. cit.*, pp. 16f.

[5] *Cross and Altar*, London, n.d., p. 110.

when he equates justification with 'the acquittal of the sinner through the (forensically) substituted bloodshedding of Christ'.[1] We conclude this list of citations with one from A. Schlatter who comments on 2 Cor. v. 21: '. . . he suffers what God does to sin, and makes visible what happens when man has God against him'.[2]

This brief list of citations makes it clear that, while a substitutionary view of justification may not be widely popular today, at least it may not be dismissed as obscurantist. It still makes its appeal to minds both devout and profound. Admittedly when we have said 'substitution' we have not described justification, much less the atonement; for a full understanding of either much more is necessary. But what we maintain is that we cannot enter into such an understanding unless we lay hold on that aspect of the truth which is expressed by the word 'substitution'. There is no condemnation now for them that are in Christ Jesus, and the reason for this may be stated, at least in one aspect, by saying that Christ bore our condemnation so that we bear it no more. But this is nothing less than to say that we are justified by a substitutionary process.

---

[1] *Redemption and Revelation*, London, 1942, p. 235.

[2] *Op. cit.*, p. 568.

CONCLUSION

IN THE foregoing pages we have surveyed some of the more important words used in the New Testament to describe the atoning work of the Son of God in the belief that modern research has much light to shed on the meaning of these terms, enabling us to see more clearly what they conveyed to those first Christian writers and readers. We have made no attempt to deal systematically with the bulk of the New Testament evidence, and there are other categories of considerable importance which we have not even noticed. But these studies are in the nature of a preliminary approach wherein we have cleared some of the ground, and begun to appreciate some of the metaphors which the men of New Testament days found helpful when they wished to draw attention to one aspect or another of a divine action they found it impossible to describe fully.

Our examination of the evidence has, we think, demonstrated that there is much support for objective as opposed to subjective views of the atonement, and none of the concepts we have considered fits naturally into a subjective view. Something happened on Calvary quite objective to man, and it is because of this that we can have the completest assurance of our salvation. In the last resort it depends on what God has done, and not upon some effect of that action upon the human heart (which is not to deny that there is such an effect, and that it is important). Thus redemption points us to a price paid, and we saw that the contention that it means no more than deliverance will not stand examination. It points us to the evil plight in which man finds himself as a result of his sin, in that he is in a state of slavery from which he cannot break free, and also in that he is under the condemnation of God, for it was in connection with disasters like these that the ancient world made use of the redemption terminology. But no less is our attention drawn to the price paid, for price was of the very essence of redemption, and was in point of fact that which distinguished it from other methods of deliverance. Even though the process might be used metaphorically to describe God's action in saving His people from Egypt, or from exile, yet even here there is the thought of cost; and so is it also in the New Testament. The salvation which Christ effects is not thought of as something brought about with effortless ease, but as something purchased only at the price of His blood. There seems not the slightest doubt that the New Testament writers thought of redemption as an objective thing, a process whereby Christ paid the price which brought them into salvation, and the idea that this means no more than that His example inspired them to be better men seems hopelessly inadequate. Whatever redemption is, it is something purchased by Christ; and in the first place it is outside of man, though the application of redemption to the individual, of course, calls for the exercise of faith, and hence to something subjective.

The people of God on the scriptural view are those who have entered into covenant with Him, and this might well be viewed as an activity of man as well as of God. But the initiative is always thought of as resting with God, and man's part is only the accepting of a covenant whose terms have been laid down by God. Thus the very idea of covenant, as the Bible understands it, puts the stress on the divine activity, and this is reinforced by the fact that the covenant in the New Testament is established only because the Son of God died for man and thus put away his sin. There is very little place for human activity in this way of viewing Calvary, and once again we see that atonement is essentially something wrought for, rather than in, man.

It is not otherwise with the use of the term 'the blood', which is often used by modern writers as indicating that in some sense it is the life of Christ that saves men. This is an idea which may be stated in various ways, some of which may demand some sort of subjective view of the atonement, although there are others which find a bigger place for the objective. But our examination of the evidence leads us to think that the view that 'the blood' directs our attention primarily to 'the life' is erroneous, and that, in point of fact, the Scriptures of both Old and New Testaments stress the death when they make use of this expression. While it is not impossible to understand the death in the Abelardian fashion, yet the impression left by those biblical passages which refer to the blood of Christ is that they are pointing us to the death of the Lord considered as the means whereby sin is dealt with, not merely the means whereby man may be inspired to deal with it.

We found it necessary to make a rather full examination of the passages speaking of propitiation, because there is a tendency to think that those scholars who have equated the Greek term with expiation have said the last word. We saw that the Bible has a great deal to say about the wrath of God, and that it leaves us in no doubt as to the fact that, although God is a God of love, yet He does not regard sin complacently, as something which does not matter greatly. On the contrary, sin calls forth the implacable hostility of His holy nature, and until something is done about it this puts the sinner in an unenviable position. If, then, we are correct in thinking that propitiation signifies the removal of the divine wrath by the offering of the Son, then this is strong evidence that the essential process of atonement is something which is done on behalf of man by his Saviour. We get something of the same idea from the concept of reconciliation which implies a state of enmity between God and man, and the removal of this state of enmity by the death of the Christ. The New Testament indicates that the reconciliation was effected by the removal of the cause of the enmity, namely, sin, and this was done in some way by the death of the Lord. These two conceptions, then, alike indicate that the essential process of atonement took place on Calvary, and that it was more than simply man's acquiescence in God's judgment on sin and his turning away from evil to serve God.

When we came to deal with justification we saw that this is essentially a legal term signifying a verdict of acquittal, and that this may be understood to come about in various ways, many of them congruous with a process of salvation by works as, for example, it was understood among the Jews. But the particular manner in which the New Testament understands justification to come about is by the way of the cross. Man is justified because Christ died, and this seems to include the thought that He bore man's penalty. At any rate it signifies, from another angle, that something took place exterior to man in the process whereby man's salvation was effected.

Thus each of the concepts we have examined bears its testimony to the fact that subjective views of atonement are inadequate.

Again we repeat that this is not to deny that they do draw attention to important truths, or that there is a subjective aspect to the atonement no matter how objective the theory we prefer. But we affirm that the essential process took place once for all on the cross, and such evidence as the concepts we have been investigating points strongly to something which was done quite outside of man, but in some way for his benefit.

The majority of scholars would agree today on some such statement, but there remains the further question of how we are to understand this objective factor, and in particular of whether we are to say that Christ's death was representative only, or that it was also substitutionary. That Christ died as our representative is widely recognized, but most scholars would affirm that there is no need of the substitutionary idea, all that is valuable in it being preserved in the concept of representation. That is to say, it is accepted that He died on our behalf, but not that He took our place.

In the preceding pages we have drawn attention to certain aspects of our subject which bear on this problem. In the light of what has already been adduced it is difficult to resist the conclusion that the idea of substitution must be included in our understanding of the atonement. The concepts of propitiation and justification in particular seem almost to demand that we understand them in a substitutionary manner and, to say the least of it, the other concepts are congruous with this interpretation. We have also seen that there are able scholars who feel that some such way of viewing the atonement is necessary. While it would be out of place to undertake a full examination of the concept of substitution in this place yet a few observations may be in order.

First may we go back to a statement of James Denney: 'God condones nothing: His mercy itself is of an absolute integrity. He is a righteous God, even in justifying the ungodly; and the propitiation which He sets forth in Christ Jesus, dying in His sinlessness the death of the sinful, is the key to the mystery.

'Once more, is not the word which spontaneously rises to our lips to express this the word substitution?'[1] In these words Denney reminds us of a fact which we must always bear in mind

---

[1] *The Expositor*, Sixth Series, III, p. 449.

in dealing with the atonement, namely that the forgiveness sinners receive is not at the expense of ignoring sin's consequences. 'God condones nothing', and we must not theorize as though He has become indifferent to the wages of sin. While admittedly it raises problems, substitution does emphasize this aspect of atonement, and alternative concepts do not always do so.

Then let us notice that there is more than one way of understanding substitution, and some ways are more worthy than others. Thus Moberly says: 'A stranger, hired for money to undergo a loss of limb or liberty, would always be an insult to true equity. But one who was very closely identified with the wrong-doer in condition, or blood, or affection; a tribesman dedicating himself for a tribal wrong; the willing representative of a conquered nation, or army; the father, on behalf of his own child; the husband, for the sake of his wife; is it impossible to conceive circumstances under which a willing acceptance of penalty on the part of some one of these, would as truly be the deepest hope of the transformation of the guilty, as it would be the crown of his own nobleness?'[1] He goes on to develop the thought that we never do see such a close substitution here on earth; but the question remains whether we do not see the circumstances he speaks of perfectly fulfilled in Jesus Christ. At any rate when we speak of substitution in connection with His death, we should bear in mind that He made Himself one with those for whom He suffered, so that the substitution which results is not the substitution of a casual stranger, but of one who stands in the closest possible relationship with those for whom He died.

A very suggestive treatment of the subject is given by P. Althaus in his essay in *Mysterium Christi*, where he distinguishes between what he terms 'exclusive' and 'inclusive' substitution. He finds the former in such spheres as the miners working underground for the community, substituting for them, and the latter in such activities as the mother who suffers for the sin of her lost son and longs to lead him to repentance. 'The substitute watching over the danger and distress of his people desires to lead them to a share in that watch. The significance of substitution here is clearly not that of gain through the relief resulting from the stronger

---

[1] *Atonement and Personality*, London, 1924, p. 78.

undertaking an act for the weaker, but rather giving those thus represented the active fruitful power which characterizes the representative.'[1] Without committing ourselves to believing that Althaus has solved all the problems of substitution we may yet feel that there is something very valuable in the thought that substitution, as we see it in the atonement, is not some purely external thing, which stops when it sees the wages of sin borne by the Substitute, but something which only reaches its consummation when the sinner comes to view sin with the same mind as his Substitute.

'God condones nothing'; 'one . . . very closely identified with the wrong-doer'; 'inclusive substitution'. These three expressions do not represent an 'Open Sesame' to the problems of atonement, but at least they do indicate, when taken together, that a rightly understood substitution is a very fruitful concept, and one we can ill afford to overlook when estimating what Christ did for us on Calvary.

[1] *Op. cit.*, p. 214.

INDEX OF GREEK WORDS

λύτρον, 9 ff. 17 n., 19 ff., 22 ff., 26 ff., 45 n. 1, 48
λυτρόω, 9, 11, 13, 17 n. 1, 24, 26, 35 f., 38 f.
λύτρωσις, 10 f., 17 n. 1, 24, 36 f., 44
λυτρωτής, 11
λυτρωτός, 10
λύω, 9, 51 n.

μεσίτης, 105 f.

νόμος, 82

ὁμοιόω, 225
ὀργή, 162, 164, 175 n. 3
ὁσιόω, 225

παλαιός, 90
πενθέω, 176
περί, 154, 176
περιποίησις, 57

περιποιοῦμαι, 9, 56 f.
πίστις, 240
πρόσταγμα, 82
προσηύξατο, 17 n. 1
προτίθημι, 171
πρωτότοκος, 24

ῥύομαι, 17 n. 1

συνθήκη, 81 f.
σωτηρία, 45 n. 2

τιμή, 50

υἱοθεσία, 56
ὑπέρ, 59, 154
ὑπομιμνήσκω, 176

φέρεσθαι, 87

ψυχή, 32

GENERAL INDEX

INDEX OF SCRIPTURE PASSAGES

I. THE OLD TESTAMENT

II. THE APOCRYPHA

III. THE NEW TESTAMENT